History
for the IB Diploma

PAPER 3

The People's Republic of China (1949–2005)

Allan Todd

CAMBRIDGE
UNIVERSITY PRESS

University Printing House, Cambridge CB2 8BS, United Kingdom

One Liberty Plaza, 20th Floor, New York, NY 10006, USA

477 Williamstown Road, Port Melbourne, VIC 3207, Australia

4843/24, 2nd Floor, Ansari Road, Daryaganj, Delhi – 110002, India

79 Anson Road, #06–04/06, Singapore 079906

Cambridge University Press is part of the University of Cambridge.

It furthers the University's mission by disseminating knowledge in the pursuit of education, learning and research at the highest international levels of excellence.

www.cambridge.org
Information on this title: www.cambridge.org/9781316503775

© Cambridge University Press 2016

This publication is in copyright. Subject to statutory exception and to the provisions of relevant collective licensing agreements, no reproduction of any part may take place without the written permission of Cambridge University Press.

First edition 2016

20 19 18 17 16 15 14 13 12 11 10 9 8 7 6 5 4 3 2 1

Printed in the United Kingdom by Latimer Trend

A catalogue record for this publication is available from the British Library

ISBN 978-1-316-50377-5 Paperback

Cambridge University Press has no responsibility for the persistence or accuracy of URLs for external or third-party internet websites referred to in this publication, and does not guarantee that any content on such websites is, or will remain, accurate or appropriate.

....

NOTICE TO TEACHERS IN THE UK

It is illegal to reproduce any part of this work in material form (including photocopying and electronic storage) except under the following circumstances:
(i) where you are abiding by a licence granted to your school or institution by the Copyright Licensing Agency;
(ii) where no such licence exists, or where you wish to exceed the terms of a licence, and you have gained the written permission of Cambridge University Press;
(iii) where you are allowed to reproduce without permission under the provisions of Chapter 3 of the Copyright, Designs and Patents Act 1988, which covers, for example, the reproduction of short passages within certain types of educational anthology and reproduction for the purposes of setting examination questions.

This material has been developed independently by the publisher and the content is in no way connected with nor endorsed by the International Baccalaureate Organization.

Dedication

For our daughters, Megan and Vanessa.
And again for Cyn:
And they are gone: ay, ages long ago
These lovers fled away into the storm
(John Keats, *The Eve of St. Agnes*)

Contents

1	**Introduction**	**7**
2	**The consolidation of the Communist State, 1949–55**	**35**
	2.1 How did the Communists establish their political rule in the years 1949–55?	39
	2.2 What were the main economic policies during the period 1949–55?	58
	2.3 What social reforms did the Communists implement during the years 1949–55?	73
3	**Mao's revolution, 1956–61**	**83**
	3.1 Why was the Hundred Flowers campaign launched?	86
	3.2 What were the main features of the Great Leap Forward, 1958–61?	96
	3.3 What were the immediate consequences of the Great Leap Forward?	110
4	**Power struggles and the Cultural Revolution, 1962–71**	**126**
	4.1 How did Mao begin to re-establish his political leadership after 1961?	129
	4.2 What were the main features of the Cultural Revolution?	141
	4.3 Why was there another power struggle after the Cultural Revolution?	150
5	**Foreign policy, 1949–76**	**158**
	5.1 What were the main features of Communist China's early foreign policy?	162
	5.2 Why did a serious rift develop between China and the Soviet Union in the 1960s?	176
	5.3 What was the significance of Communist China's rapprochement with the USA in the 1970s?	185

6	**The struggle for power, 1972–82**	**198**
	6.1 Why were there tensions within the CCP from 1972 to 1975?	201
	6.2 What was Mao's legacy?	208
	6.3 What were the main stages of the power struggle, 1976–82?	213
7	**Deng's economic revolution, 1976–89**	**235**
	7.1 What economic policies were followed by Hua in the period 1976–78?	238
	7.2 What were the main features of Deng's 'Revolution', 1979–89?	246
	7.3 How successful were Deng's economic reforms?	262
8	**Political developments under Deng, 1976–89**	**279**
	8.1 What was Deng's political approach in the period 1976–79?	283
	8.2 Why did political unrest re-emerge in the period 1980–88?	289
	8.3 What led to the Tiananmen Square Massacre of June 1989?	302
9	**Developments in China, 1989–2005**	**322**
	9.1 How did China's politics change after 1989?	326
	9.2 What were the main economic developments after 1989?	338
	9.3 How far have China's leaders created a 'Harmonious Society'?	346
	9.4 How did China's relations with the rest of the world develop after 1989?	355
	9.5 To what extent was China still communist by 2005?	359
10	**Exam practice**	**366**
	Further reading	**384**
	Index	**386**
	Acknowledgements	**394**

Introduction

1

1 The People's Republic of China (1949–2005)

This book is designed to prepare students for *People's Republic of China (1949–2005)*. This is Topic 14 in HL Option 3, History of Asia and Oceania for Paper 3 of the IB History examination. First, it will examine the consolidation, after 1949, of the rule of the Chinese Communist Party (CCP) under Mao Zedong. The major economic, political and social challenges – both internal and external – facing China in the period 1949–76 will then be explored, along with the nature and impact of Mao's responses to those challenges.

Finally, the main political and economic developments in post-Mao China from 1976 to 2005 will also be examined – in particular, the changes arising from the rule of Deng Xiaoping. Under him, and successive leaders, China has experienced a combination of economic reform and rapid industrial growth – making China the world's second largest economy – and political repression which has, so far, enabled the CCP to contain challenges to its regime and so remain in power.

Figure 1.1: A Democracy protestor – known only as the 'Unknown Rebel' or 'Tankman' – confronts tanks in Tiananmen Square the day after the government's violent suppression of the Tiananmen Square protests in Beijing, June 1989.

Introduction

> **ACTIVITY**
>
> The identity of the Tiananmen Square protestor in Figure 1.1 is still not clear – but he is believed to have been arrested and given a long prison sentence. Go to YouTube to see for footage of the protest and write an account of events.

Themes

To help you prepare for your IB History exams, this book will cover the main themes and aspects relating to *The People's Republic of China, 1949–2005* as set out in the *IB History Guide*. In particular, it will examine China in the period 1949–2005 in terms of the major areas shown below:

- the consolidation of the communist state under Mao Zedong, and his main reforms and policies in the period 1949–57
- Mao's political and economic reforms from 1958 to 1962, which were intended to achieve China's transition to socialism
- the main social reforms and developments in Mao's China
- the struggle for power within the CCP from 1962 to 1976
- China's changing foreign policy under Mao, 1949 to 1976, and China's emergence as a regional power
- the struggle for power in Communist China that broke out after Mao's death in 1976
- the main economic and political developments in China under Deng Xiaoping from 1981 to 1992
- China's economic growth and emergence as a global power under Deng's successors, 1992–2005

1 The People's Republic of China (1949–2005)

> **ACTIVITY**
>
> Carry out some research on the rise to power of the Chinese Communist Party from 1921 to 1949 – including the Civil War between the CCP and the Chinese Nationalists of the Guomindang (GMD). Then make some brief notes on these main issues. This will help you better understand many of the arguments and events which took place after 1949.

Key Concepts

Each chapter will help you focus on the main issues, and to compare and contrast the main developments that took place during the various periods of Chinese history post 1949. In addition, at various points in the chapters, there will be questions and activities that will help you focus on the six Key Concepts – these are:

- change
- continuity
- causation
- consequence
- significance
- perspectives.

Theory of Knowledge

In addition to the broad key themes, the chapters contain Theory of Knowledge (ToK) links, to get you thinking about aspects which relate to History, which is a Group 3 subject in the IB Diploma. The *People's Republic of China* topic has several clear links to ideas about knowledge and history. The subject is highly political, as it concerns, among other things, aspects of ideology -- namely a logically connected set of ideas that form the foundation of a relatively coherent system of political beliefs and/or political theory. As far as this book is concerned, the main

Introduction

ideologies which are relevant to your study are Communism and Capitalism.

At times, the highly political issues that it covers have influenced the historians writing about the leaders involved, and the policies and actions taken. Thus questions relating to the selection of sources, and to interpretations of them, by historians, are extremely relevant to the IB Theory of Knowledge course.

For example, when trying to explain aspects of the policies implemented by leaders, their motives, and their success or failure, historians must decide which evidence to select and use to make their case – and which evidence to leave out. But to what extent do the historians' personal political views influence their decisions when they select what they consider to be the most important or relevant sources, and when they make judgements about the value and limitations of specific sources or sets of sources? Is there such a thing as objective 'historical truth'? Or are there just a range of subjective historical opinions and interpretations about the past, which vary according to the political interests and leanings of individual historians?

You are therefore encouraged to read a range of books giving different interpretations of the situations and events, the theory and practice, and the policies and leaders, covered by this book, in order to gain a clear understanding of the relevant historiographies.

IB History and Paper 3 questions

Paper 3

In IB History, Paper 3 is taken only by Higher level students. For this paper, IB History specifies that three sections of an Option should be selected for in-depth study. The examination paper will set two questions on each of the eighteen sections – and you have to answer three questions.

1 The People's Republic of China (1949–2005)

Unlike Paper 2, where there are sometimes regional restrictions, in Paper 3 you will be able to answer *both* questions from one section, with a third chosen from one of the other sections. These questions are essentially in-depth analytical essays. It is therefore important to ensure you study all the bullet points set out in the *IB History Guide*, if you wish to give yourself the widest possible choice of questions.

Exam skills

Throughout the main chapters of this book, there are activities and questions to help you develop the understanding and the exam skills necessary for success in Paper 3. Your exam answers should demonstrate:

- factual knowledge and understanding
- awareness and understanding of historical interpretations
- structured, analytical and balanced argument.

Before attempting the specific exam practice questions that come at the end of each main chapter, you might find it useful to refer *first* to Chapter 10, the final Exam Practice chapter. This suggestion is based on the idea that if you know where you are supposed to be going (i.e., in this instance, gaining a good mark and grade), and how to get there, you stand a better chance of reaching your destination!

Questions and mark schemes

To ensure that you develop the necessary skills and understanding, each chapter contains comprehension questions and examination tips. For success in Paper 3, you need to produce essays which combine a number of features – in many ways, these require the same skills as the essays in Paper 2.

However, for the Higher Level Paper 3, examiners will be looking for greater evidence of *sustained* analysis and argument – linked closely to the demands of the question. They will also be seeking more depth and precision with regard to supporting knowledge. Finally, they will be expecting a clear and well-organised answer, so it is vital to do a rough plan *before* you start to answer a question. Not only will this show you early on whether you know enough about the topic to answer the question, it will also help maintain a good structure for your answer.

So, it is particularly important to start by focusing *closely* on the wording of the question, so that you can identify its demands. If you simply take

Introduction

the view that a question is *'generally about this period/leader'*, you will probably produce an answer that is essentially a narrative, with only vague links to the question. Even if your knowledge is detailed and accurate, it will only be broadly relevant – if you do this, you will get half-marks at the most.

The next important aspect of your answer is that you present a *well-structured* and *analytical argument that is clearly linked to all the demands of the question*. Each aspect of your argument/analysis/explanation then needs to be supported by carefully selected, precise and relevant own knowledge.

In addition, in order to access the highest bands and marks, you need, where appropriate, to show awareness and understanding of relevant historical debates and interpretations. This does not mean simply paraphrasing what different historians have said. Instead, try to *critically evaluate* particular interpretations: for example, are there any weaknesses in some arguments put forward by some historians? What strengths does a particular interpretation have?

Examiner's tips

To help you develop these skills, most chapters contain sample questions, with examiner tips about what – and what not – to do in order to achieve high marks. These chapters will focus on a specific skill, as follows:

- Skill 1 (Chapter 2) – understanding the wording of a question
- Skill 2 (Chapter 3) – planning an essay
- Skill 3 (Chapter 4) – writing an introductory paragraph
- Skill 4 (Chapter 5) – avoiding irrelevance
- Skill 5 (Chapter 6) – avoiding a narrative-based answer
- Skill 6 (Chapter 7) – using your own knowledge analytically and combining it with awareness of historical debate
- Skill 7 (Chapter 8) – writing a conclusion to your essay

Some of these tips will contain parts of a student's answer to a particular question, with examiner comments, to help you to understand what examiners are looking for.

This guidance is developed further in the Exam Practice chapter, where examiners' tips and comments will help you focus on the important aspects of questions and their answers. These will also help you to avoid

1 The People's Republic of China (1949–2005)

the kind of simple mistakes and oversights which, every year, result in some otherwise good students failing to gain the highest marks.

For additional help, a simplified Paper 3 mark scheme is provided in the Exam Practice chapter. This should make it easier to understand what examiners are looking for in examination answers. The actual Paper 3 IB History mark scheme can be found on the IB website.

The content covered by this book will provide you with the historical knowledge and understanding to help you answer all the specific content bullet points set out in the *IB History Guide*. Also, by the time you have worked through the various exercises, you should have the skills necessary to construct relevant, clear, well-argued and well-supported essays.

Background to the period

China before 1949

A general understanding of the background history of China before 1949 will help put the developments in China after 1949 into context.

The 1911 Revolution

Before 1911, China was ruled by emperors and the political system was extremely undemocratic. Economically, China was an undeveloped agricultural society, in which most of the population were poor peasants. There were frequent famines, in which millions died. Because of its limited economic development and relative military weakness, China was often at the mercy of stronger, more developed states, such as Britain, the US, Germany, France and Japan. In particular, China's resources and people were frequently exploited by foreign companies.

As a result of all these problems, groups of would-be political reformers emerged in China during the 19th century. These groups tried to push for reforms to modernise and democratise Chinese society, but they were usually brutally crushed by the Chinese government – or by the forces of Western powers. The lack of success of these reformers eventually led some to believe that revolution – violent, if necessary – was the only way things could be improved.

Introduction

However, those wanting reform – or revolution – often found it hard to agree on which strategy offered the best way forward. At first, groups in China wanting radical change adopted liberal and nationalist ideologies rather than those based on socialist or communist ideas. Soon, though, Marxism began to appeal to a small number of reformers and revolutionaries. Although there was a nationalist revolution in China in 1911 (known as the 'Double Tenth', as it began on 10 October 1911) which overthrew the emperor and established a republic, Marxism was still relatively insignificant in China. The preponderance of nationalism among China's youth was shown, for instance, by the May Fourth Movement, which university students began on 4 May 1919, to protest against the treaties that had ended World War One, and which – despite China being on the Allied side – had allowed Japan to retain some Chinese ports.

After the Bolshevik Revolution in Russia in 1917, however, Marxist ideas began to spread more widely in China. In 1921, the Chinese Communist Party (CCP) was formed – one of its founder members was **Mao Zedong**.

> ### Mao Zedong (1893–1976):
> Mao came from a relatively prosperous peasant family. In 1913, he decided to train as a teacher and, in 1918, he helped establish a 'Society for the Study of Marxism'. In 1919, he became a library assistant in Beijing University and studied Marxism. In 1921, he became a founder-member of the Chinese Communist Party (CCP); he became its leader in 1935, and held this position until his death in 1976. He resented Soviet attempts to influence developments in China – both in the years before and after the victory of the CCP in 1949 – and, from the 1960s, a serious split developed between these two Communist states. During the Cultural Revolution in the 1960s, his ideas were spread by young Chinese activists organised in units of Red Guards.

At first, Communism in China was heavily influenced by developments in the Soviet Union – in fact, the formation of the Chinese Communist Party had been encouraged by the Communist leaders in Soviet Russia. At the time, the Chinese Nationalist Party (the Guomindang, or GMD) – under its founder and leader, Sun Yat-sen – was attempting to establish a democratic and modern China free of foreign control and influence,

The People's Republic of China (1949–2005)

and which would introduce social reforms. As most Soviet leaders believed the CCP was too small to play an independent role in Chinese politics, they instructed the Chinese Communists to join the GMD.

Civil War

However, in 1925, Sun Yat-sen died and the leadership of the GMD was taken by **Jiang Jieshi** – unlike Sun Yat-sen, Jiang was strongly anti-Communist.

> **Jiang Jieshi (1887–1975):**
> Jiang became leader of the Guomindang (GMD) in 1925 and, from 1928–48, was the president of the government of Nationalist China. He was determined to destroy the CCP and even after Japan invaded mainland China in 1937, he still used his forces against the Chinese Communists. His government was corrupt and inefficient, and his limited opposition to Japan's invasion of China in 1937 resulted in his increasing unpopularity. After the Communist victory in 1949, he fled to the Chinese offshore island, Taiwan, which he ruled until his death.

At first, though, as Jiang wanted to continue receiving military advice and supplies from the Comintern (Communist International) – which had been established in Soviet Russia in 1919 to further world revolution, and was increasingly dominated by Stalin after 1928 – the GMD and CCP worked together in an attempt to create a national government by defeating the various warring warlords that, after the overthrow of the emperor, had come to dominate different areas of China.

By 1927, most of the warlords had been defeated, and Jiang became leader of China in 1928 – though warlord rebellions still kept much of China in chaos after that date. Yet, even before he became leader, Jiang turned on his former allies in 1927 and began a massacre of Communists in areas controlled by his armies. As a result, a full-blown civil war was soon raging between the GMD and the CCP.

In 1930, Jiang launched the first of five 'Extermination Campaigns' that aimed to wipe out the CCP and their Red Army. By then, the CCP had established several 'Soviets' in some of China's southern and western provinces – the main one being the 'Chinese Soviet Republic' in Jiangxi province. Mao was the main leader of this Jiangxi Soviet, and the CCP had gained the support of millions of peasants by a series of reforms that included land redistribution, reducing land taxes, literacy campaigns, establishing schools for both males and females, providing medical services and abolishing traditional practices such as arranged marriages. The Communists also established Peasant Councils, which gave peasants a say in how their communities were run.

At first, the Red Army had been able to survive Jiang's Extermination Campaigns by avoiding major battles and, instead, adopting guerrilla warfare tactics. However, this often allowed GMD forces to briefly capture Communist-controlled villages – as a result, over a million peasants had been killed or starved by GMD actions. Many members of the CCP had thus criticised Mao's tactics and – following the advice of a military adviser from the Soviet Union – Mao was expelled from the Party's Central Committee.

In the autumn of 1933, with the help of two military advisers from Nazi Germany, Jiang began the Fifth Extermination Campaign. This involved a GMD army of over 500 000 troops, which attempted to encircle the Communist areas and starve them out. This new tactic forced the Communists to attempt an escape to other areas.

The Long March, 1934–35

Over 85 000 soldiers of the main Red Army forces in Jiangxi began their retreat on 16 October 1934. This became an epic journey of almost 6000 miles (9000 kms), over rough terrain, which lasted approximately a year, and became known as the 'Long March'. Eventually, after losing over half of their original number during their retreat as a result of fighting many pitched battles using the tactics favoured by the Soviet Union's military adviser, the survivors reached the town of Zunyi on 9 January 1935.

Many of the Red Army commanders blamed their losses on the Soviet adviser and, at a special conference, the CCP elected Mao as the new leader of the Party, and returned military control of their Red Army to him. The Communists then decided to move in a series of different directions, in order to confuse the GMD, with the ultimate aim of retreating to the northern province of Shaanxi, which was far away from the areas controlled by Jiang's GMD. Eventually, in October 1935, they reached Yan'an, a town in Shaanxi province. Of the 87 000 soldiers who had set out a year before, fewer than 10 000 had survived.

The People's Republic of China (1949–2005)

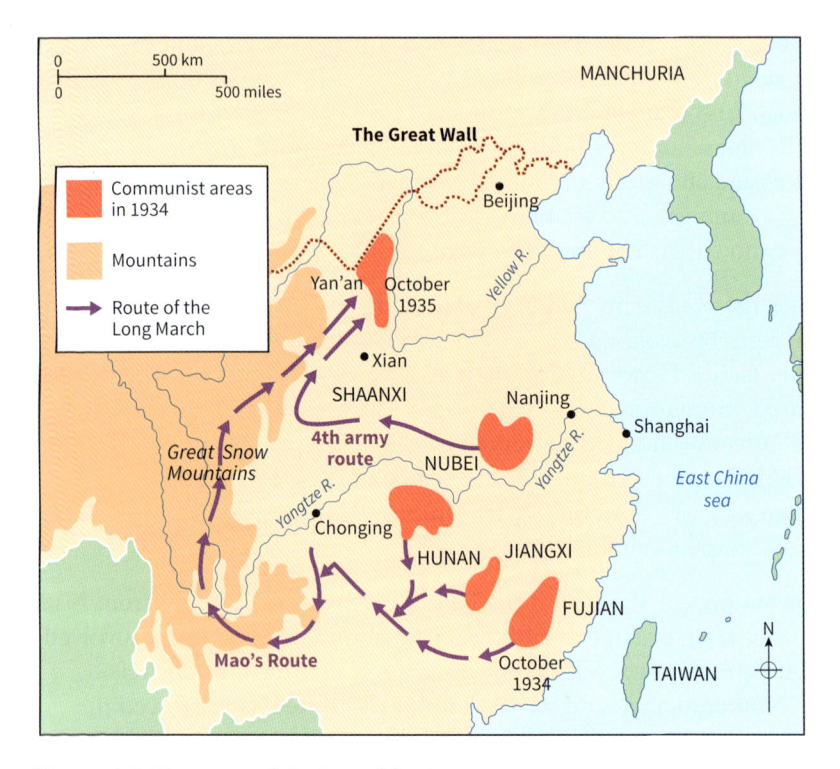

Figure 1.2: The route of the Long March.

The 'Spirit of Yan'an'

Here, as in their earlier soviets in the provinces of Jiangxi and Hubei, the Communists began to carry out the reforms that had made them popular. Such policies won them new recruits, and they were also reinforced by other Communist forces that had escaped from the south. As a result, their Red Army soon numbered over 80 000.

In 1937, Japan invaded China, so beginning the Second Sino-Japanese War – though Japanese incursions into northern China had been increasing since their seizure of the Chinese province of Manchuria in 1931. As Jiang had been much more concerned to destroy the CCP, GMD forces had done little to oppose these Japanese incursions. However, the CCP's Red Army had soon used their guerrilla tactics to resist the Japanese.

As a consequence, despite suffering further losses, the CCP's Red Army gained much support from the peasants; eventually, in December 1936, Jiang's own troops had forced him to form a 'United Front' with the

Introduction

Communists against the Japanese invaders. However, Jiang turned once again on the Communists in 1938. In later years, the 'Spirit of Yan'an' – and the Long March – were frequently invoked to remind the Party and the people of the sufferings, sacrifices and heroism of the first-generation leaders of the CCP.

The final stages of the Civil War

After Japan's surrender and the end of the Second World War in 1945, Mao's Red Army was re-organised as the People's Liberation Army (PLA) and, in December 1945, a truce between the GMD and the CCP had been arranged by the US and the Soviet Union.

Mao's earlier resentment of the Soviet Union's attempts to 'advise' the CCP on what tactics to adopt in the civil war was increased by the pressure that Stalin (partly as a result of his agreements with the US and the West about spheres of influence) placed on the CCP to form a coalition government with the GMD. However, civil war broke out again in 1946, when Jiang launched a major offensive against the Communists. Despite US aid to the GMD, the Communists were strong enough by 1948 to move from guerrilla warfare to direct attacks on Jiang's armies. During 1948–49, large numbers of GMD troops then began to desert to the PLA and Jiang even lost control of Nanjing, his capital. Eventually, in October 1949, Mao and the CCP were able to claim victory and announce the formation of the People's Republic of China (PRC).

Government in China today

Communist China – still officially known as the People's Republic of China (PRC) – is a one-party state, run by the Chinese Communist Party (CCP). In theory, power is shared between the CCP, the People's Government and the People's Liberation Army (PLA).

Although the CCP did have a General-Secretary, at first the most important Party post in practice was that of Party Chairman – the first one being Mao Zedong, who held the post until his death in 1976. This post, however, was later abolished under Deng Xiaoping, and the role of General Secretary became more important. The CCP also has a Politburo, which contains the top leaders of the CCP, and a Central Committee. The Politburo's smaller Standing Committee meets almost continually and comprises the most powerful and influential leaders. The government – known as the State Council – is headed by a premier

The People's Republic of China (1949–2005)

(prime minister). There is also a President (head of state) of the National People's Congress, which is elected every five years – this latter body is the equivalent of a parliament.

Terminology and definitions

The history of modern China can often seem extremely complicated. In part, this is the result of the range of political terms involved in studying and understanding the various arguments and developments during this period.

To complicate things further, different historians have at times used the same terms in slightly different ways. To understand the various ideas, which at times came to the fore in the history of modern China, you will need to be familiar with concepts such as 'left-wing' and 'right-wing', and a few basic terms relating to Communism and to Capitalism.

'Leftists' and 'Rightists'

Although Communist parties are seen as being 'on the left' in political terms, in practice Communist parties – like all parties – are themselves divided into left, centre and right-wings or factions. The origins of these political terms can be traced back to the early stages of the French Revolution in 1789. At this time, the most radical/revolutionary groups sat on the left side of the National Convention, while the most conservative ones sat on the right; the moderate political groups sat in the middle.

In fact, the French Revolution also gave rise to various terms and developments that were occasionally used during political conflicts within Communist China after 1949. One such term was 'Thermidorian', which refers to events in 1794, when the more radical Jacobins were overthrown by more conservative leaders, who then proceeded to undo some of the earlier policies. The other term was 'Bonapartism' – this refers to when Napoleon Bonaparte used his control of the army to make himself the overall leader of France.

Introduction

Figure 1.3: The Political Spectrum: Left/Centre/Right.

In addition, during the years leading up to the French Revolution, reformers and radicals had often met in the salons of sympathetic members of the upper-middle and upper classes (often led by women) to discuss political, economic and social ideas. Members of the pro-democracy movement in China in the 1980s often held similar meetings to discuss how to achieve political reform. In part, these pro-democracy discussions – and economic debates within the leadership of the CCP – were influenced by developments in the Soviet Union where, since 1985, Gorbachev, the new Soviet leader, had begun to introduce economic and political reforms. His ideas of *glasnost* (openness, and greater media freedoms) and *demokratizatsiya* (democracy), in particular, appealed greatly to many of China's students and intellectuals. However, for many CCP leaders, his economic policies of *perestroika* (restructuring), which involved reducing state control of the economy, and the introduction of market mechanisms, were of much more interest.

The existence of different wings or factions helps explain the arguments and power struggles that have taken place at various times between members of the CCP – in particular, those surrounding Mao's attempts to build a 'socialist' China, and the economic policies favoured by later leaders such as Deng Xiaoping.

The People's Republic of China (1949–2005)

During these political debates and struggles, opposing factions were often referred to as either 'conservative' Leftists (who basically wanted to retain state control of the economy) and 'liberal' Rightists (who wanted to 'free' the economy from state control by adopting market mechanisms). According to the Leftists, the Rightists (also referred to at times as 'revisionists', who wanted to 'revise' Communist principles) were taking China away from socialism and, instead, taking it down the 'capitalist road'.

Communism

When studying modern Chinese history, you may face special difficulties with the terminology connected to Communism. Apart from the fact that not everyone means the same thing when they use the term 'communism' – there are various other terms that also do not necessarily mean the same thing either. The five main ones you will encounter, in addition to Communism, are: Marxism, Leninism, Marxism-Leninism, Stalinism and Maoism.

In theory, Communism is a social and economic system in which all significant aspects of a country's economy are socially owned and self-managed – either by the state or by local communities or cooperatives. Unlike in capitalist countries, where land, industries and banks are privately owned, social ownership is intended to result in a classless society. Such ideas came to prominence with the writings of **Karl Marx** and Friedrich Engels.

> ### Karl Marx (1818–83):
>
> Marx was a German philosopher and historian who developed the materialist conception of history (meaning that historians should look to social and economic aspects rather than 'ideas' as the main causal factors in history). He argued that class struggle and conflict were the most (but not the only) important factors behind social and economic – as well as intellectual and political – change. He also identified various stages in the development of human societies. He worked closely with his friend and collaborator, Friedrich Engels (1820–95), and together, in 1847, they wrote *The Communist Manifesto*. He then went on to write an in-depth study of the workings of capitalism, entitled *Capital (Das Kapital)*.

Marx and Engels urged the industrial working classes in the developed capitalist countries (mainly Britain, Germany and the US at the time) to bring about socialist revolutions that would result in societies where – for the first time in human history – the ruling class would be the majority of the population. From this new form of human society, Marx believed it would be possible to move eventually to an even better one: communism. This would be a classless society but, because it would be based on the economic advances of industrial capitalism, it would be a society of plenty, not of scarcity. Such a society would also be based on greater freedom and abundance – and would eventually see a real decline in state power.

The transition period from capitalism to socialism would be marked by a form of political rule that Marxists called the 'dictatorship of the proletariat'. This specialist – but very important term – is explained in more detail below. However, Marx did not write much about the political forms that would be adopted under socialism and communism. On these, he said only that, as the majority of the population would be in control, it would be more democratic and less repressive than previous societies. He argued that after the workers' revolution, measures should be adopted from day one to bring about the eventual 'withering away' of bureaucracy and the state.

Marx, however, did not believe that 'progression' through the stages of society that he had identified was inevitable. He also argued that, in special circumstances, a relatively backward society could 'jump' a stage – but only if that state was then aided by sympathetic advanced societies. He certainly did not believe that a poor agricultural society – such as China in 1949 – could move to socialism on its own, as socialism required an advanced industrial base.

1 The People's Republic of China (1949–2005)

- Communism
- Socialism
- Industrial capitalism
- Agricultural capitalism
- Feudalism
- Slave society
- Primitive communism

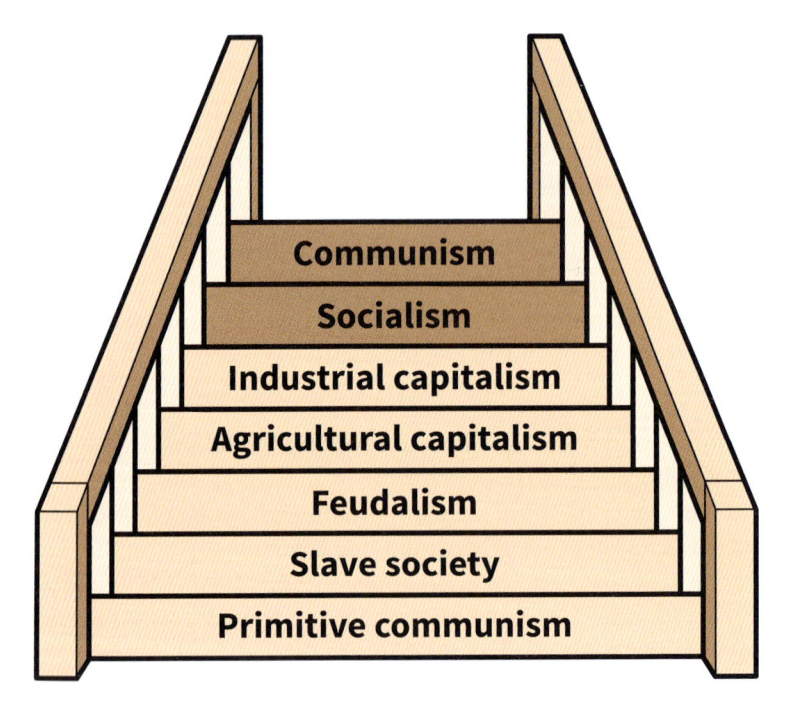

Figure 1.4: The Marxist 'stages of history' theory.

ACTIVITY

Before you begin to work your way through this book, try to find out a bit more about Marxism and its aims before Mao came to power in China. When you have done so, write a couple of sentences to explain to what extent you think its aims are: (a) achievable and (b) desirable.

Marx's ideas inspired many revolutionaries – including Mao in China. The first attempt to put them into practice was made in Russia, following the November 1917 Revolution. After the Communist Revolution in 1949, Mao tried to adapt and apply these ideas to China. However, practice turned out to be very different from theory – and many have argued that the ideals of Communism have never yet been implemented anywhere.

Introduction

Marxism

This refers to the political and economic writings of one man, Karl Marx (1818–83) – or two men, if Marx's close collaborator, Friedrich Engels (1820–95), is included. Marx's writings were based on the materialist conception of history that he developed, and on his theory that human history was largely determined by the 'history of class struggles' between ruling and oppressed classes which, fundamentally, had mutually exclusive or conflicting interests.

Figure 1.5: Front cover of *The Communist Manifesto*.

Marx believed that if the workers were successful in overthrowing capitalism, they would then be able to construct a socialist society. This would still be a class-society but one in which – for the first time in human history – the ruling class would be the majority of the population. From this new form of human society, Marx believed it would be possible to move eventually to an even better one: communism. This would be a classless society but, because it would be based on the economic advances of industrial capitalism, it would be a society of plenty, not of scarcity. However, Marx did not write much

The People's Republic of China (1949–2005)

about the political forms which would be adopted under socialism and communism, other than to say that, as the majority of the population would be in control, this society would be more democratic and less repressive than previous societies.

After the short-lived Paris Commune (in which a revolutionary provisional government took over Paris from April to May 1871, following the Franco-Prussian War of 1870–71), Marx added to his views on the nature of the state and politics after a workers' revolution. He argued that the democratic organisation of the Commune showed that, after the workers' revolution, measures should be adopted from day one to bring about the eventual 'withering away' of the state. Marx shared this aim with many anarchists, who also believed the state prevented people from governing themselves. This aim was a long way from states such as Communist China and the Soviet Union that actually came into existence after 1900.

Marx did not believe that this 'progression' in the stages of society was inevitable. However, he also argued that, in special circumstances, a relatively backward society could 'jump' a stage – but only if that state was then aided by sympathetic advanced societies. He certainly did not believe that a poor agricultural society could move to socialism on its own, as socialism required an advanced industrial base. Such questions became important at various stages in the history of Communist China – especially during Mao's Great Leap Forward in 1958.

Leninism

Marx did not refer to himself as a 'Marxist'. He preferred the term 'communist', as in the title of the book he and Engels had written in 1847, *The Communist Manifesto*. However, many of Marx's followers preferred to call themselves 'Marxists' as well as communists. In this way they distinguished themselves from other groups which claimed to be 'communist', and emphasised that Marxism and its methods formed a distinct philosophy.

One such Marxist was the Russian revolutionary Vladimir Ilyich Lenin (1870–1924). Lenin developed some of Marx's economic ideas, but his main contribution to Marxist theory related to political organisation. His main ideas, based on the extremely undemocratic political system operating in Tsarist Russia, were what became known as 'democratic centralism', and included the need for a small 'vanguard' party (a leading group) of fully-committed revolutionaries.

Introduction

The concept of 'democratic centralism' was one of Lenin's main adaptations of Marx's ideas. Lenin believed that all members of the party should be able to form factions ('platforms') to argue their points of view (the 'democratic' part of 'democratic centralism'). However, the repressive nature of Tsarist Russia meant the Party could only operate effectively in a centralised way. So he argued that once the Party had made a decision, all Party members – even those who had voted against it – should fully support it, even if the decision resulted from the votes of the 'centralism' part. Under Lenin, freedom of debate among members of the Communist Party continued at least until 1921–22.

Like Marx, both Lenin and **Leon Trotsky** believed that Russia could not succeed in carrying through any 'uninterrupted revolution' without outside economic and technical assistance. When this assistance failed to materialise, despite their earlier hopes of successful workers' revolutions in other European states after 1918, Lenin proved to be an extremely pragmatic – or opportunistic – ruler who was quite prepared to adopt policies that seemed in total conflict with communist goals and even with those of the 'lower' socialist stage. Similar arguments and policies developed at various times in Communist China after 1949.

> **Leon Trotsky (1879–1940):**
>
> Trotsky was a leading Russian Marxist, who disagreed with Lenin. From 1903–17, Trotsky argued that the system of 'democratic centralisim' would allow an unscrupulous leader to become a dictator over the party. Nevertheless, both Lenin and Trotsky believed in the possibility of moving quickly to the socialist phase. This idea was similar to Marx's idea of 'permanent revolution', which argued that as soon as one revolutionary stage had been achieved, the struggle for the next would begin almost immediately.

Marxism-Leninism

The term 'Marxism-Leninism', invented by Stalin, was not used until after Lenin's death in 1924. It soon came to be used in Stalin's Soviet Union to refer to what he described as 'orthodox Marxism', which increasingly came to mean what Stalin himself had to say about political and economic issues. Essentially, Marxism-Leninism was the 'official' ideology of the Soviet state and all communist parties loyal to Stalin and his successors – up to 1976 and beyond.

1 The People's Republic of China (1949–2005)

However, many Marxists – and even members of the Communist Party itself – believed that Stalin's ideas and practices (such as 'Socialism in One Country' and the purges) were almost total distortions of what Marx and Lenin had said and done. 'Socialism in One Country' is an aspect of Stalinist ideology, based on the belief that even an economically backward country could construct socialism without any outside help – contrary to the views held by Marx and Lenin. This view contributed to the rapid industrialisation of the USSR as it stimulated national confidence and pride in what the Soviet people could achieve by their own efforts.

The term 'purges' is usually applied to the massive and brutal purges Stalin initiated in the Soviet Union in the 1930s, during which most of the Communist leadership were executed. They were accompanied by show trials, in which the accused 'confessed' to their 'crimes' – such as plotting against Stalin and the Soviet Union – often after sleep deprivation, beatings and threats to family members. These purges were very different from previous 'cleansings', which had merely expelled members for such things as drunkenness or political inactivity.

The Chinese Communist Party also followed the ideology of Marxism-Leninism at first – until it adopted its own version, which became known as 'Maoism'. The struggle between supporters of Stalin and Trotsky in the Soviet Union during the second half of the 1920s was, to an extent, mirrored within the CCP, with Mao taking a clear 'Stalinist' stance. Two early leaders of the CCP, Chen Duxiu (the CCP's first general-secretary), and Peng Shuzhi, independently developed ideas similar to those of Trotsky. Consequently, they often disputed Stalin's advice, and then organised a Left Opposition within the CCP that supported Trotsky's ideas about revolution – and, in particular, his advice that the CCP should not be too closely tied to the GMD. In 1929, they were expelled from the CCP, and established a small Trotskyist movement within China. After 1949, both Stalinists in the Soviet Union and Maoists in China often accused their Marxist critics of being 'Trotskyists'.

Stalinism

The term Stalinism is used both by historians and by those politically opposed to Stalin to describe the views and practices associated with Stalin and his supporters – and with the Chinese Communists. Historians and political scientists use it to mean a set of beliefs and a type of rule that are essentially deeply undemocratic and even dictatorial.

Marxist opponents of Stalin and post-Stalin – and Mao and post-Mao – rulers used the term in some of the ways used by historians. However, they were also determined to show that Stalinism was not an adaptation of Marxism but, on the contrary, a qualitative and fundamental aberration from both Lenin and Marx, and from revolutionary communism in general. In particular, they stress the way in which Stalin and his supporters – and later Mao and his successors in China – rejected the goal of socialist democracy in favour of a permanent one-party state.

By 'socialist democracy', revolutionary socialists and Marxists mean a form of democracy in which government is in the hands of the people, who have the right to immediately recall any elected representatives who break their promises. In this system, all parties that accept the goal of ending capitalist exploitation should be allowed to exist and the state makes newspaper facilities available to all groups with sufficient support. A limited version of this had operated in the Soviet Union from 1917–21 but, under Stalin, the USSR became in both practice and theory a one-party state. This continued until Gorbachev began to introduce democracy after 1985. They also emphasise how Stalinism in practice and in theory, in both the Soviet Union and China, placed national interests above the struggle to achieve world revolution.

Maoism

Maoism is a particular form of Stalinism that originated with Mao in China, and was given a more definite form during the 1950s and 1960s. It was the official ideology of the CCP until Deng Xiaoping took over in the late 1970s. It differed from official Marxism-Leninism in that it placed the peasantry at the head of the revolutionary movement, rather than the industrial working class (known as the proletariat). Maoism also based its political strategy on guerrilla warfare: according to Maoist theory, the 'revolutionary countryside' was supposed to encircle and capture the 'bourgeois/capitalists towns', and then carry out a socialist revolution.

Although Maoism seemed to contain a greater democratic element – because it often tried to involve large numbers of people in their campaigns – in practice the CCP was just as authoritarian as Stalin's CPSU. The CCP also often resorted to purges of those who had

The People's Republic of China (1949–2005)

different ideas from the leadership. During the late 1950s and early 1960s, China accused the Soviet Union of being 'revisionist': meaning that it had 'revised' (or abandoned) the revolutionary aspects of Marxism in favour of a more moderate, less revolutionary approach. After Nikita Khrushchev became leader of the Soviet Union, he began carrying out a limited 'de-Stalinisation' in the USSR, and also tried to achieve 'peaceful coexistence' with the West. This led the CCP to believe that the Soviet Union was departing from 'orthodox' Marxism, especially regarding foreign policy, and doing deals with capitalist states. These arguments eventually split the international communist movement into pro-Moscow and pro-Beijing parties. However, in the early 1970s, Mao was also prepared to do deals with the 'imperialist' USA, thus showing that Maoism's strong nationalist sentiments at times meant he put China's national interests above those of Communist principles and the goal of world revolution. Just like the Soviet Union's leaders, Mao often put national interests before ideology.

Capitalism

Essentially, this is an ideology based on the belief that the most important parts of a country's economy – such as banks, industries and the land – should be owned and controlled by private individuals and/or companies. An important part of this belief is the view that the state, or government, should not be involved in the economy. In fact, in its early 'liberal' or 'classical' phase in the Industrial Revolution, it was believed that, apart from providing an army and (grudgingly) a police force, the government should not even provide social welfare. This, it was argued, helped ensure 'freedom'.

Although most capitalist states eventually developed as liberal political democracies, this was not always the case. Several capitalist states – such as Hitler's Germany in the 1930s and 1940s, or Pinochet's Chile in the 1970s and 1980s – were decidedly undemocratic. An indication of how capitalism can be decidedly undemocratic is provided by terms such as 'state capitalism', 'bureaucratic capitalism' or 'authoritarian capitalism' – all three of these terms have been applied to China since 1949.

Neo-liberal capitalism

In the 1980s, a more extreme version of capitalism emerged, which rejected Keynesian economics and which, in several ways, harked back to the early form of 'classical' unregulated capitalism. In most Western states, the 'welfare capitalism' that had emerged by the mid 20th. century came increasingly under attack. In opposition to the welfare state, a return to 'liberal' capitalism was called for instead.

These moves involved calls for a 'small' state – i.e. one that allowed private firms to take over the provision of various public utilities and welfare services; in which taxation of profits was reduced; and the rights of trades unions were restricted. At first, the economic policy associated with this 'rolling back' of the state was often called 'Monetarism', and was quickly adopted by Reagan's governments in the US, and by Thatcher's in Britain.

Such policies were based on the ideas of Friedrich Hayek and Milton Friedman, and other theorists linked to the Chicago School of Economics, who increasingly argued for an unrestricted capitalism and the privatisation of most publicly owned social services. During the 1990s, these policies were applied in post-Soviet Russia (and in the former East European states), and this application was often called economic 'shock therapy'. Since then, these kinds of ideas and policies have usually been referred to as 'neo-liberalism', and have been associated with the austerity and privatisation programmes in many Western states following the 2008 banking failures. These ideas have also been closely associated with the spread of economic globalisation.

'Dictatorship of the proletariat'

This Marxist term has three main specialist meanings – which, in many ways, are very different from the usual meaning of 'dictatorship'. Firstly, in relation to the revolutionary period immediately following the overthrow of capitalism, it refers to the 'dictatorship' that would need to be exercised over the old minority ruling class. This would involve repression of 'counter-revolutionaries' and 'class enemies' to ensure they did not try to overthrow or undermine the revolution and so regain their power.

However, a more significant meaning is 'dominance' or 'hegemony' – not harsh and repressive rule. According to Marxist theory, in any class-divided society, the dominant ideas are always those of the dominant class or classes. In a capitalist society, these were the private owners of banks, factories and land. Thus, Marx described the parliamentary democracy of late 19th-century Britain as the 'dictatorship of the

The People's Republic of China (1949–2005)

bourgeoisie' (the capitalist class) – even though most males (but no women) had won the right to vote by then.

In a socialist society (midway between capitalism and communism), the dominant class would be the industrial workers: the 'proletariat.' Unlike the bourgeoisie (which comprises a small minority of the population in any capitalist society), the proletariat – because they would be the overwhelming majority – would be able to rule in a much more democratic way in the post-revolutionary period.

This meaning is related to its third meaning – the idea of an entirely new form of government. This would be based on a form of popular (or mass) participation and rule at the grassroots – almost amounting to direct democracy – with regional and local councils, and other democratic institutions, exercising much of the decision making and implementation of policy previously done by the central state. This is what is meant by the phrase 'the withering away of the state'.

This notion of popular power in the post-capitalist period also includes the idea that the previous state functionaries – the bureaucracy – should either be replaced with officials in sympathy with the revolution's aims, or be supervised closely by popular institutions to ensure they do not try to frustrate revolutionary policies. Such measures would be essential for the transition to socialism and then communism.

It is these aspects of the 'dictatorship of the proletariat' within the post-capitalist state that seem to have been behind Mao's various actions and policies in the period 1949–76. For instance, the Anti-Rightist Campaign in the 1950s, or the Cultural Revolution launched in 1966, can be seen as attempts to control conservative bureaucrats opposed to the creation of a socialist China, and to involve mass participation in politics – as well as ways of defeating his political opponents within the CCP.

'Generations'

Promotion within the CCP has mainly been by seniority/age, and it is thus possible to discern specific 'generations' of Party leaders – or 'leadership collectives'. These individuals were mainly those who belonged to the powerful Politburo's Standing Committee. This method of identification of leaders was formalised by Jiang Zemin (who became the leader of China in 1993), and was announced in 1999 – partly to bolster his own position within the CCP. Jiang also identified a 'core

Introduction

leader' for each generation – but subsequent leaders of the CCP have just identified leadership collectives.

This system now recognises six 'generations' in all – since 2002, the 'generations' relate to Party elections and fixed terms of office – the fifth followed the 2012 elections, and the sixth will be decided by the 2020 elections. This book covers four of these generations:

- First generation (1949–76) – Mao, Zhou Enlai, Zhu De, Chen Yun, Liao Shaoqi, Peng Dehuai. Originally, it also included Lin Biao and the 'Gang of Four' – but, after 1976, these have been 'removed' from the official list.
- Second generation (1976–92) – Deng Xiaoping, Hua Guofeng, Hu Yaobang, Zhao Ziyang, and the 'Eight Elders' (which included Chen Yun).
- Third generation (1992–2003) – Jiang Zemin, Li Peng, Zhu Rongji, Qiao Shi, and Li Ruihuan.
- Fourth generation (2003–12) – Hu Jintao, Wu Bangguo, Wen Jiabao, Jia Qinglin, Zeng Qinghong and Li Changchun.

Summary

By the time you have worked through this book, you should be able to:

- understand and explain how Mao and the CCP's political reforms and initiatives – such as the Hundred Flowers campaign – were able to establish and maintain a communist state in China following their victory in 1949.
- evaluate the success Mao's various economic policies – such as land reform, Five-Year Plans and the Great Leap Forward – in relation to the building of a socialist society by 1962.
- assess the impact of Mao's social reforms on the position of women, the education of young people, and the health of Chinese people in general.
- understand and explain the reasons for the power struggle that emerged after 1962, and which culminated in the Cultural Revolution; and account for the changing foreign policy followed by Mao and Communist China from 1949 to 1976 – including the split with the Soviet Union.

The People's Republic of China (1949–2005)

- show an awareness of the different reasons for the power struggle that emerged in China following the death of Mao in 1976.
- evaluate the significance of the economic and political reforms implemented under Deng Xiaoping, and show an awareness of the challenges faced by Communist China after 1976.
- understand the main developments in Communist China from 1992 to 2005.

The consolidation of the Communist State, 1949–55

2 The People's Republic of China (1949–2005)

Introduction

The Civil War between the nationalist Guomindang (GMD) and the Chinese Communist Party (CCP) had resumed in 1945, shortly after the defeat of Japan. By the end of 1948, it was clear that the GMD were losing that civil war. In January 1949, the GMD suffered a massive defeat that allowed the CCP's People's Liberation Army (PLA) to take Beijing in April. Further Communist successes led Jiang Jieshi to flee – with China's entire gold reserves – to the Chinese island of Taiwan (known as Formosa at the time).

On 1 October 1949, Mao and the Communists held a massive rally in Beijing, at which a crowd of 300 000 heard them announce the creation of the People's Republic of China (PRC). However, Jiang – who still claimed to be the true leader of China – called Taiwan the 'Republic of China', and threatened to overthrow the recently proclaimed PRC in the very near future. Thus, despite having won the Civil War, the CCP's most immediate challenge was how to consolidate their new state. To do this, they quickly launched a series of political measures, along with several economic and social reforms.

TIMELINE

1949 Sep: CPPCC meets and agrees Common Programme

Oct: The People's Republic of China (PRC) is established with Mao as its chairman

1950 Jan: Treaty of Friendship, Alliance and Mutual Assistance with USSR

Apr: Marriage Law

Jun: Start of Korean War; Agricultural Reform Law

Jul: Suppression of Counter-Revolutionaries campaign is launched

1951 Aug: The Three-Anti campaign is launched

1952 Jan: The Five-Anti campaign is launched; all political parties except CCP are banned

Nov: State Planning Commission established to draw up First Five-Year Plan

1953 Mar: Election Law

1954 Feb: Purge of Gao Gang and Rao Shushi

Sep: New constitution is adopted

The consolidation of the Communist State, 1949–55

1955 Mar: Start of Sufan Movement
May: Start of new campaign against intellectuals
Jul: Mao's 'High tide of socialism' announcement
Oct: Move to APCs rapidly stepped up

KEY QUESTIONS

- How did the Communists establish their political rule in the years 1949–55?
- What were the main economic policies during the period 1949–55?
- What social reforms did the Communists implement during the years 1949–55?

Overview

- The CCP's sudden victory in 1949 meant it had no firm proposals for a new constitution. At first, it established a United Front approach, based on cooperation with elements who had not been strong GMD supporters and had not collaborated with the Japanese.
- A Consultative Committee, with representatives from several smaller parties, drew up a Common Programme and appointed a coalition government. But the CCP dominated, and their PLA was used to help re-establish central control.
- A series of 'rectification campaigns' against 'counter-revolutionary' elements – including some members of the CCP – was used to establish the CCP's political control so that it could create a 'New' China.
- Early measures included land reform that ended the domination of traditional rural élites and distributed land to the peasants. Many landlords were executed following 'speak bitterness' meetings.
- In industry, the largest firms were nationalised but, until 1952, the government cooperated with smaller owners to help build a 'national capitalism'.

2 The People's Republic of China (1949–2005)

- In 1953, the CCP launched moves towards socialism. With help from the USSR, a Five-Year Plan was launched – this resulted in joint private-state ownership of industries, and the creation of cooperatives in rural areas. From 1955, these developments were extended.
- Social reforms included laws to give women equal rights; improve working conditions and employment benefits for industrial workers; and develop education and health provision – especially in rural areas.

Figure 2.1: Mao Zedong announces the creation of the People's Republic of China in Beijing on 1 October 1949. The man to his left is Liu Shaoqi, one of the Deputy Chairmen of the CCP.

The consolidation of the Communist State, 1949–55

2.1 How did the Communists establish their political rule in the years 1949–55?

In many respects, the CCP enjoyed more favourable conditions in 1949 than those Lenin and the Bolsheviks had faced in Russia in 1917 for consolidating their revolutionary victory, and for establishing the necessary preconditions for the eventual transition to socialism. In particular, as most of China's old state bureaucracy had been destroyed by war and civil war before 1949, the CCP had the opportunity to create new political institutions to secure the future of their revolution.

SOURCE 2.1

Whereas the Bolsheviks were forced to wage a materially and spiritually debilitating civil war after the October Revolution, in China the civil war had been fought and won during the revolutionary years; when the Communists established state power in 1949, they faced only scattered counter-revolutionary resistance. Moreover, decades of revolutionary struggle had permitted the Communists to develop their own organizational forms and administrative structures and had provided them with considerable governmental experience and many experienced administrators; they were thus much less dependent on the bureaucratic apparatus left over from the old regime than the Bolsheviks had been. And perhaps most significantly, the Chinese Communists came to power with far greater popular support than had their Russian predecessors, especially, of course, in the countryside where 80 per cent of the Chinese people lived; unlike Lenin, Mao was not confronted with the problem of a hostile peasantry in a largely agrarian society.

Meisner, M. 1999. **Mao's China and After: A History of the People's Republic.** *New York, The Free Press, pp.57–8*

2 The People's Republic of China (1949–2005)

> **QUESTION**
>
> What, according to Source 2.1, were the advantages the Chinese Communists enjoyed in 1949, when they began constructing their new China?

The New Democracy

The sudden collapse of the GMD regime in 1949 had taken the CCP by surprise. This is one of the reasons why it had no formal document to propose as a new constitution – in the end, the new constitution did not appear until 1954. At first, the CCP announced its intention – in the spirit of the 'United Front' approach – to form a coalition government with several smaller parties.

The Chinese People's Political Consultative Conference

In September 1949, before the formal proclamation of the PRC, the CCP called a Chinese People's Political Consultative Conference (CPPCC) in Beijing. The 662 delegates included delegates of the Left GMD (a more radical section that had broken away from Jiang's GMD in 1927), along with some representatives of small democratic political groups. However, as Source 2.2 shows, GMD members who had supported Jiang, and those who had collaborated with the Japanese invaders, were excluded. Significantly, though, the proceedings of the CPPCC were clearly dominated by the Communists.

The consolidation of the Communist State, 1949–55

SOURCE 2.2

Although its military units were taking control of the key towns and cities, the senior leadership of the Chinese Communist Party was working to establish its political authority and attempting to make common cause with political, religious and intellectual leaders who were not committed to supporting the Guomindang Nationalists. This reflected the United Front policy which characterised the early years of the People's Republic but which began to disintegrate in 1956 when Mao became aware of the depths of distrust that many educated Chinese felt for his government. The first instrument of the United Front policy was the Chinese People's Political Consultative Conference…, usually referred to by its initials, CPPCC. The conference opened on 21 September 1949 in one of the halls of the Forbidden City in Beijing and closed on 30 September… The United Front Bureau of the CCP had contacted potential sympathisers and had organised a Preparatory Committee for the CPPCC. This committee… was given the responsibility of setting the date and time for the meeting, drawing up an agenda and drafting a Common Programme…, the first statement of national policy under the new Communist government.

Dillon, M. 2012. **China: A Modern History.** *London. I. B. Tauris. pp.261–2*

The CPPCC passed the Organic Law of the People's Central Government of the People's Republic of China (see Source 2.3). Mao was elected as Chairman of the Republic (head of state), and a coalition Government Administrative Council (GAC) was elected to rule China until a new constitution had been drafted and adopted. Mao then appointed **Zhou Enlai** as the new China's first premier (prime minister).

2 The People's Republic of China (1949–2005)

SOURCE 2.3

CHAPTER 1. GENERAL PROVISIONS

ARTICLE 1. The Chinese People's Political Consultative Conference… is the organization of the democratic United Front of the entire Chinese people. Its aim is to unite all democratic classes and all nationalities throughout China by establishing the unity of all democratic parties and groups and people's organizations. This will enable them to put forward their combined efforts in carrying out New Democracy, opposing imperialism, feudalism and bureaucratic capitalism, overthrowing the reactionary rule of the Guomindang, eliminating open and secret remnant counter-revolutionary forces. It will also enable them to heal the wounds of war, rehabilitate and develop the people's economic, cultural and educational work, consolidate national defence, and unite with all nations and countries which treat us on a footing of equality. All this is for the express purpose of establishing and consolidating an independent, democratic, peaceful, unified, prosperous and strong People's Republic of China of the People's Democratic Dictatorship, led by the working class and based on the alliance of workers and peasants.

Extract from 'The Organic Law of the Chinese People's Political Consultative Conference', *Beijing, 29 September 1949. Quoted in: Mimmack, B., Senés, D. and Price, E. 2010.* Authoritarian and Single-Party States. *Harlow. Pearson. p.157*

Zhou Enlai (1898–1976):

Zhou Enlai worked closely with Mao, and was premier (prime minister) from 1949 to 1976. Zhou played important roles in the economy (where he mainly supported Deng Xiaoping's ideas) and in foreign policy (until 1958, he was also foreign minister, favouring 'peaceful coexistence' with the West). During the Cultural Revolution, his attempts to moderate the more violent activities of the Red Guards (see Chapter 4) made him a popular and much-respected leader – his death in 1976 led to thousands of ordinary Chinese showing their respect in huge demonstrations.

The consolidation of the Communist State, 1949–55

> **QUESTION**
>
> In the context of China in 1949, what was meant by the term 'Democratic Dictatorship', mentioned in Source 2.3?

The Common Programme

The CPPCC also passed the Common Programme – parts of which can be seen in Source 2.4. This announced that the new government of China would be a 'People's Democratic Dictatorship': a democracy for the majority of the population, but a dictatorship for 'reactionaries' who had exploited the people before 1949 and who remained opposed to the new China.

SOURCE 2.4

The People's Republic of China strives for independence, democracy, peace unity… prosperity, and the strength of China… It must systematically transform … the land ownership system into a system of peasant land ownership… It must steadily transform the country from an agricultural into an industrial one… The people shall have freedom of thought, speech, publication, assembly, religious belief and the freedom of holding processions and demonstrations. The People's Republic of China shall abolish the feudal system which holds women in bondage. Women shall enjoy equal rights with men…. All nationalities in the People's Republic shall have equal rights and duties…

The People's Republic of China shall suppress all counter-revolutionary activities, severely punish all Guomindang counter-revolutionary war criminals and other leading counter-revolutionary elements… Feudal landlords, capitalists and reactionary elements in general shall be deprived of their political rights.

Extracts from the Common Programme, quoted in Brooman, J., 1988. **China Since 1900.** *Harlow, Longman. p.28*

Theory of Knowledge

History, language and bias:

According to the Marxist political sociologist Ralph Miliband (1924–94), *'The term 'democracy', which is*

2 The People's Republic of China (1949–2005)

always used to describe Western-style regimes, carries a strong ideological and propagandist charge...' So is it possible for historians to arrive at a common definition of 'democracy' that is not influenced by cultural values? Does 'democracy' refer only to political aspects such as multi-party parliamentary systems, with regular elections? Or – as Sources 2.3 and 2.4 seem to suggest – does democracy also depend on other additional factors, such as a general equality of social conditions (including income, wealth, and education and health opportunities) between citizens?

Government, the CCP and the PLA

The new Government Administrative Council (GAC) (known as the State Council after 1954) had a Central Military Commission, answerable to the National People's Congress, to oversee the military. However, as with other civil government structures and posts, the CCP also had its own Military Affairs Commission, which was accountable to the Party's Central Committee.

Given the Party's predominating influence, this dual government and Party oversight over the PLA gave the CCP, in practice, overall control. This Party control was further increased by the fact that, in 1949, the PLA was led by **Zhu De**, who was one of Mao's firmest supporters.

Zhu De (1886–1976):

He joined the CCP while in Germany in the early 1920s, and was a close supporter of Mao from 1928. As chairman of the Central Revolutionary Military Commission, he was largely responsible for the Red Army's military organisation during the Civil War, eventually becoming its Commander-in-Chief. He retained this position in the re-named People's Liberation Army from 1949 until 1954; in 1955, he became one of the PLA's ten Marshals. Although he remained loyal to Mao, his refusal to strongly condemn Peng Dehuai at the Lushan Conference in 1959 (see Chapter 3) led to the loss of several of his positions. In 1969, during the Cultural Revolution, he was temporarily purged but Zhou's support meant he was not imprisoned. In 1973, he was rehabilitated.

The consolidation of the Communist State, 1949–55

China's eighteen provinces were merged to form six large – essentially military – regions, each made up of smaller units ranging upwards from administrative villages and towns to districts, cities, counties and provinces. At each of these levels, there were Communist committees that, among other things, had to ensure that each unit carried out government decisions.

Figure 2.2: The six administrative regions and the provinces of the PRC, as established after 1949.

From 1949 until the 1954 constitution, the civilian administration was overshadowed by the military, as the PLA was used to help re-establish law and order via several 'reunification campaigns'. As the Civil War and the Japanese invasion had greatly disrupted China's administrative and communications systems, the PLA was also used to establish central control.

Reunification campaigns

Although the Communists had won the Civil War in 1949, they did not yet control the whole of China. Many outlying border provinces in China still contained GMD or warlord armies that continued armed resistance to the new government. Several 'bandit' groups also operated in some areas. In addition, US support for Jiang – which increased after

2 The People's Republic of China (1949–2005)

the outbreak of the Korean War in June 1950 – made Jiang's intention to invade a real threat to the newly established government on mainland China.

The PLA quickly established control of Guangdong province in October 1949; and, by early 1950, the provinces of Guizhou, Guangxi and Hainan Island, and Yunnan were under Communist control. There was considerably more GMD resistance in Xianjiang province until March 1950, by which time all organised GMD military actions were ended on mainland China.

Finally, there was the question of Tibet, which had been part of the Chinese empire since 1720. After 1911, Tibet's religious and political ruler, the Dalai Lama, had taken advantage of the turmoil of revolution to unilaterally declare independence from China. In 1949, most Chinese nationalists – whether communist or non-communist – wanted to restore Chinese control. Using a combination of negotiation, compromises and military force, the PLA restored Chinese control during 1950–51.

> **DISCUSSION POINT**
>
> Since the mid 20th century, Tibet has been a matter of international controversy. Do you think the case of Tibetan nationalists for independence is overwhelming – or do you think Chinese nationalist arguments have any significant validity? Do some extra reading on this topic to help you come to some conclusions.

Government and the CCP

It soon became apparent that real power lay with the CCP which, in 1949, numbered almost 5 million. The Party institution that, in principle, was most powerful was the National Party Congress (NPC). Among other things, it was the NPC that chose the top Party leaders. The NPC also elected the Central Committee (CC) of the CCP which, in 1949, consisted of the 44 most important Party leaders. It was the CC that, in practice, wielded more power than the NCP, as the CC was in session all year round, whereas the NCP only met, at irregular intervals, for about two weeks.

The consolidation of the Communist State, 1949–55

The meetings of the CC – known as plenums – made many important decisions about policies and Party posts. However, there were other top party bodies which were even more powerful than the CC: these were the Political Bureau (Politburo) and the Standing Committee of the Politburo. In 1949, the Politburo consisted of the fourteen most senior CCP leaders; while its Standing Committee – which was in virtual permanent session – was made up of the five most important Party leaders. These were: Mao, **Liu Shaoqi**, Zhou Enlai, Zhu De and **Chen Yun**. For most of the 1950s, Mao was usually able to dominate this small but very powerful group.

Liu Shaoqi (1898–1969):

In 1921, Liu became a founder-member of the CCP, while being educated in the Soviet Union; from the late 1930s, he became the main theoretician of the CCP. After 1949, he had several leading Party and state posts and, by 1956, was seen by many as Mao's heir apparent. Following the disaster of the Great Leap Forward (see Chapter 3), he became president of China in 1959, when Mao resigned from that post. Liu supported economic reforms involving limited 'market mechanisms' for rebuilding the economy. As a result, in 1968, he was accused of being a 'capitalist roader' during the Cultural Revolution and was purged from all his posts. He was imprisoned and died as a result of being badly treated. He was posthumously rehabilitated in 1980.

Chen Yun (1905–95):

Chen joined the CCP in 1924, and received economic training in the USSR, and soon became prominent in Mao's China. As one of the 'first generation' of leaders, he helped draft China's First Five-Year Plan in 1952, but frequently attempted to moderate Mao's more radical economic policies. After Mao's death in 1976, he was one of those calling for Deng's rehabilitation. In 1979, he was appointed head of the National Economic and Financial Commission, and became one of the 'Eight Elders'. However, while favouring the use of some capitalist aspects, he was concerned that socialism should not be abandoned and, in 1981, attacked what he called 'bourgeois liberalisation'. In 1982, he resigned from the Politburo and the Central Committee, and began to raise concerns that Deng's economic reforms were undermining socialist principles.

The People's Republic of China (1949–2005)

Because many leading CCP members also held government and administrative posts, and because the Party had a system of committees that paralleled the government and administrative structures, the CCP had tremendous influence over the government.

'Rectification' campaigns and CCP control

In the early years, the CCP followed a general policy based on cooperation with the 'national' and 'petty bourgeoisie'. However, Mao – and several other CCP leaders – remained concerned by the influence of 'counter-revolutionary elements' and 'class enemies'. So, from 1949, they initiated a series of mass political campaigns to strengthen the Party's political control.

Particularly important was to establish political control of China's towns and cities from which, since the late 1920s, the CCP had been largely expelled by the civil war unleashed by Jiang and the GMD. In the main, the urban areas were where those most opposed to the CCP lived: these were the members and supporters of the GMD: industrial capitalists, and the middle classes.

> **ACTIVITY**
>
> With a partner, carry out some additional research on the groups that, according to the CCP, were 'counter-revolutionaries' and 'class enemies'. Then draw up a table listing the different categories, and what was done to them. Finally, discuss with another group the extent to which such groups might have posed a threat to the new government.

After 1949, therefore, propaganda was conducted to overcome 'bourgeois individualism'. This was accompanied by several self-criticism and rectification campaigns designed to get individuals to alter or 'rectify' their ideas, thoughts and actions to those more supportive of the aims of the revolution. During the Korean War, from 1950 to 1953, these campaigns became increasingly bitter.

The consolidation of the Communist State, 1949–55

Consequently, during 1950–51, mass rallies were organised, at which people were encouraged to bring 'enemies' and 'reactionaries' to account. These were mostly people who had collaborated with the Japanese or GMD. In all, such People's Courts condemned almost 1 million 'reactionaries' to death. Later in 1951, the Communists also began a movement for 'thought reform' of intellectuals, based on a study of Mao's writings. One way to try to achieve this was to get them to 'self-criticise' their pre-revolutionary ideas at public meetings.

SOURCE 2.5

On the pretext of defending the people from their enemies, it was not long before Mao and the CCP began to resort to terror as a basic method of control. It soon became clear that China was to be turned into a one-party state. At the time of the Communist success in 1949 there had been over ten separate political parties in China. These included the Left GMD and the Democratic League, splinter parties that had broken away from Chiang Kaishek's [Jiang Jieshi's] Nationalists. By 1952 they had disappeared, destroyed in a set of repressive moves which denied the right of any party to exist other than the Chinese Communist Party.

The political purges were accompanied by a series of mass campaigns aimed at extending the CCP's authority over the people of China. A concerted attack was launched against 'counter-revolutionaries and imperialists', catch-all terms that were used to condemn anyone who showed signs of disapproving of the Communist regime.

Lynch, M. 2008. **The People's Republic of China 1949–76**. London. Hodder. p.23

QUESTION

Compare and contrast what Sources 2.5 and 2.6 say about the purposes of the 'Rectification' campaigns launched by the CCP in the early 1950s.

2 The People's Republic of China (1949–2005)

> **SOURCE 2.6**
>
> Once political and economic stability had been achieved, the Communists moved quickly to end their reliance on what they regarded as the least politically reliable members of the urban population. Beginning in late 1951, this took the form of three politically repressive campaigns: the thought reform movement directed primarily against intellectuals; the Sanfan ('three anti') campaign against bureaucratic corruption and inefficiency; and the Wufan ('five anti') campaign which was essentially an attack on the bourgeoisie. Unlike the preceding campaign against 'counterrevolutionaries,' which attempted to eliminate political dissent in society in general, the new movements had specific goals aimed against particular élite groups in the cities. And unlike the concurrent land reform campaign which served to destroy the rural gentry, a class which had nothing to offer the new society, the urban campaigns aimed not to destroy social groups but rather to establish firmer political control over them. The thrust was to politicize people with expertise while preserving them and their talents to serve society. Unlike the gentry and the counterrevolutionaries, the people to be politicized were still regarded as members of 'the people.'
>
> Meisner, M. 1999. **Mao's China and After: A History of the People's Republic.** *New York, The Free Press, pp. 85–6*

The earliest mass campaign was that associated with the Land Reform programme (see Section 2.2) – but this was as much an economic campaign as it was a political one. Another of these campaigns – the 'Resist America and Aid Korea' campaign was clearly closely linked to the Korean War, and is dealt with in Chapter 5. The three most important political campaigns were launched to win over and control the urban population, and were closely linked – in fact, they often overlapped.

The 'Suppression of Counter-Revolutionaries' campaign, 1950–51

This was focused on 'active counter-revolutionaries': these included leading members and officers of the GMD and its army, senior police officers and GMD spies. However, as the campaign unfolded, it also affected thousands of minor officials.

Between January and October 1950, almost 4000 people were arrested as counter-revolutionary agents and, in July 1950, Zhou signed an order for the campaign – which soon became known as 'Eliminate Counter-Revolutionary Elements' – to be stepped up. Mao gave his official support and, in February 1951, the government issued the Regulations. These were based on the Common Programme, and defined 'counter-revolutionary crimes' as those which tried to disrupt or overthrow the newly established People's Democracy.

This campaign was also directed at the secret societies of various religious sects – such as the Buddhists – and members of the criminal gangs that had long operated in urban areas and had often collaborated with the GMD to eliminate trade union and communist militants.

Those found guilty faced life imprisonment or execution. The harshness of these Regulations reflected, in large part, the CCP leadership's concerns over the threats posed by Taiwan and the US, which openly backed the GMD as the legitimate rulers of China. In addition, the scale of this campaign is not too surprising, given that it followed closely on from an extremely bitter and violent civil war lasting more than 20 years. However, there were many cases where those accused of counter-revolution were released, while many others were given short prison sentences or sent to labour camps.

The campaign involved large numbers of people – according to historian Michael Dillon, up to 80 per cent of the population were involved in what became a mass movement. Factories, schools, government offices and neighbourhood organisations formed committees to root out counter-revolutionaries. As Source 2.7 shows, mass meetings were held in which people were encouraged to denounce to the security forces and police those who had supported the GMD.

2 The People's Republic of China (1949–2005)

> **SOURCE 2.7**
>
> A great number of people have denounced counter-revolutionaries. Wives have denounced their counter-revolutionary husbands; children have denounced their fathers. Young students have caught counter-revolutionaries and brought them to the security offices. This shows that the great propaganda has moved the masses to struggle against the counter-revolutionaries and that the People's Government and the People struggle together. Accusation meetings have been held in many quarters of Beijing, and a total of 200 000 people have taken part in them. Many have written letters to the police… The government will eradicate the counter-revolutionaries totally. In recent days we have examined the cases of 500 persons. Most of them were denounced by others; 221 will be executed.
>
> *Extracts from an address made by Luo Ruiqing, the Security Minister, to a mass meeting in Beijing in May 1951. Quoted in: Dillon, M. 2012.* **China: A Modern History.** *New York. I. B. Tauris. p.269*

Accurate estimates of the total number of executions have proved difficult – in part, because of propaganda and counter-propaganda between the PRC and Taiwan. In addition, the pressures of forced confessions at mass meetings led to large numbers – possibly several hundreds of thousands – of those accused committing suicide.

The 'Three-Anti' campaign, 1951

The main aim of this campaign – the *Sanfan* campaign – was to end corruption, waste and obstruction arising from the emerging culture of bureaucracy. It, too, was essentially urban, and was directed primarily at CCP cadres, state officials, managers and members of the police. It was particularly aimed at those working in financial and economic departments, who were suspected of corruption as a result of their connections to the pre-1949 commercial and banking élites. The campaign was initially begun in August 1951 by **Gao Gang**, on a trial basis in Northeast China – it was then launched as a national campaign in early December.

The consolidation of the Communist State, 1949–55

> **Gao Gang (1905–54):**
> Gao joined the CCP in 1926, and during the 1930s had controlled a communist soviet in Shaanxi province, where the Long March ended in 1935. In 1943, he was appointed to the Politburo of the CCP, and later became Party chairman in Manchuria, where he also controlled the army. In 1952, he had been put in charge of the Central Planning Commission, where he had supported Mao's ideas for a five-year plan. However, he was purged in 1954, when he tried to undermine the positions of leading Communists such as Zhou Enlai and Liu Shaoqi.

This was definitely aimed at communists as well as non-communists – a Party report issued in 1957 stated that the aim had been to purge 25 per cent of Party members, and had just about achieved that target. Significantly, future mass campaigns also set targets for the number of offenders to be identified and punished. Government leaders, including Zhou, had been encouraged to launch this new campaign by the success of the 'Resist America – Aid Korea' campaign. By the end of December 1951, the 'Three-Anti' campaign took over from other political campaigns – including an internal Party 'rectification' campaign – as an important way to curb corruption while trying to manage the developing urban economy.

In January 1952, Mao intervened to step up the pace of the campaign. Meetings, articles and cartoons in the press, and displays in shop windows, stressed the financial temptations that businesses used to corrupt Party and state officials. Soon, 'mass struggle meetings' were held in workplaces: individuals suspected of corruption were forced to confess in public and otherwise humiliated. Though some 'struggle sessions' also involved physical violence, the main aim was to use a combination of peer pressure and humiliation to bring such people 'into line'. As the campaign unfolded, it spread from workplaces associated with the financial and business sectors to institutions of education.

The 'Five-Anti' campaign, 1952

While the 'Three-Anti' campaign was still taking place, another campaign was launched in January 1952 against five other 'evils': theft of state property, fraud on state contracts, bribery, tax-evasion and leaking state and economic secrets. This campaign – the *Wufan* campaign – was essentially directed against the 'national bourgeoisie' – especially the

2 The People's Republic of China (1949–2005)

wealthiest industrialists and merchants – and affected all the main urban areas. By 1952, the CCP had come to see such classes as blocking the aim of moving to a socialist economy.

Workers' organisations were encouraged to investigate employers' business affairs, and many employers were forced to undertake self-criticisms and 'thought reform'. Those accused faced fines and property confiscations, and several were then sent to labour camps. If they cooperated and confessed their faults, and paid the necessary fines – sometimes, the government loaned the victims the necessary money – they were usually allowed to return to their businesses.

Very often, this campaign pushed private owners to agree to 'state-private' arrangements. This meant they had to sell part of their business to the state, and accept the appointment of a state manager who then worked alongside them. These new 'middle managers' were often appointed from among the ranks of those who had played an active part in the campaign.

> **QUESTION**
> What was the main aim of these mass campaigns?

Purging the CCP

As well as dealing with 'rightists' of various sorts, Mao was also concerned with ensuring that members of the CCP – including the leadership – had the 'right' political attitudes. In late 1953, he launched what turned out to be the first of several major purges of leading members of the CCP. This purge was linked to the intense political debates that had broken out within the CCP leadership when Mao had first announced his intention of launching a five-year plan for industry (see Section 2.2).

The Gao Gang Affair

The two main victims were Gao Gang and **Rao Shushi**. Gao had backed Mao's plans for moving towards a fully socialist economy, which were being opposed by Zhou Enlai and Liu Shaoqi. Then, supported by Rao, Gao began to put himself forward to some senior members of the CCP as a replacement for Zhou as vice-chairman of the CCP. He

The consolidation of the Communist State, 1949–55

also began attempts to undermine Liu's position in the government. Gao believed Mao would support his plans as, during late 1952 and early 1953, Mao had expressed concerns to him about the caution being shown by Zhou and Liu.

> **Rao Shushi (1903–75):**
>
> Rao joined the CCP in 1925, and was a political commissar during the Civil War. In 1949, he was given several key appointments in the administrative region of East China: chairman of the Military and Political Committee, general secretary of the local bureau of the CCP and governor. In 1953, he became the minister in charge of party organisation. His decision to support Gao led to his downfall.

However, Chen Yun and Deng Xiaoping revealed his plans to Zhou and Mao, as they believed Gao was undermining Party unity. In December 1953, both Gao and Rao were accused of 'underground activities', and Mao accused them of forming an 'antiparty alliance'. Gao was also accused of having very close ties to the Soviet Union's leadership. This was probably his main 'crime', as most CCP leaders – while grateful for Soviet financial and technical assistance – had no intention of allowing the USSR to increase its political influence in China.

In February 1954, Mao appointed Liu to organise a meeting to discuss party unity. Gao committed suicide in August 1954, while Rao was arrested. In 1955, both of them were expelled from the CCP, and Rao was imprisoned; he was then sent to work on a farm until his death in March 1975.

ACTIVITY

Using whatever additional sources are available to you, try to find out more about the 'Gao Gang Affair'. Then write a short paragraph to explain what you consider to have been its main cause.

# 2

The People's Republic of China (1949–2005)

The *Sufan* Movement

In March 1955, the CCP Conference called for a more extensive purge of all Party cadres (officials) – the *Sufan* Movement, or the 'Campaign to Wipe Out Hidden Counter-revolutionaries'. This was endorsed by the CC in July and began in August.

Initially, this was intended to identify other supporters of Gao and Rao; it continued until early 1956, and was aimed at 'reactionary' cadres posing as 'Marxist-Leninists'. Those accused were interrogated and – like during the earlier 'rectification' campaigns – forced to make written or oral 'confessions'. During 1955, as many as 150 000 Party and government cadres were detained – those designated as counter-revolutionaries were sent to labour re-education camps. Yet, the following year, most were released and reinstated.

However, the main thrust of this campaign seems to have been designed to reassert Party control over the large numbers of economic and political experts and bureaucrats required for the implementation of the Five-Year Plan (see Section 2.2). Later, the attempt to strengthen Party control was extended to China's intelligentsia.

China's intelligentsia and the CCP

Many of China's intelligentsia (or intellectuals) – usually defined as the 'educated levels' who had been to colleges or universities and were employed in the professions – had had a generally positive attitude towards the CCP because of its resistance to the Japanese invaders before 1949, and because of its intention after 1949 to create a modern 'New' China.

However, Communist attempts during the 1950s to establish a good working relationship with intellectuals increasingly encountered several problems. In part, this reflected the limited contact the mainly rural-based CCP had had with intellectuals before 1949. Many leading Communists – especially Mao – were very suspicious of this group and their determination to maintain intellectual independence.

The first real signs of conflict came in 1950 when, because of the start of the Korean War, the Party decided that university lecturers, writers, artists and other professional and cultural workers (such as secondary school teachers) needed to undergo a period of 'thought reform'. In particular, this was applied to anyone who had studied in Europe or the US. At the same time, libraries and bookshops were instructed to weed

The consolidation of the Communist State, 1949–55

out 'counter-revolutionary' texts – especially certain books from the classical Chinese tradition and works by foreign writers.

In the second half of 1954 – after the Gao Gang Affair had been resolved – a clash emerged between the Party and intellectuals involved in cultural and artistic matters. In particular, the clash revolved round two individuals: **Feng Xuefeng** and **Hu Feng**. The CCP leadership decided that a campaign against 'bourgeois idealism' and 'individualism' was needed, in order to establish the Party view that the primary function of literature and art was to serve the revolution and the people, rather than just expressing individual thoughts and feelings. Feng was dismissed for having published an article by a literary historian whose views were condemned as being too 'individualistic'.

Feng Xuefeng (1903–76):

Feng was a poet, literary theorist and translator and, for a time, was a spokesperson for the CCP. In 1952, he became editor of the official literary and art magazine, *Wenyibao*. However, his criticisms of the Party's attempts to enforce some political control over literature and art, led to his dismissal for being a 'rightist'. He took part in the Hundred Flowers campaign in 1957, but was again accused of being a rightist and was sent for 'reform through labour'. His last years were spent doing manual labour during the Cultural Revolution.

Hu Feng (1902–85):

Hu had been an early supporter of the CCP, and had joined its Youth League as early as 1923. In 1933, he had joined the League of Left-Wing Writers in Shanghai and, by 1949, was an established writer and a respected literary and art critic. However, in the 1930s, he had clashed with Zhou Yang who, since 1949, had been vice-minister for culture and the Party's propaganda commissar. In 1955, Zhou Yang decided to attack him, along with Feng Xuefeng. Hu was imprisoned for his refusal to subordinate literature to Party views about 'socialist realism' (which identified the topics writers should deal with, and how they should deal with them), and was not released until 1979; in 1988, he was rehabilitated posthumously.

2 The People's Republic of China (1949–2005)

The dismissal of Feng prompted Hu to criticise the Party's cultural policy. Zhou Yang, the Party's cultural chief, decided Hu should be particularly singled out in this new cultural campaign against intellectuals. He was forced to make a formal self-criticism in May 1955; he was then denounced as a counter-revolutionary by Mao. He was dismissed from all his posts and imprisoned. The CCP then widened the campaign into a general campaign against 'hidden counter-revolutionaries'. Periodic attacks – involving mass campaigns, self-criticism and imprisonment – on intellectuals, writers and artists then followed after 1955, culminating in the Cultural Revolution (see Chapter 4).

2.2 What were the main economic policies during the period 1949–55?

Apart from various political steps, the Communists also consolidated their rule by passing a series of economic and social reforms. In 1949, when the CCP came to power, most of China's economy was essentially a pre-modern agricultural one. The use of old-fashioned basic agricultural equipment still predominated, and the scarcity of arable land and inefficient farming methods – along with a growing population – had resulted in frequent famines before 1949.

Since 1911, China's agriculture and industry had been greatly disrupted by civil and international war. In both urban and rural areas, there were serious food shortages. In addition, urban areas suffered from high inflation, unemployment, corruption, gambling, prostitution and drug addiction. The CCP thus implemented economic policies designed to resolve some of these fundamental problems.

Early reforms, 1949–52

The new government concentrated on policies for tackling the twin problems of providing sufficient food for China's population of 500 million (increasing rapidly by 15 million a year); and for stimulating the national economy. The CCP did not, at this stage, envisage a rapid

The consolidation of the Communist State, 1949–55

transformation of China into a socialist society. Instead, they spoke of *'Three years of recovery; then ten years of development'*.

Land reform

In 1949, grain production in China was just 113 million tons – an amount totally inadequate to feed China's population. Initially, the new Communist-dominated government extended many of the policies that had been implemented in the Communist soviets and the areas that the Communist Red Army had 'liberated' from GMD rule before 1949. Especially important was taking land from wealthy landowners and sharing it among the peasants – many of whom, before 1949, had had to pay high rents or were too poor to rent any land at all.

Before 1949, only about 20 per cent of China's villages had had any experience of the CCP's land reform. By then, peasants made up about 70 per cent of China's population of 500 million, and the Communists had long promised to distribute 'land to the tiller'. However, in addition to honouring their promise to the peasants – and so retain their support – the CCP saw land reform as a way of destroying a class of potential counter-revolutionaries, and enhancing their own political control. Furthermore, such reform would increase agricultural production, which – as well as feeding China's rising population – would pave the way for China's industrial development.

The Agrarian Reform Law, 1950

On 14 June 1950, the Agrarian Reform Law was presented to the CPPCC by Liu Shaoqi and, at the end of the month, was adopted by the government. The main points of this were agreed by most of the CCP leaders – including Mao. In 1950, wealthy landlords (around 4 per cent of the rural population) owned over 30 per cent of all cultivated land.

Almost 20 million people were classified as members of landlord families. Those who it was decided had more land than they needed had their surplus land confiscated and distributed to landless and poor peasants. However, most landlords were left with enough land on which they could work to feed themselves and their families. After five years of such 'reform through labour', ex-landlords could have their 'landlord class' status officially removed. In addition, land belonging to temples, monasteries and churches was also confiscated and redistributed. From

2 The People's Republic of China (1949–2005)

1950 to 1953, around 40% of all farmland was taken away and given to over 300 million peasants.

However, land and other properties used by landlords for industrial and commercial enterprises were not confiscated. Also protected was the land held by 'rich' peasants – even those who employed labourers. This was because they produced almost 50 per cent of total agricultural production, despite being only 6 per cent of the total population. Rich peasants were also allowed to continue renting land to tenants.

To carry all this through, the CCP relied on the middle peasants who, although only 20 per cent of the rural population, soon provided over a third of the leaders of peasant associations. None of their land was subject to confiscation, and they were allowed to obtain as much as 25 per cent of their income from hiring labourers or renting out land.

This disappointed the poor peasants, as the CCP had previously promised a more equal distribution of land. The failure to honour this promise in the first few years was mainly the result of the government's fear of too much social disruption in the countryside leading to a drop in production. However, Mao and other leaders saw this moderate policy as just the first stage towards the eventual collectivisation of agriculture.

ACTIVITY
Write a couple of paragraphs to explain why many peasants were disappointed by aspects of the first phase of land reform.

Within three years, the CCP brought about a massive social revolution in the countryside as regards landownership. By 1952, the rural élites that had dominated China for over two thousand years had been dispossessed. By expropriating the landlord class and redistributing the land among the peasantry, the Communists in effect carried out a 'bourgeois' revolution by creating a massive class of small-scale capitalist peasants. This created massive peasant support for the CCP, which was already high in areas that had experienced their land reforms in Communist-controlled areas before 1949. Later, the CCP was able to use this support to begin moves towards collectivisation without too much opposition. However, although land was taken from the larger landowners and distributed to individual peasant families, the basis of

The consolidation of the Communist State, 1949–55

land ownership remained private. Thus this was not a *socialist* revolution, which would require the social – as opposed to private – landownership of land.

'Speaking bitterness'

The new law encouraged peasants to decide who were landlords or 'rich' peasants, and which ones had treated people harshly. However, unlike the often uncontrolled violence that had accompanied pre-1949 land reform, the new government tried to curb this, in the hope that a more orderly land transfer would not disrupt production. Unlike the urban bourgeoisie whose skills the government needed to carry through industrial modernisation and development, the rural landlord class contributed very little to agricultural production.

Yet, despite the government's hopes for an essentially peaceful reform process, there was great bitterness in many rural areas against those who had ruthlessly exploited them before 1949 – as shown by Sources 2.8 and 2.9. As a result, a bitter class struggle (made worse by the impact of the Korean War) often took place at mass 'struggle meetings', which CCP cadres could not always control. Lucky landlords had to apologise for their past behaviour at these mass meetings – the unlucky (approximately 1 million) faced summary execution; many more were sent to labour camps, after mass public trials.

SOURCE 2.8

Rather than simply distribute land to the landless, CCP workers, or cadres, were assigned to villages across China. After identifying the biggest landholders, or landlords, in the village, their task was to organize meetings of the villagers to discuss the 'bitterness' of the past and denounce the landlords as a symbol of the villagers' past oppression. Only after such 'speak bitterness meetings' ended in a verdict on the landlords was the actual land reform carried out. In some instances, landlords judged by the villagers to be exploiters or bullies faced execution; those not considered enemies of the people were denounced and then released with only enough land to support themselves and their families. It is estimated that during the period of the land reform, some 2–3 million landlords were executed by peasant tribunals led by Party representatives.

Benson, L. 2002. **China Since 1949.** *Harlow, Longman, p.25*

2 The People's Republic of China (1949–2005)

Figure 2.3: A 'speak bitterness' meeting of a People's Court trying a landlord as part of the first stage of land reform. The landlord is the person kneeling before the committee.

SOURCE 2.9

When the final struggle began Ching-ho [a local landlord] was faced not only with those hundred accusations but with many many more. Old women who had never spoken in public before stood up to accuse him. Even Li Mao's wife – a woman so pitiable she hardly dared look anyone in the face – shook her fist before his nose and cried out, 'Once I went to glean wheat on your land. But you cursed me and drove me away. Why did you curse me and beat me? And why did you seize the wheat I had already gleaned?' Altogether over 180 opinions were raised. Ching-ho had no answer to any of them. He stood there with his head bowed. We asked him whether the accusations were false or true. He said they were all true. When the committee of our Association met to figure up what he owed, it came to 400 bags of milled grain, not coarse grain… We went to register his grain and altogether found but 200 bags of unmilled millet – only a quarter of what he owed us… So then we began to beat him… Then Ching-ho admitted that he had hid 110 silver dollars…

The consolidation of the Communist State, 1949–55

> Altogether we got $500 from Ching-ho that night… All said, 'In the past we never lived through a happy New Year because he always asked for his rent and interest then and cleared our houses bare. This time we'll eat what we like,' and everyone ate his fill [of Ching-ho's food] and didn't even notice the cold.
>
> *A villager's account of a 'speak bitterness' meeting, quoted in Hinton, W. 1968.* **Fanshen: A Documentary of a Revolution in a Chinese Village.** *New York, Random House, pp.137–8*

As the Korean crisis worsened, the CCP became concerned to speed up the reform process, in order to more quickly eliminate a potential counter-revolutionary class. The various political repression campaigns of 1951 also added to the atmosphere of fear and violence.

Peasant cooperation

Because most peasants had no equipment, and because their farms were very small, many formed Mutual Aid Teams, made up of about 10 cooperating families. Although labour and tools were pooled, the latter remained the property of individual families. In fact, many areas of China already had a similar tradition of helping each other during busy times. The CCP favoured this development as it fostered a collective spirit.

Results

By and large, the land reform from 1950 to 1952 had succeeded in eliminating the landlord class, without disrupting production. In fact, total annual production increased by an average of 15 per cent each year. In part, this was also the result of the new irrigation and flood-control projects begun in 1949, campaigns against pests, increased use of fertilizers and taking some uncultivated lands into production.

However, total grain production (as opposed to all foodstuffs) in 1952 was, according to official figures, only 9 per cent higher than in pre-war years – this was not just insufficient for feeding China's growing population, but was also unable to provide the surplus funds needed for industrial development. Thus, for these – and other – reasons, the CCP decided it needed to begin the 'transition to socialism', in both industry and agriculture.

2 The People's Republic of China (1949–2005)

> **QUESTION**
> Why, by 1952, did the CCP feel that its land reform programme had to be stepped up?

Industrial reforms

In 1949, China's urban population was about 20% of the country's total population. Initially, the Communist-dominated coalition government moved slowly to develop its industry. In 1949, most of China's – not very extensive – industry was owned by foreign companies. One of the government's first steps was to nationalise, without compensation, the largest industrial firms and commercial enterprises owned by the 'bureaucratic bourgeoisie', and those owned by foreign companies and GMD supporters. Most of the latter had fled with Jiang to Taiwan.

In March 1950, the government began to deal with inflation by centralising finance and taxation, and restricting the circulation of foreign currencies. The banks were also nationalised and, in 1951, a People's Bank was set up, which by 1955, had ended inflation by taking control of all financial transactions and by limiting the issue of bank notes. Thus, as early as 1950, much of the most modern elements of China's urban economy were already 'socialist'.

'National Capitalism'

The 'United Front' approach saw the government prepared to cooperate with small-scale Chinese capitalists – known as the 'national bourgeoisie' – in what was known as 'National Capitalism'. These were mainly commercial entrepreneurs, owners of small factories and workshops, shopkeepers, and managers of industrial and commercial enterprises. While these people were suspicious of the long-term aims of the victorious CCP, they were won over by their stated policy of controlling but not immediately eliminating capitalism. This was done in order to avoid further disrupting the already fragile and devastated economy.

According to Mao, it would be necessary to use elements of urban and rural capitalism to improve and modernise the national economy and that, therefore, the policy of Communists would be to 'control not eliminate capitalism'. As a result, most small firms were left in the hands of their private owners, in what was an urban mixed economy, comprising both state- and private-owned firms.

The consolidation of the Communist State, 1949–55

In fact, the 'national bourgeoisie' were assisted by the new government: by 1953, the number of privately owned industries had increased from 123 000 to 150 000, while the number of workers in private firms rose from 1.6 million to 2.2 million. In all, this private sector accounted for almost 40 per cent of China's industrial output. The government even used nationalist pleas to encourage some of those who had fled in 1949 to return to aid economic reconstruction, and help develop and modernise China's economy.

The Communists concentrated on dealing with unemployment by placing large state contracts with private firms, and improving workers' pay and rights by insisting that firms paid a minimum wage and gave paid holidays to workers. In addition, the government controlled access to raw materials. However, private firms still operated as capitalist ventures – receiving profits (though these were controlled) that were big enough to give these 'national capitalists' a very comfortable life-style.

'The transition to socialism', 1953–55

As a result of the Treaty of Friendship, Alliance and Mutual Assistance signed between the Soviet Union and China in January 1950, China was to receive financial and technical assistance from the USSR for the next 15 years. Further agreements were made in 1953, 1954 and 1956. Although the financial assistance mainly consisted of short-term credits rather than loans, over 10 000 Soviet engineers were sent to China – all this helped create 300 modern industrial plants.

By 1952, the leaders of the CCP felt they had achieved sufficient economic recovery to move on to their promised 'ten years of development'. In November 1952, acting on Soviet advice, Mao set up a State Planning Commission – headed by Gao Gang – to design a Five-Year Plan to expand and modernise China's economy in both agriculture and industry. Initially, however, China's involvement in the Korean War until 1953 (see Chapter 5) meant there was little surplus funding for this project.

When the Plan was first announced in late 1952, total industrial and agricultural production – despite the revival of China's war-wrecked economy – was still only at mid 1930s levels; while modern transportation systems were still largely lacking. Nonetheless, in January 1953, it was announced that the 'bourgeois-democratic' phase of the

The People's Republic of China (1949–2005)

revolution was over, and that its socialist phase was now beginning. On 1 October, on the fourth anniversary of the founding of the PRC, the government set out its aims for the 'transition to socialism'.

Mao and his supporters saw the development of industry as allowing for the eventual collectivisation of agriculture, while the latter would then allow for the completion of the socialist revolution. Thus, both industry and agriculture were to be tackled at the same time.

The First Five-Year Plan and industry

The First Five-Year Plan was designed to build up heavy industry (such as steel, machinery, chemicals, coal, electricity) over the period 1953–57. This was to be largely financed by surpluses coming from a more efficient agriculture. At first, it was implemented in the Northeast Administrative Area, headed by Gao Gang – who then rolled the Plan out to the rest of China.

The main thrust of the Five-Year Plan was towards the 'socialist transformation of industry' via a process of nationalisation and the development of heavy industry. To begin with, many private businesses were converted into 'joint private-state enterprises', with most of the investment – and control – coming from the government. Many other owners were persuaded to sell their companies to the government, in return for generous compensation. Many owners and directors remained in executive positions on the boards of these companies, and continued to receive dividends from their shares from the company profits – this continued until 1962.

By the end of 1955, the private sector of China's urban economy had been eliminated, with all medium and large-scale factories and commercial enterprises nationalised. However, many smaller handicraft industries and workshops remained either privately owned, or became cooperatives.

Soviet assistance

It was planned to build almost 700 new major heavy-industry enterprises – with nearly 500 to be located in the interior, so that they were nearer to the necessary raw materials. The Soviet Union was to provide 156 industrial units, which were seen by the Chinese planners as 'the core' of their Plan. In fact, though, the Russians financed less than one-third of the costs of these units; while Soviet financial aid was very

The consolidation of the Communist State, 1949–55

limited, amounting to about 3 per cent of China's total investment in the Plan.

However, more significant was the technology, expertise and training provided by the Soviet Union. Over 12 000 Soviet and East European experts were sent to China in the 1950s, and over 6000 Chinese students and 7000 workers travelled to the USSR to be trained in modern science and technology.

Figure 2.4: The steelworks at Anshan, which became China's most important iron and steel complex under the First Five-Year Plan. Much of the initial equipment was provided by the Soviet Union.

Results of the First Five-Year Plan

The targets for industrial growth set by the Plan was 14.7 per cent a year. In fact, Chinese industry grew even more rapidly than this. According to Nicholas Lardy, the annual increase was 18.1 per cent. This was more or less what was claimed by official statistics. However, even more conservative Western estimates calculate that the overall annual

The People's Republic of China (1949–2005)

growth rate was 16 per cent. At the same time, national income grew at an average annual rate of 8.9 per cent.

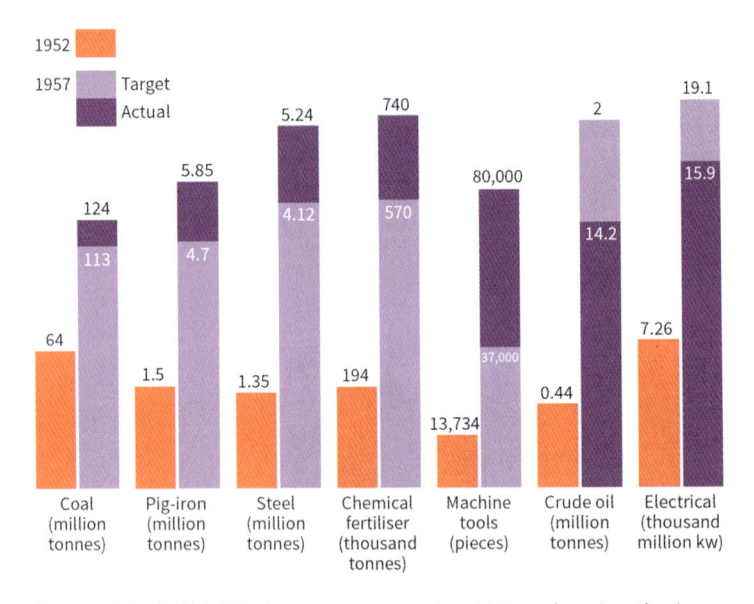

Figure 2.5: Official Chinese government statistics, showing the increased industrial production achieved under the First Five-Year Plan begun in 1953. Although the accuracy of these statistics is questioned, most historians are agreed that tremendous increases were nonetheless achieved.

There were particularly large increases in rolled steel production, cement, coal and electric power. At the same time, China – for the first time – began producing its own trucks, tractors, jet planes and merchant ships. In addition, the number of industrial and construction workers increased from about 6 million to 10 million by the end of the Plan, while China's urban population increased from 70 million to 100 million during the same period.

Overall, total industrial output more than doubled, growing at an average 6.5 per cent per capita each year – this rate, if it had been sustained, would have resulted in a doubling of national income every eleven years. These results compared very favourably for those of other newly independent developing countries – for instance, the figures for India (which had economic conditions similar to those of China) in the 1950s was well under 2 per cent per capita.

The consolidation of the Communist State, 1949–55

Yet, despite these dramatic increases in production, the concentration on heavy industry and rapid industrialisation caused shortages of goods and housing in the towns.

Nonetheless, most contemporary analysts – Communist and non-Communist – judged the results of the Five-Year Plan as broadly successful.

> **KEY CONCEPTS ACTIVITY**
>
> **Significance:** Carry out some additional research on the CCP's industrial reforms, and then write a couple of paragraphs to show how important financial and technical assistance from the Soviet Union was in the early successes of China's First Five-Year Plan.

Impact on industrial workers

However, for China's industrial workers, the rapid industrialisation meant increasing subjection to strict codes of labour discipline. It also led to greater wage and status differentials – and thus inequalities – based on skills and outputs. Before 1952, trade unions had been relatively independent but, by 1955, had largely become state instruments geared to increasing workers' productivity. In addition, the rapid industrialisation required many more administrators, managers and technical experts. As has been seen, this led to concerns about an emerging non-revolutionary bureaucracy. There was also growing inequality between urban and rural areas. This latter problem was something Mao decided to address from 1956 onwards, and eventually led to the Great Leap Forward (see Chapter 3).

The First Five-Year Plan and agriculture

Initially, CCP leaders believed that the move to full collectivisation (i.e. full social ownership) and the abolition of private land ownership, would not be for several years. Mao himself at first believed that for this to happen, industrial development via three Five-Year Plans would be needed. Those Party members who, at the time, urged much more rapid progress were criticised for advocating 'utopian agrarian socialism' – i.e. for believing that China could become socialist just by transforming agriculture.

2 The People's Republic of China (1949–2005)

Mutual Aid Teams

In 1952, a new Land Reform Act proclaimed the need for three further stages of agrarian reform. The first stage began in early 1953, with the government encouraging more peasants – on a voluntary basis – to form Mutual Aid Teams (MATs), which many peasants had begun to set up after 1949. These involved about 6–20 families, with families retaining their own private farms, but assisting each other at busy times. By mid 1953, 40 per cent of peasant families were part of MATs and, by early 1955, this had risen to 65 per cent.

Agricultural Producers' Cooperatives

The second stage, again voluntary, saw peasants encouraged by local Party cadres to organise their farms into larger collectives by combining several MATs into Agricultural Producers' Cooperatives (APCs). These APCs – known as lower-stage (or semi-socialist) cooperatives – each involved between 30 and 100 families, and were intended to improve efficiency and output. Under this system, the land was farmed cooperatively – but still belonged to individual peasant families, which received rent from the cooperatives in return for the use of their land. Families were also allowed to retain some land for their own use – approximately 5 per cent.

Early problems

Initially, the government planned that, by the end of 1957, only one-third of peasant farms would be organised in these APCs. By mid 1953, almost 15 per cent of rural households were members of APCs, and this reform continued during 1953–54. However, the harvests of 1953 and 1954 were relatively poor, which had serious implications for the industrial aspects of the Five-Year Plan. This had calculated that the move to APCs would result in a 30–50% increase in agricultural productivity within two or three years.

According to official statistics, the annual increase in the production of food grains was 3.8%. However, foreign estimates put the growth rate at 2.7% – this barely kept pace with China's population growth of 2.2% annually. In order to feed the growing numbers of industrial workers, the government imposed a relatively high grain tax on peasants, along with high quotas of grain, which peasants had to sell at low fixed prices to the state.

The consolidation of the Communist State, 1949–55

In addition, in 1954, the government banned the sale of surplus grain on the private market – instead, peasants had to sell all surplus grain at the lower prices fixed by the state. This led to food shortages as the drop in peasant incomes led many peasants to flock to the towns instead of growing food in the countryside. While some found employment in factories, many joined the ranks of the unemployed – a problem made worse following the demobilisation of much of the PLA as a result of the end of the Korean War in 1953.

Mao and his supporters then became concerned that the pace of land reform was too slow and was, in fact, undermining plans for developing the national economy. Fears were also expressed about signs of an increased tendency towards rural capitalism, with rising numbers of 'rich' and 'middle' peasants who were reluctant to pool their land with 'poor' peasants. As a result, many 'poor' peasants remained in relative poverty. Finally, there was evidence that rural cadres themselves were becoming more concerned with making money from their farms than with implementing Party policy.

As early as October 1954, the Party's Politburo began to call for a more rapid move towards APCs. The pace was stepped up, and the number of APCs quickly rose. However, there was evidence of mounting peasant dissatisfaction in some areas. As a result, in March 1955, the State Council ordered a temporary halt to further expansion, in case it disrupted food production. Although, in May, the CC ordered a resumption of the APC campaign, it was to be at a more gradual pace.

Stepping up the pace

Mao considered this inadequate and, in July 1955, he spoke of the need to step up the pace, and launch a 'high tide of socialism' in the countryside which, he said, should result in all peasant households being in APCs by 1960. Mao's argument – that conservative Party cadres were holding back the peasant's desire for further reform – was a clear break with the Party consensus up to that date. He bypassed the CC (in which he was in a minority) by presenting his ideas to provincial and regional Party leaders who were in Beijing for a session of the National People's Congress. Mao's plans were then formally ratified by the CC in October 1955.

2 The People's Republic of China (1949–2005)

The pace of cooperativisation was then quickly stepped up: by November 1955, the proportion of households involved increased to 60%. By the end of the year, almost 2 million lower-stage cooperatives had been organised – this marked an increase four times bigger than the figures for mid 1955. By and large, there was no significant opposition to this policy. By then, farming families got about 50% of their income from rent, and 50% from 'work points' (exchanged for food and goods) for their work within the cooperatives – this encouraged many families with larger landholdings to participate.

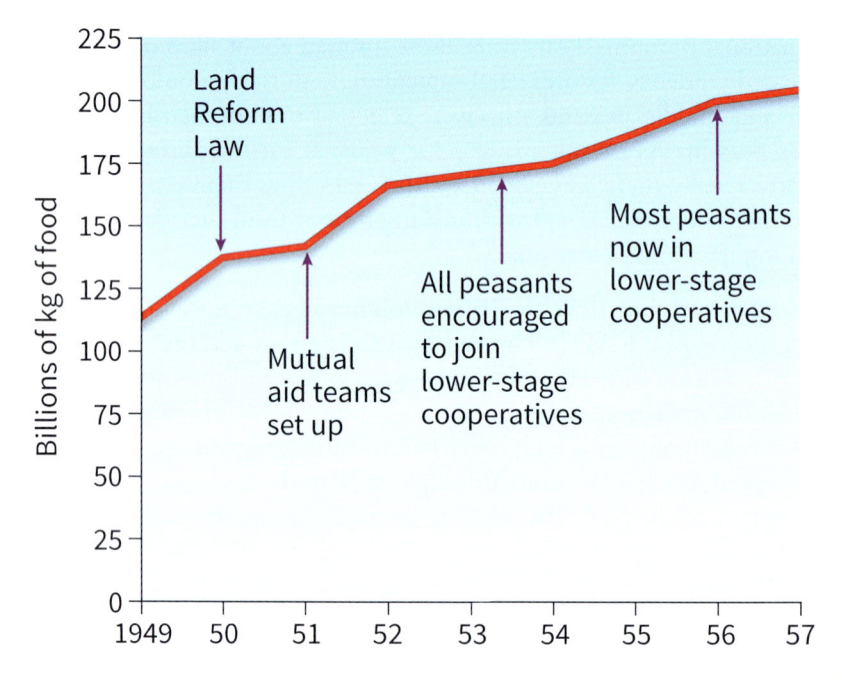

Figure 2.6: The increase in agricultural production achieved in China between 1949 and 1957.

Encouraged by this success, Mao spoke of the 'victory of socialism' by the end of the year and, in December 1955, new targets were set: to complete the semi-socialist stage by the end of 1956, and then to move towards fully socialist collectives by 1960. As in the early history of the CCP, Mao was now identifying the peasantry as crucial for China's 'transition to socialism'.

The consolidation of the Communist State, 1949–55

2.3 What social reforms did the Communists implement during the years 1949–55?

The first six years of the PRC were a time of great change that affected virtually all Chinese people. In particular, there were great changes that affected the rights of the 270 million females who constituted half of China's population. In addition, there were health and social welfare reforms which significantly altered the lives of China's inhabitants.

Greater equality for Chinese women

Women had had very few rights in pre-revolutionary China, which had been a very patriarchal (male-dominated) society.

For centuries, the drowning of female babies had been allowed, and girls could be sold to wealthy men as servants or concubines ('other women' or mistresses). Marriages were usually arranged: as early as 1919 (following the case of a young women who had committed suicide rather than be forced to marry a wealthy man she did not like), Mao had publicly condemned this practice as being, for women, 'indirect rape'. In addition, only men could demand a divorce; and women could be beaten by their fathers, husbands and mothers-in-law.

Women were also not allowed to own property, which was solely in the hands of their husbands. The painful upper-class practice of foot binding – keeping women's feet small was traditionally seen as sexually attractive by many men – had, by the late 19th century, spread to the lower classes. Though, in this case, it was more to make running away from abusive situations more difficult. The Communists were determined to end all of these inequalities.

Communist attitudes

The CCP had long advocated equality for women and the ending of their second-class status. Mao himself had once said that 'Women hold up half the sky'. During the Civil War in the 1930s and 1940s, the CCP under Mao insisted that women were the equal of men, and many women had played leading roles in the Jiangxi and Yanan soviets.

2 The People's Republic of China (1949–2005)

However, some leading Chinese feminist writers – such as **Ding Ling** – have suggested that, in practice, Mao's commitment to women's equality was often limited. Several foreign visitors to the Yanan soviet observed how most of the domestic chores were carried out by female members of the CCP.

> ### Ding Ling (1904–86):
> Ding was an intellectual and writer, had joined the CCP in 1932, and was an early supporter of Mao. Arrested by the GMD in 1933, she escaped in 1936 and joined the CCP's soviet in Yanan. She was linked for a time with the PLA general Peng Dehuai, and Mao had admired her cultural and literary contributions. She became one of China's leading feminist writers, but later openly accused Mao and other CCP leaders of double standards: operating an essentially male-dominated system, and often exploiting women Party members in order to enjoy more comfortable domestic lives. She eventually concluded that Mao's version of communism was not compatible with complete women's liberation. She was expelled from the CCP as a 'rightist' in 1957, and was imprisoned during the Cultural Revolution. She was released in 1975 and, in 1979, her Party membership was restored.

Another feminist writer, Xiufen Lu, claims that the Communists exaggerated the extent of the subordination of women in pre-revolutionary China in order to make their reforms after 1949 seem more significant.

The Marriage Law, 1950

One of the government's first acts was to introduce a Marriage Law in April 1950, which gave equal rights to women, and made illegal practices such as:

- arranged marriages
- child marriages
- the paying of dowries and bride-prices
- bigamy
- the killing of unwanted girl babies.

The consolidation of the Communist State, 1949–55

After 1950, all marriages had to be officially recorded, and women were also given equal ownership of family property, and the right to apply for divorce.

> **SOURCE 2.10**
>
> GENERAL PRINCIPLES:
>
> Article 1. The arbitrary and compulsory feudal marriage system, the supremacy of man over woman, and disregard of the interests of children is abolished.
>
> The new democratic marriage system, which is based on the free choice of partner, on monogamy, on equal rights for both sexes, and on the protection of the lawful interests of women and children, is put into effect.
>
> Article 2. Bigamy, concubinage, child betrothal, interference in the re-marriage of widows, and the extraction of money or gifts in connection with marriages, are prohibited.
>
> THE MARRIAGE CONTRACT:
>
> Article 3. Marriage is based upon the complete willingness of the two parties. Neither party shall use compulsion and no third party is allowed to interfere.
>
> Article 4. A marriage can be contracted only after the man reaches twenty years of age and the woman eighteen years of age…
>
> *Extracts from a 1950 Chinese government pamphlet, published in connection with the 1950 Marriage Law. Quoted in Johnson, K. A. 1983.* **Women, the Family and Peasant Revolution in China.** *Chicago, University of Chicago Press, pp.235–7.*

Further reforms

The rights of women were also increased by the expansion of education in the 1950s, as girls – as well as boys – were now expected to go to school. In February 1951, the government introduced maternity benefits equivalent to two months' wages after the birth of a child.

In addition, women were actively encouraged to train for jobs formerly held only by men; and nurseries were set up so that women could play a more important part in the reconstruction and development of China's economy.

2 The People's Republic of China (1949–2005)

In March 1953, the Election Law gave women the right to vote and to be elected. Women had long played an important part in the CCP and, during the early 1950s, a few women were given government posts and important positions in the PLA. During the land redistributions of the land reform campaign against landlords, some women were even granted land in their own right; while further laws were passed granting women the right to own and sell land and property.

Figure 2.7: A young Chinese woman operating a precision machine at a factory in Beijing in October 1955.

Yet, there were limitations to the effectiveness of these reforms for many Chinese women. In many rural areas – especially Muslim ones – government attempts to ban traditional practices (such as arranged marriages and polygyny) were often ignored or even resisted.

In addition, despite the 1953 Election Law, the percentage of women within CCP and representative bodies remained well below 50 per cent. Finally, although many more women in urban areas were able to find employment outside the home, most still had to carry out all household chores.

> **KEY CONCEPTS QUESTION**
>
> **Change and continuity:** To what extent did Communist reforms in the period 1949–55 succeed in achieving equality for Chinese women?

Education

In 1949, 90 per cent of China's adult population was illiterate; only about 20 per cent of children went to primary school, and only 1 per cent to secondary schools. The CCP was determined to eradicate illiteracy and to massively expand educational provisions.

Tackling illiteracy

Literacy programmes for adults were begun in many villages, though many of the instructors – often Party cadres – had only basic elementary education themselves. At the same time, study groups and evening classes were established; and a 'little teacher' scheme was developed, under which secondary school students shared their learning with illiterate adults.

To make it easier to eradicate illiteracy, the system of Chinese characters was simplified in the 1950s, and a more standardised written version – known as Pinyin – replaced Mandarin. This was increasingly used on posters produced during the various 'mass campaigns' of the 1950s – this helped spread a rudimentary form of literacy, especially in rural areas.

Expansion of education

The growth in formal education – especially under the First Five-Year Plan – after 1949 was impressive. The number of primary schools rose dramatically: as a result, the number of primary school students more than doubled, from approximately 26 million to over 64 million. Secondary schooling also expanded greatly, initially helped by teachers and textbooks supplied by the Soviet Union; and the number of university students increased even more rapidly, going from almost 120 000 to 440 000.

2 The People's Republic of China (1949–2005)

The new education system was initially heavily influenced by the Soviet model of education. In particular, it was geared to the drive for industrial development, with the greatest emphasis on science and technology. As a result, a privileged technological intelligentsia soon emerged, widening the separation between intellectual and manual work.

Other social inequalities – despite the CCP's formal commitment to equal opportunities for all – also appeared. Educational expansion was greater in urban than rural areas; in addition, admissions to schools beyond the primary level tended to favour the children of Party cadres, government employees and technicians.

Although the government aimed to provide free and universal primary education throughout China, the lack of surplus finance meant this had by no means been achieved by 1955. Nonetheless, by the mid 1950s, most village children had some primary education, and the numbers in secondary education had almost tripled.

ACTIVITY

Carry out some additional research on the educational reforms of the period 1949–55. Then write a couple of paragraphs to explain why full educational equality was not achieved by these reforms.

Health and living standards

During the 1950s, there were important advances in health care which, before 1949, had been almost completely absent from rural areas. The CCP quickly established clinics in most counties, and health workers were sent to deal with the most common diseases. Young people were trained to help people in rural areas identify and report contagious diseases, and to give instruction in the importance of hygiene and sanitation.

As regards living standards, attempts were made to improve housing conditions in towns, and real wages and consumption in urban areas increased. However, the rural economy was largely stagnant during the 1950s – in large part because of the transfer of funds from agriculture to finance industrialisation – and thus there were no significant improvements in most rural areas. Despite this inequality between urban and rural areas as regards living standards, and the fact that China in 1949 had had extremely limited financial resources to spend on providing anything more than basic health services, life expectancy nonetheless increased: from 36 years in 1949, to 57 by the mid 1950s.

2 The People's Republic of China (1949–2005)

Paper 3 exam practice

Question

Evaluate the **successes and failures** of **Mao's economic policies** during the period from **1949–55**. **[15 marks]**

Skill

Understanding the wording of a question.

Examiner's tips

The first step in producing a high-scoring essay is to look closely at the wording of the question. Every year, students throw away marks by not paying sufficient attention to the demands of the question.

It is therefore important to start by identifying the key or 'command' words in the question – with this one the key words are as follows:

- evaluate
- successes and failures
- Mao's economic policies
- 1949–55

Key words are intended to give you clear instructions about what you need to cover in your essay – hence they are sometimes called 'command' words. If you ignore them, you will not score high marks, no matter how precise and accurate your knowledge of the period.

For this question, you will need to cover the following aspects:

- **evaluate:** requires an analytical and structured argument that assesses the overall outcomes of Mao's economic policies. This will involve, where relevant, consideration and evaluation of different historical interpretations/perspectives.
- **successes and failures:** *both* the positive *and* the negative aspects of Mao's industrial and agricultural policies will need to be considered. An answer that considers *only* successes *or* failures that will not score more than half marks, even if the argument and knowledge is excellent.

- **Mao's economic policies:** as well as briefly establishing the state of China's economy in 1949, and outlining Mao's aims, the focus here must be on the outcomes of aspects such as the land reform, the Laws of 1950 and 1952, the Five-Year Plan and the move to lower-stage cooperatives in agriculture.
- **1949–55:** the period from 1949 to 1955 is the focus here. Be careful to focus on the time period specified in the question – i.e. don't go beyond 1955.

Common mistakes

Under exam pressure, two types of mistakes are particularly common.

One is to begin by giving some pre-1949 context, but then to continue giving a detailed account of the Civil War, and GMD rule and policies from 1927–49. It is true that a brief reference to the situation just before 1949 will be relevant for putting your answer into context. However, the period before 1949 must not be any significant part of your answer. As the question is focused on Mao's economic policies from 1949–57, such an answer would only score the very lowest marks, no matter how detailed and accurate your knowledge of Jiang Jieshi's economic policies might be.

The other – more common – mistake is to focus entirely on the dates. This is almost certainly likely to end in the production of a general and descriptive account of the economic policies during this period, with students tending to put down all they know about this period, rather than dealing with the specific focus of the question, and selecting relevant facts from what they know. Such a narrative-based account will not score highly, as it will not explicitly offer a considered evaluation of successes and failures, which is a central part of the question.

Both of these mistakes can be avoided if you focus carefully on the wording of the question.

For more on how to avoid irrelevant and narrative answers, see Chapters 5 and 6.

2 The People's Republic of China (1949–2005)

Activity

In this chapter, the focus is on understanding the question and producing a brief essay plan. So, look again at the question, the tips and the simplified mark scheme in Chapter 10. Now, using the information from this chapter, and any other sources of information available to you, draw up an essay plan – perhaps a spider diagram – which has all the necessary headings for a well-focused and clearly structured response to the question.

Paper 3 practice questions

1 Examine Mao's success in establishing the authority of the Communist Party in the years, 1949–55.

2 To what extent had Mao's policies modernised Chinese agriculture by 1955?

3 Discuss the impact of Mao's domestic policies on the position of women in the period 1949–55.

4 Examine the initial results of Mao's Five-Year Plan in the period 1953–55.

5 'The Gao Gang Affair and the purge of Party cadres that followed was mainly designed to limit Soviet influence in China.' To what extent do you agree with this statement?

Mao's revolution, 1956–61

3

3 The People's Republic of China (1949–2005)

Introduction

By the beginning of 1956, many CCP leaders – not just Mao – seemed to believe that China was on the verge of completing 'the transition to socialism.' Zhou Enlai, for instance, was just one of many who spoke publicly of the 'high tide of socialist transformation'. Thus, although the changes that took place in China from 1956 to 1961 are seen very much as Mao's work, it is important to realise that other CCP leaders also had similar views in 1956.

In January 1956, Mao announced that the successes achieved during the second half of 1955 had been decisive in determining the eventual outcome of the struggle between capitalism and socialism. On the basis of those achievements, he stated that by the end of 1956, the victory of socialism in China would be beyond doubt. From 1956, China's Communist leaders began a series of political and economic initiatives to bring this 'socialist transformation' about.

TIMELINE

1956 Jan: CCP relaxes ideological controls on intellectuals

May: The Hundred Flowers campaign is launched; move to HAPCs begins

Sep: Hundred Flowers campaign endorsed by CCP Congress

1957 Feb: Mao's speech on constructive versus antagonistic criticism

Jun: Spread of protests from universities to schools

Jul: Hundred Flowers campaign ended; the Anti-Rightist campaign begins

Sep: Anti-Rightist campaign extended to Party 'conservatives' and bureaucrats

Oct: Party leaders accept Mao's call for 'simultaneous development'

1958 Jan: Great Leap Forward first mentioned by Mao

Feb: Mao claims Great Leap Forward will see China overtake British economy in 15 years

May: 'Simultaneous development' launched at 8th Party Congress

Jun: High Great Leap Forward targets set – especially for 'backyard steel' furnaces

Mao's revolution, 1956–61

Aug: Second Five-Year Plan abandoned by Politburo; plans for GLF and Rural Communes agreed

Nov: Some leaders voice criticisms at Zhengzhou meeting

Dec: CC meeting at Wuhan temporarily halts Urban Communes and reduces targets; Mao offers to resign as chairman of PRC

1959 Mar: Second Zhengzhou meeting confirms slowdown of GLF; insurrection in Tibet

Apr: CC and National People's Congress accept Mao's resignation as Chairman of PRC; Liu takes his place.

Jul-Aug: Mao accepts the 'backyard steel' plan has been a 'great catastrophe' at Lushan Conference; critical letter from Peng leads to new purge; harvests hit by severe floods and drought.

1960 Jul: Soviet Union ends aid and withdraws experts from China; GLF effectively abandoned

KEY QUESTIONS
- Why was the Hundred Flowers campaign launched?
- What were the main features of the Great Leap Forward, 1958–61?
- What were the immediate consequences of the Great Leap Forward?

Overview

- From 1956, Mao and his supporters came to believe that China was about to complete its 'transition to socialism'.
- As a first step, the CCP decided to allow people to express their views on the reforms and policies introduced since 1949. However, this Hundred Flowers campaign was quickly ended because of widespread criticisms.
- In 1957, there was a new mass political campaign against 'rightwingers' – including members of the smaller parties that had been part of the United Front.
- From 1958, Mao and his supporters – unhappy about some of the consequences of the Soviet model of economic development – launched the Great Leap Forward.

3 The People's Republic of China (1949–2005)

- The Great Leap Forward saw large communes established across China, and the ending of private ownership of land in rural areas. These communes were then encouraged to create their own industries and steel furnaces.
- Despite some early successes, the lack of clear plans led to increasing problems, including some protests.
- As a result of bad weather and poor administration, many areas of China experienced famine, and 1959–61 became known as the 'Three Bitter Years'.
- Mao's influence within the CCP was reduced, and his opponents – such as Liu and Deng – were able to bring an end to the Great Leap Forward in 1961.

3.1 Why was the Hundred Flowers campaign launched?

By 1956, Mao and other CCP leaders concluded the economic and social reforms that had been carried out since 1949 had put China firmly on the road to socialism. So they felt they could allow both Party cadres and intellectuals – a term which included teachers and, at times, anyone with secondary-level education, as well as writers, academics and scientists – greater freedom to express their views.

The Hundred Flowers campaign, 1956–57

Zhou Enlai in particular was concerned that, since the attack on Hu Feng in 1954–5, China's intellectuals had become estranged from the Party. In an attempt to regain their support, the Party's Cultural Committee met in January 1956 and decided that ideological controls on intellectuals should be relaxed. The 'clash of ideas' that this would encourage was seen as an essential step to ensure the success of the final push to build a fully socialist society, which would need a massive development of science and technology.

Zhou argued that as most intellectuals had, in practice, become government 'workers', they should be given the tools necessary to help China modernise and become a fully socialist society. To that end, they should be given more resources, better housing and pay, and not be unduly over-burdened with political study sessions. He also wanted restrictions on intellectuals joining the CCP removed. By the end of 1957, there were was a 50 per cent increase in the number of intellectuals in the Party: this resulted in there being more intellectuals in the Party than industrial workers.

While Mao had serious misgivings about some of these proposals – especially those that would transform intellectuals into a new privileged professional and technical élite within China – he certainly agreed that a great improvement was needed in science and technology. As well as speeding up the transition to socialism, he was beginning to see this as a way of reducing China's dependence on the Soviet Union. For a time, the issue of the role and position of intellectuals in socialist China overshadowed emerging differences within the CCP leadership over the economic policies to be pursued after 1955.

The new approach to intellectuals was based on an idea first put forward by the Central Committee's Propaganda Department. This was a call – to scientists and to writers and artists, respectively – to 'let a hundred flowers bloom and a hundred schools of thought contend'. The slogan was linked to classical Chinese philosophy, and suggested to intellectuals that the Party would allow a plurality of views to exist.

The new constitution of the PRC – which had been published in September 1954 – among other things, had promised freedom of speech, association and the press. Yet, by 1956, because of the earlier 'rectification' campaigns against intellectuals and critics during 1954–45, it was clear to many intellectuals that in practice such rights were often restricted. In addition, many loyal CCP members were reluctant to criticise policies and actions – especially those associated with Mao.

3 The People's Republic of China (1949–2005)

SOURCE 3.1

What came to be called the 'blooming and contending' of 1956–1957 was a time when the most critical questions about the present and future of socialism in China were raised and debated. Questions about the relationship between state and society, between leaders and led, and questions involving human and intellectual freedom were discussed more openly and candidly than ever before in the People's Republic…

It was not the case that the Communists suddenly had come to appreciate the virtues of intellectual freedom. The purpose was largely economic (although Mao Zedong's own motives were rather more complex…). As industrialization proceeded, a more rapid development of scientific and technological research – and the creation of a larger and better trained technological intelligentsia – were required… An intelligentsia terrified into silence and driven into political hostility was not likely to provide the cooperation or intellectual creativity that was required. Intellectual repression was becoming an economic liability.

Meisner, M. 1999. **Mao's China and After: A History of the People's Republic.** New York. The Free Press. pp.158–9.

QUESTION

What do you think was meant by the last sentence in Source 3.1?

Consequently, very few at first took up the opportunity to express their views until the new policy was publicly endorsed by Mao in a speech in May 1956. This relaxation of censorship restrictions in art, literature and academic research, he said, would be the best way to promote 'progress in the arts and the sciences, and a flourishing socialist culture' in China.

The campaign was officially – though rather reluctantly – endorsed by the Eighth Party Congress in September 1956. Further encouragement of intellectuals, to comment on and constructively criticise the Communist government's performance and policies since 1949, came in February 1957, when Mao announced in another speech – 'On the Correct Handling of Contradictions Among the People' – that the government would allow criticisms as long as they were 'constructive' or 'non-antagonistic' ('among the people') rather than 'hateful and destructive' or 'antagonistic' ('between the enemy and ourselves').

Significantly, Mao's speech was not delivered at a Party meeting, but at an enlarged session of the Supreme State Council. This was similar to his use of a non-Party forum for announcing his plans for agricultural collectivisation in July 1955. In both cases, he had failed to receive majority support among CCP leaders for his ideas, so he appealed over their heads to 'the people'. In particular, he raised concerns about emerging contradictions between Party and government leaders on the one hand, and the people on the other.

By then, because of growing disagreements over the direction and pace of economic policies within the CCP leadership, Mao had come to see the campaign as a way of using the intellectuals to 'rectify' the Party and state bureaucracy which he and his supporters felt was blocking further progress in continuing with revolutionary policies. According to historians such as Maurice Meisner, this new element was introduced by Mao as an attempt to overcome his increasing powerlessness within the Party leadership.

Following extensive personal visits to many areas of rural China, Mao was concerned about what he said was the 'heavy-handedness' with which many Party cadres were applying national and local policies. Thus he urged Communist and government officials to be prepared to undergo criticism from the people. Not surprisingly, most CCP leaders objected to this aspect. A series of articles then appeared in newspapers that repeated and expanded on Mao's call for such criticisms.

However, some of the changes and problems associated with the Five-Year Plan had caused much discontent. During 1956 and early 1957, there were several strikes by industrial workers, peasant demonstrations and student protests in many colleges and universities.

To an extent, dissatisfaction with government policies was only to be expected: not only because of the radical nature of the changes implemented since 1949, but also because many Party cadres were relatively inexperienced and/or poorly educated and trained.

3 The People's Republic of China (1949–2005)

After several more calls for people to comment on the achievements of China's revolution so far, criticisms began to emerge in the spring of 1957. Thousands of articles and posters criticised government policies, Party leaders – including Mao – and even the goal of socialism itself. These criticisms by intellectuals then encouraged wider protests. Soon, there were rallies in the streets, and the government began to receive a flood of letters. Critical remarks were also made by many Party members, who complained about bullying and abuses of power by senior Party cadres.

Students at Beijing University created a 'Democracy Wall', and produced posters and unofficial journals that criticised political and economic corruption, low living standards, Russian influences, censorship – and even the privileged lifestyle enjoyed by many of the leadership of the CCP. They also began to hold rallies and demonstrations. In addition, lecturers complained about the state of education, and attacked the idea that Mao's thoughts should be part of the curriculum.

Protests then spread to other universities, in what became known as 'the storm in the universities'. Semi-political organisations – such as the 'Hundred Flowers Society' – were formed to distribute leaflets and unofficial newspapers. Particularly prominent was **Lin Xiling**, a Marxist studying at the Chinese People's University. She argued that a 'new class' was emerging and that China could not become genuinely socialist until it also became genuinely democratic. By June, this student movement had spread down to middle schools, and occasional violence broke out as students occupied state and Party buildings.

Lin Xiling (1935–2009):

Lin was a committed revolutionary communist who placed the people's rights at the top of her socialist agenda. As a result, she was opposed to the top-down version of communism that emerged in China after 1949. In one of her speeches in 1957, she attacked the 'three nuisances' of the CCP: dogmatism, bureaucratism and sectarianism. She was one of the many 'rightists' punished for her part in the Hundred Flowers campaign. She was imprisoned from 1958 to 1969, and was then sent to a *laogai* camp. She was finally released in 1973; in 1983, she went into exile in France. She was never politically rehabilitated.

Mao's revolution, 1956–61

The minor democratic parties, which had been allowed to continue after 1949 began to demand greater participation in decision-making, while journalists condemned the censorship controls. Marxist critics pointed out that the Marriage Law of 1950 was not being fully observed – even by some Party leaders. While others criticised wage differentials, and the lack of free trade unions and workers' control in factories.

> **QUESTION**
> What were the main features of the Hundred Flowers campaign?

The 'Anti-Rightist' campaign, 1957

The explosion of criticisms, protests and strikes that emerged during 1956 and early 1957, led Mao and the CCP to announce, in June 1957, that such actions had gone beyond 'healthy criticism', and that 'right-wingers' were abusing their freedom in order to attack socialism and the Party. What appears to have been at first a genuine attempt to agree a greater role for the intelligentsia in a socialist China soon became a political witch-hunt. Many ordinary Party members were deeply disappointed by those comments, and by the clamp-down that followed.

However, many CCP leaders and officials were relieved that the calls to criticise Party bureaucrats was about to end. In part, the severity of the repression in 1957 reflected concerns that had first emerged among CCP leaders following the Hungarian Revolt of October 1956: leading roles in that rising against a communist government had been played by intellectuals. In fact, from as early as late 1956, CCP officials had been trying to limit the Hundred Flowers campaign.

From July, the campaign was called off and, instead, censorship and central control were re-imposed, and another mass campaign – this time against the most outspoken critics —— began. Those identified as 'rightists' were vilified at public 'struggle meetings' in their workplaces. Many were sacked; while others were directed to undergo 'thought reform' or 're-education through labour' on farms or in special labour camps.

3 The People's Republic of China (1949–2005)

Figure 3.1: A public rally in Beijing in July 1957, at which Zhang Bojun, the minister of transportation (communications), was subjected to a 'mass criticism' conducted by his own staff. He was identified as 'China's number one rightist' during the Anti-Rightist campaign, and was sacked from his post.

> ### QUESTION
>
> What are the value and limitations of Figure 3.1 for historians studying the 1957 Anti-Rightist campaign?

Overall, approximately 500 000 intellectual critics were branded as 'rightists' and 'anti-party'. About 1000 of the most outspoken critics were publicly executed – including three student leaders who were executed in August 1957. Thousands of other critics were arrested as 'criminals' or 'vagrants' and sent to prison or to *laogai* camps.

Mao's revolution, 1956–61

While the failure of the Hundred Flowers campaign can be seen, in one way, as a defeat for Mao and a victory for the Party bureaucrats, Mao was soon able to use the Anti-Rightist campaign to eliminate the last vestiges of capitalism in rural areas, and then to turn on the 'rightists' in the party itself.

In September 1957, the CC reluctantly sanctioned attacks against bureaucratism and conservative resistance to socialism. By the time this had come to an end in 1958, over 1 million Party members had been expelled or sent to rural areas for 're-education' by China's peasants.

Even some of the CCP's main leaders were affected: Zhou Enlai, the prime minister, made a self-criticism in front of a large Party meeting for having been too slow in putting Mao's industrialisation plans into effect. Not surprisingly, most Party members drew the conclusion that any criticism of the party and government – and especially of Mao and other main leaders – should be avoided.

Repression and 're-education through labour'

The aim of 're-education through labour' was that making intellectuals live among peasants and workers would 'cure' them of their bourgeois values. The special labour camps – known as *laojiao* – to which Party members were sent for 're-education' through work on farms, soon became part of the national *laogai* system, which was very similar to the gulag system in Stalin's Soviet Union.

In the *laogai* camps, to which convicted criminals were sent, conditions were often harsh, and many of those sent there died or committed suicide before their release. Although conditions on the *laojiao* camps were better, most intellectuals – not surprisingly – never trusted Mao or the CCP again. Interestingly, given future developments in China, this repression was overseen by **Deng Xiaoping**, who ensured that this became a long-term national system.

3 The People's Republic of China (1949–2005)

> **Deng Xiaoping (1904–97):**
> Deng joined the CCP in the 1920s while in France. After studying in Moscow, he became a military leader of the CCP's Red Army during the Civil War. In 1952, he became deputy premier and, in 1956, was appointed general-secretary of the CCP. He was associated with the more 'pragmatic' policies of centre-right CCP leaders, such as Liu Shaoqi and Zhou Enlai, rather than Mao's more 'leftist' approaches. As a result, he was purged in 1966 at the start of the Cultural Revolution. After the fall of the 'Gang of Four', he re-emerged to become the 'paramount leader' from 1978 to 1992, and played the decisive role in determining economic developments in China.

This repressive campaign, however, was not restricted to intellectuals – the CCP decided to use the campaign as an opportunity to deal with all sorts of political opposition. Members of the various democratic parties that had been part of the United Front, were particularly targeted. Between August and September 1957, about 12 000 members of these parties were sacked and sent for re-education through labour. By the end, any influence these parties had had since 1949 was destroyed. Though they continued to exist, not surprisingly, they found it difficult to attract new members.

Motives behind the Hundred Flowers campaign

Historians are divided over Mao's reasons for launching the Hundred Flowers campaign. Some historians – and writers such as Jung Chang – believe that, from the outset, it was a cynical attempt by Mao and the CCP leadership to flush out intellectuals critical of, or opposed to, developments in post-revolution China.

Many, however, such as Jonathan Spence, argue that it was a genuine, if muddled, attempt to allow intellectuals and others to express their views – about the pace and type of development that was best for China – as a way of venting concerns.

Mao's revolution, 1956–61

Figure 3.2: What is the message of this cartoon concerning Mao's motives for launching the Hundred Flowers' Campaign?

Other historians, such as Philip Short, believe it was essentially designed to create some kind of 'democratic check' on those in the Party who Mao believed had, since 1949, begun to lose revolutionary values and commitment. Another possible influence was the 'secret speech' made by the Soviet leader, Khrushchev in February 1956, in which – as well as revealing the extent of Stalin's murderous purges of the 1930s – he had attacked the 'cult of personality' that had grown up around Stalin. Given Mao's predominant position in the PRC, the encouraging of criticism might have been a way of deflecting such accusations against himself.

Some historians – such as Maurice Meisner and Lee Feigon – go further, and see Mao's speech in February 1957 (which revived the Hundred Flowers campaign, despite growing misgivings among the Party's leadership) as an attempt to use the intellectuals to weaken his political opponents in the Party and government. These had, at the Eighth Party Congress in September 1956, reduced Mao's political influence in favour of a more collective leadership, by re-establishing the post of General Secretary (abolished in 1937) and giving it to Deng.

This Congress had also ignored Mao's radical plans for rapid economic development (later implemented as the Great Leap Forward) in favour of a more orthodox Soviet-style Second Five-Year Plan. According to historians such as Meisner and Feigon, the campaign can thus be

3 The People's Republic of China (1949–2005)

seen as an attempt by Mao to use the people to weaken Party and government bureaucrats and, instead, encourage them to work harder to create a socialist China. However, whatever the motives behind the Hundred Flowers campaign were, the main outcome was that – as stated in Source 3.2 – Mao had been able to isolate those Party members opposed to his ideas.

SOURCE 3.2

In the event, whatever Mao's motives may or may not have been, it was the scale of the criticism that the Hundred Flowers unleashed that took him aback. He had not realised the scale of the dissatisfaction with the party that the campaign had revealed. In practical terms there was little difference as to whether he intended from the beginning to flush out opponents or whether he decided to do this once he had discovered the extent of the opposition. The outcome was the same. Mao crushed those he thought were opposed to him.

Lynch, M. 2008. **The People's Republic of China 1949–76.** London. Hodder Education.p.40

Whatever the reasons behind the Hundred Flowers campaign, the amount of criticism that emerged in 1956–57 showed that the CCP had seriously underestimated the degree of dissatisfaction that existed in China. This gave extra urgency to Mao's arguments that, after the events of 1957, the PRC needed to move more rapidly to complete the transition to a fully socialist society.

3.2 What were the main features of the Great Leap Forward, 1958–61?

From January 1958, Mao and his supporters began to argue for a form of 'permanent revolution'. By this, Mao meant that continued industrial development, on its own, would not lead to socialism. What was needed was a serious of radical breaks – or 'leaps' – as part of a continuous revolutionary process. At this stage, other CCP leaders seemed to go along with this – in May, Liu also referred to 'permanent revolution' as always having been a principle of the CCP. Mao's plans soon became known as the Great Leap Forward.

Impact of the First Five-Year Plan

During 1956, Mao – and some other CCP leaders – had become concerned about several of the effects of the First Five-Year Plan. While the economic results were generally pleasing, some of the social, political and ideological consequences were not. These negative effects included:

- the growth of bureaucracy
- the emergence of privileged professional élites
- new economic inequalities
- a growing gulf between urban and rural areas.

Thus, although it was possible, on one level, to describe China as a 'socialist' economy – or, at least, as a post-capitalist one – on another level, China seemed to be moving further from, rather than closer to, a socialist and communist future. Following the Anti-Rightist campaign of 1957, Mao then decided it was time to push ahead more quickly with plans for the rapid transition to socialism. As he saw it, the answer to all these problems was to industrialise the countryside. As a result, several steps towards this new policy were taken before 1958, especially in agriculture.

Higher Agricultural Producers' Cooperatives, 1956–58

Because the Five-Year Plan required many more industrial workers, the government decided in 1956 to further improve agricultural output by merging the lower-stage cooperatives into larger higher-stage cooperatives – known as Higher Agricultural Producers' Cooperatives (HAPCs) – involving 200 to 300 families, or about 1200 people. These were then subdivided into production brigades of between 30 to 40 families – most were based on the earlier APCs. The idea was to increase agricultural efficiency, so that more food could be produced by fewer peasants. This would then release many more peasants for work in factories.

3 The People's Republic of China (1949–2005)

The creation of HAPCs began in the spring of 1956, and continued until August 1958. The aim of these HAPCs was to achieve a socialist agricultural system, by making virtually all land collectively owned, with individual peasant families only retaining a small proportion of their land (about 7 per cent of cultivated land by the end of 1957). They were no longer paid rent for their land, which became the property of the cooperative. Instead, they were paid wages out of the profits of the cooperative, based on work points earned by their labour in the cooperative.

This new system gave a bigger role to the local CCP bodies, which were charged with ensuring that plans were implemented in their areas. However, many peasants were unhappy about losing most of their land, and there was a general reluctance to join the new HAPCs. In addition, many of the local administrators struggled to cope with some of the practical issues involved with larger-scale planning.

> ### KEY CONCEPTS ACTIVITY
>
> **Change and continuity:** Write a couple of paragraphs to show how the HAPCs were (a) different from and (b) similar to the earlier lower-stage APCs.

Consequently, although the assumption had been that these new cooperatives would result in higher agricultural production, the levels actually reached for 1956 and 1957 were lower than planned. It was this situation that led Mao, initially, to consider new approaches in 1957. He reluctantly agreed that state taxes and compulsory grain purchases should be reduced, and that peasants should be allowed to spend more time on their private plots and sell such produce on the private market.

The Second Five-Year Plan

A Second Five-Year Plan was ready to run from 1958 to 62, which was intended to expand light industry, improve workers' living standards, and develop science and technology. However, Mao had become increasingly concerned during 1955 that agriculture was growing too slowly, and so wanted to increase the pace of economic development. To do this, the First Plan had assumed that, as in the Soviet Union, the task of 'primitive socialist accumulation' (obtaining capital funds to finance

Mao's revolution, 1956–61

industrial development which would create a socialist society) would be achieved by 'exploiting' the countryside.

In fact, at the same time that the CCP was beginning to formulate what became the Hundred Flowers campaign, Mao was already arguing for economic developments that would drop the traditional Soviet model of Five-Year Plans. These ideas eventually became the basis of Mao's Great Leap Forward. However, while he wanted a break from Stalinist industrial approaches, he did not intend to abandon Stalinist methods as regards the political methods of the CCP. As Source 3.3 shows, having sidelined his opponents within the Party, Mao was determined to launch a radical and massive transformation of China's economy.

SOURCE 3.3

Having effectively silenced all real and potential critics [via the Anti-Rightist campaign], Mao moved forward with plans for the rapid shift of all China to the commune system. An opportunity for open discussion and realistic appraisal of the Party's achievements was lost. Instead, Mao announced that China would now begin a 'great leap forward' to catch up with European powers like Britain in just 15 years. What was to become the first great cataclysm to hit the PRC was thus launched by Mao and his supporters in 1958.

Benson, L. 2002. **China since 1949**. Harlow. Pearson Education. p.31

The Great Leap Forward

In February 1958, Mao and his supporters proposed that there should be a simultaneous development of industry and agriculture. In the document *'Sixty Points on Working Methods'*, Mao described his plan as a 'Great Leap' which, he predicted, would result in China's industrial production overtake developed Western economies such as Britain within 15 years.

This was the signal for what, in 1958, became known as the Great Leap Forward (GLF) – this was a dramatic departure from the Soviet model of gradual economic development. It was also a significant shift in the way the Party thought China should be governed.

3 The People's Republic of China (1949–2005)

Technically, the Great Leap was just one part of a new CCP policy known as the 'Three Red Banners'. These were:

- The General Line for Building Socialism (for the simultaneous development of both industry and agriculture)
- The Great Leap Forward (the mobilisation and organisation of labour)
- The creation of People's Communes.

These policies were developed by Mao, and were pursued against strong opposition from many leading CCP leaders. To overcome this opposition, Mao used regional and provincial leaders to begin the reforms he wanted to see put into operation. Particularly important were 'model' communes such as the Qiliyang People's Commune in Henan province, and the Yangyi Commune in Hebei province. Once these had begun, Mao pushed for them to be set up across the whole country.

ACTIVITY
Using those resources available to you, carry out some additional research on the reported achievements of 'model' communes. Then write a couple of paragraphs to explain the extent to which such claims were reliable.

The main focus of the GLF was the countryside, where under-employment (because of 'slack' seasons) meant that peasants could also be harnessed for small and medium-scale industrial production. This was sometimes referred to as 'walking on two legs'. The idea was that basic consumer goods factories, small chemical and fertiliser plants, and tool workshops could be built in rural areas, without peasants having to move to urban areas. These would also be more responsive to local conditions and needs, and would more quickly create the funds necessary for the development of heavy industry in the cities.

Though later the GLF was sometimes presented as showing that Mao was opposed to modern technology, he in fact saw the GLF as a way of developing China's technological base more quickly than the traditional Soviet approach. However, he was concerned about how to develop technology without giving rise to a privileged technocratic élite. He hoped this could be done by making ordinary Chinese people 'masters

Mao's revolution, 1956–61

of culture and science' and thus not overly-reliant on a technological élite. Several CCP leaders were also aware that the problems of under-employment in rural areas – which had led to peasants moving into towns and so causing unemployment in the cities – had not been fully solved by the First Five-Year Plan.

Mao's aim was to turn China into a modern industrial – and fully socialist – state in a very short time. Although the draft Second Five-Year Plan was never formally abandoned, this is what in practice happened. Instead, the Great Leap Forward became the new Second Five-Year Plan. Yet it soon became clear that this Great Leap Forward had no clearly drawn-up blueprints for how this transformation was to be achieved in practice.

'Revolutionary romanticism'

However, in order to achieve this transformation, Mao did not think merely in terms of financial investments and raw materials – he also saw the right political attitudes and determination as crucial. Voluntarism and revolutionary utopianism were strong strands within what became known as Maoism. The planners began to speak about 'General Grain' and 'General Steel' – these two would bring about the changes Mao and his supporters wanted. What counted, it was said, was not so much skill as enthusiasm and commitment. People were to be enthused by slogans such as: 'more, faster, better, and cheaper'.

In fact, as early as May 1956, Mao had made a speech – 'On the Ten Great Relationships' – in which he stated his aim of distancing China from the Soviet Union by abandoning the centralised Soviet development model of concentrating on industry. Mao began to argue for rapid industrial and agricultural growth via a mass campaign. Instead of basing this on greater levels of capital expenditure, Mao believed that China's huge population could be harnessed to achieve the necessary surplus funds required for rapid development.

For instance, as China lacked sufficient mechanical diggers, it would be necessary for many construction projects – such as dams – to be built with simple tools and labour-intensive manual labour. In many respects, Mao argued that China's under-development and relative poverty would enable it to make this Great Leap Forward. His 'revolutionary romanticism' placed great emphasis on 'revolutionary enthusiasm', and called for a concentration on agriculture, light industry and small-scale industries that required minimum capital investment.

3 The People's Republic of China (1949–2005)

Figure 3.3: A propaganda poster produced during the GLF, depicting Mao.

Mao began putting these ideas forward at the same time as the Hundred Flowers campaign was developing. As with that political campaign, Mao was concerned about the political impact on the CCP of rapid industrial development and the growing influence of urban society. In particular, he worried that the increasing implantation of cadres in urban areas might corrupt the ideological 'purity' of the Party which, before 1949, had had few urban links.

Consequently, he began to think of ways in which to re-emphasise the importance of bringing about the socialist transformation of the countryside, as a way of preventing a love of the relative luxury and easy living in towns and cities from corrupting Party cadres and administrative bureaucrats, which might result in a loss of revolutionary commitment. In many ways, Mao seemed to be wanting to revive the heroic 'Yanan spirit' displayed by the CCP during the Long March and the Civil War in the 1930s. The method chosen was to create massive urban and rural communes.

Mao's revolution, 1956–61

The GLF and the CCP

In October 1957, Mao's idea of 'simultaneous development' – which was the central core of his Great Leap Forward – was formally adopted by the Party, and was officially approved and launched during the Eighth Party Congress in May 1958. Mao's arguments for the GLF reflected the debates which had surrounded the Hundred Flowers campaign – when Mao had contended that a 'class struggle' was taking place between socialist and bourgeois/capitalist attitudes and ideas.

By implication, this 'class struggle' between proletarian and bourgeois ideas could also be within the leadership of the CCP itself, as well as in society as a whole. His policies, it was said, were vital to secure China's progress on the 'socialist road'.

To secure his position at the top of the Party – where one of his biggest opponents was **Peng Dehuai** – Lin Biao was promoted to the CC and the Politburo. While Liu and Deng were doubtful, in 1958 they remained quiet.

Peng Dehuai (1898–1974):

Peng joined the CCP in 1927, and was a veteran of the Long March. During the Korean War, he was in charge of the Chinese troops sent to defend North Korea from the US/UN invasion. From 1954 to 1959, he was Minister of Defence and one of the ten Marshals of the PLA. His differences with Mao's Great Leap Forward led to an open clash in the summer of 1959. As a result, he was purged from all his posts and placed under house arrest. Briefly brought back by Liu and Deng in 1965, he was persecuted during the Cultural Revolution, and was sentenced to life imprisonment in 1970. He died in prison, but was post-humously politically rehabilitated under Deng's rule.

Party criticisms of the GLF

Debates within the CCP about the policies of what became the Great Leap Forward eventually brought to a head a growing division within the leadership between the centre-rightists and leftists over the way in which China should be developed in the future. This had already begun before the end of 1955, with the centre-right increasingly seeing Mao and his supporters as reckless utopians, and Mao seeing these leaders as a

3 The People's Republic of China (1949–2005)

conservative bureaucracy blocking further progress on the road to socialism.

As early as November 1958, some leading members of the CCP began to criticise the unrealistic targets and the lack of sound planning. A meeting in Zhengzhou saw Mao forced to slow down the push to totally abolish a market economy in rural areas and, in December, a meeting of the Eighth CC at Wuhan confirmed the retreat from certain 'excesses' associated with the drive to establish communes, and revised downwards many of the ambitious production targets set in August.

It was at this meeting that Mao first proposed that he step down from his position as chairman of the PRC. This was accepted in principle, although he remained as chairman of the Party (see Chapter 4).

Another meeting at Zhengzhou in March 1959 confirmed these revised targets and, in April, the CC voted to return powers to the smaller units of Communes. Part of reason for this is that it was soon seen that many of the Communes lacked the facilities and trained personnel to carry out administrative and budgetary functions. Many even lacked the buildings or resources to provide the requisite schools, canteens and care facilities.

Mao's position within the CCP was further undermined by the fact that, by the end of 1958, some areas were also beginning to see resistance from peasants to his new policy. In some localities, PLA units were needed to suppress the resistance. Particularly severe was the insurgency that broke out in Tibet in March 1959. This revolt – which received limited US aid – had begun because of opposition to the 1950s' land reforms, which many Tibetan landowners and peasants saw as breaking the Seventeen-Point Agreement reached in 1951.

By the time the National People's Congress met in April 1959, the insurgency had been easily crushed by the PLA. The government then confiscated the largest landholdings and distributed them to peasants with smaller landholdings. However, these disturbances strengthened the hand of Mao's critics within the Party leadership. In fact, it was at this NPC meeting that Mao was officially replaced as chairman of the PRC by Liu Shaoqi. The divisions within the leadership of the CCP, between those who supported or opposed Mao, were now becoming increasingly apparent.

Mao's revolution, 1956–61

However, Mao remained concerned that bureaucracy within both Party and state, and the negativity of richer peasants, were undermining the scheme. In particular, this was a serious problem, as the development of industry was dependent on obtaining a growing surplus of grain and raw materials from rural areas.

Implementation of the GLF

Despite lack of funds and equipment, many new dams, bridges and canals were constructed in the early period of the Great Leap. One example was the building of Tiananmen Square in Beijing: begun in 1957, it was completed in 1959, and – important for Mao – was bigger than Moscow's Red Square. Government propaganda published these achievements, in order to inspire people to even greater achievements.

Industry and the GLF

As far as industry was concerned, a number of urban communes were established from the summer of 1958. However, because of various difficulties, this was halted in December 1958. From then until 1960, the CCP concentrated on rural areas. However, in 1960, in order to cope with signs of growing shortages, workshops and vegetable gardens on the outskirts of larger urban areas were hastily organised.

The main change was the reorganisation of urban areas into communes, which were intended as economic, administrative and military bodies. Usually, large factory or residential areas were grouped together, and each commune provided workers with accommodation, schools, hospitals and other facilities. Sometimes though, several towns were merged to form bigger communes. Once economic conditions began to improve, urban communes largely disappeared.

In addition, there was an increase in the number of State-Owned Enterprises (SOEs), and the ending of former owners receiving a share of the profits. There was also a massive increase in the production targets set, and pay differentials and bonuses were ended.

The Rural People's Communes

The main drive, though, was on the establishment of huge rural communes, which were to be formed by merging many collectives together. These were to make huge contributions to industrial production as well as increasing the amount of foodstuffs produced.

3   The People's Republic of China (1949–2005)

In particular, rural communes were expected to produce iron and steel in what became known as 'backyard furnaces'. The targets set in June 1958 were extremely high: over 30 million tons by 1959, and 50–90 million tons in 1962.

The campaign urged peasants to produce 'twenty years in a day'. Even individual families felt encouraged to build their own furnaces – this applied to some government ministers, too.

In August 1958, the Politburo also agreed the basis for establishing People's Communes in rural areas. By the end of 1958, almost all of China's peasants had been grouped into about 25 000 huge communes.

The biggest ones took over the political and administrative functions of the counties. Other communes were the size of township (*xiang*) administrations. Each commune contained about 5000 families, or about 30 000 people on average. Some, however, had fewer than 5000 members, while others had over 100 000. This involved an almost total abolition of the private ownership of land, and an expansion and intensification of collective labour.

Communes also had a military function, and the GLF was accompanied by the revival of the idea of a 'people's militia'. By the end of 1959, 220 million people had joined the militia, and over 30 million had been armed with old-fashioned rifles. This soon sparked a debate about the role of the PLA – as some Party members saw the militia as replacing a professional standing army.

This went hand-in-hand with the idea of the communes as exercising political power, and not just being responsible for economic production – with some Party cadres seeing this as a form of 'proletarian' rule. This idea, in particular, seemed to undermine the existing state and Party bureaucracies and these groups quickly took advantage of emerging economic and organisational difficulties to limit the impact of this 'proletarian' direction.

In order to build dams and irrigation systems, urban workers, technicians and Party cadres were sent to rural areas to help the peasants. With large numbers of males employed on such construction projects, it was women who filled their places in agriculture and light industry.

Mao's revolution, 1956–61

Figure 3.4: An example of the 'backyard' furnaces constructed during the Great Leap Forward.

As in the urban areas, these rural communes were to provide all the amenities people needed: such as schools, banks, health care and communal kitchens. All tools and materials possessed by the collectives were managed by each commune. The state then set quotas for each commune: the state would take a certain proportion, and the remainder was for consumption within the commune.

The people in each commune were divided up into production brigades (often basically a village) and smaller work teams. Each brigade was given a production quota, and each member was 'paid' in work points – though women were paid at a lower rate than men. These work points could then be spent to buy items in the commune stores; some families also received payment in cash.

This 'drive to produce metals locally' involved over 90 million peasants in industrial projects, which required shifting their labour from farming to build brick furnaces in order to produce crude steel. Very often, tools,

The People's Republic of China (1949–2005)

nails and metal household items were melted down and added to the ore being smelted.

It has been estimated that over 500 000 such furnaces were built – and different brigades and communes competed with each other to produce the most steel. The government announced that steel production had more than doubled – from 5.35 million metric tons in 1957 to 10.7 million tons in 1958.

	1958	1959	1960	1961	1962
Steel	8.80	13.87	18.66	8.70	6.67
Coal	270.0	369.00	397.00	278.00	220.00
Cement	9.30	12.27	15.65	6.21	6.00

Figure 3.5: Production of steel, coal and cement in million metric tons, 1958–1962.
Source: Adapted from J. Fenby, 2013, **The Penguin History of Modern China**, London, Penguin Books, p.414.

As far as food production was concerned, the government tried to increase yields by getting peasants to do 'deep ploughing' and close planting. During 1958, such methods appeared to be working – the 1958 harvest produced about 215 million tons of grain, compared to 196 million tons in 1957. However, official figures claimed 375 million tons – though this was later revised downwards to 250 million tons. This distortion was largely the result of over-reporting by local commune officials who were concerned to give the impression they had met – or even exceeded – production quotas set by the state, even when they had not. The problem was that, once the state had taken its tax, many communes were left with insufficient resources.

Grain output	Total grain (million metric tons)	Rice (million metric tons)	Wheat (million metric tons)
1957	185	86.8	23.6
1958	200	80.8	22.6
1959	170	69.3	22.2
1960	143.3	59.7	22.2
1961	147.5	53.6	14.25

Mao's revolution, 1956–61

Other crops	1958	1961
Sugar cane (million metric tons)	12.50	4.27
Beets (million metric tons)	3.00	0.80
Oil-bearing plants (million metric tons)	4.77	1.80
Cotton (million metric tons)	1.97	0.80

Livestock	1958	1961
Pigs (millions)	138.29	75.50
Draught animals (millions)	53.60	38.10

Figure 3.6: Food production in China, 1957–61.
Source: Adapted from J. Fenby, 2013, *The Penguin History of Modern China*, London, Penguin Books, p.414.

Theory of Knowledge

History and the role of the individual:

While it can be argued that an individual – such as Mao – might have considerable influence on some aspects of the course of history within their own lifetime – such as the GLF – does this also apply to long-range historical developments over several generations? Do *transgenerational* historical trends – such as long-term economic developments – have much more importance than any influence an individual might exert within the perspective of *generational* history?

3 The People's Republic of China (1949–2005)

3.3 What were the immediate consequences of the Great Leap Forward?

From 1959 to 1961, China was gripped by chaos and suffering – much, if not most, of this was the result of the rapid implementation of the 'Great Leap Forward' policies. As well as economic and social consequences, these years also saw an intensification of divisions within the CCP – and Mao temporarily losing much of his political influence.

Early problems

As early as 1958, various problems had begun to emerge about unrealistic targets. There were early signs of food shortages, while there was a marked decline in peasant enthusiasm in many areas. In large part, this was because of the 'militarisation' and discipline of labour, and the heavy emphasis on communal living. In particular, peasants from what had been richer collectives resented having to share, on an equal basis, with peasants from poorer ones. Often, they would slaughter and consume their animals, rather than hand them over to the communes.

So, in late November/early December 1958, the Wuhan Conference – which was increasingly dominated by Liu – saw the CC reduce the steel and grain targets. The CC also began to undo some of the organisational aspects of the communes, and decided to place more emphasis on rewarding peasants from the commune surplus according to work done rather than according to economic need (the ration had previously been 30:70, respectively, for work done as opposed to need). More significantly, it warned against utopian over-enthusiasm, and agreed that private ownership of tools, small domestic animals and small family plots should be restored. Further party meetings in early 1959 took additional steps to moderate some aspects – and to reassert central control.

These steps were taken largely despite the opposition of Mao and his supporters. In April 1959, the National People's Congress saw Liu formally instated as head of state. Although Mao remained as chairman of the Party, the fact that Deng was general secretary meant that

Mao's revolution, 1956–61

although Mao retained great personal authority as the leader of the 1949 revolution, he was no longer fully in charge of the party apparatus. He was later to proclaim that, as a result of the Wuhan meeting, he was treated like 'a dead ancestor'. Increasingly, however, concerns over the effectiveness of the Great Leap created further tensions within the CCP – especially as Mao remained determined to restore his influence and power. As he saw it, it was becoming a 'struggle over two roads': one leading back to capitalism, the other leading forwards to communism.

The 'Three Bitter Years', 1959–61

Both the industrial and agricultural plans of the GLF had soon begun to experience real problems. Much of this was down to lack of sufficient expertise and experience, and to inferior raw materials and machinery. These problems came to a head during 1959–61, leading to these three years being known as the 'Three Bitter Years'.

Industrial chaos

The move to urban communes, temporarily halted in 1958, was revived in 1960 as an emergency measure to cope with shortages. Party cadres constantly urged factory workers to work faster, and machines often broke down through overuse and inadequate maintenance. The end products were often substandard as a result of the long hours worked by employees, while such workers were also prone to more industrial accidents.

Finally, tensions between China and the Soviet Union – in part resulting from Khrushchev's strong criticisms in July 1959 of the GLF – led, in July 1960, to the abrupt ending of Soviet aid and the provision of spare parts, along with the withdrawal of 1400 Soviet technicians. In fact, almost from the beginning of the GLF, Khrushchev had angered Mao by his warnings of the risks he believed Mao's policy entailed.

Coming on top of the amount of wasted resources, fuel and time, this left over 250 half-finished industrial projects, and thus made things worse. However, many of the smaller industrial enterprises established during the GLF were more successful – these later formed the basis of the 'Township and Village Enterprises' (TVEs) that were set up after 1976.

3 The People's Republic of China (1949–2005)

The backyard steel campaign

Problems of inadequate technology and lack of skills were most obvious in the production of 'backyard steel'. In July 1959, Mao himself referred to it as a 'great catastrophe'. One of the worst impacts was that the campaign took too many peasants away from agricultural production, thus reducing the amount of food grown. The heavy use of coal deprived trains of fuel, which meant they could often not transport the steel produced to the factories that needed it.

Women

However, there was a positive consequence associated with the GLF. This was that, as a result of the GLF, most women entered into the workforce and so became an integral part of the national economy. This compensated for the fact that the move from cooperatives to communes, under the Great Leap Forward, ended private land ownership by either men or women. This undermined the right granted by the 1950 Marriage Law for women to own land and property in their own right.

As Linda Benson points out, the GLF needed many more full-time workers – this need was met by involving large numbers of women living in rural areas. Women had always performed agricultural work in some parts of China, but it had tended to be mainly seasonal. In most areas, women's primary roles had been as mothers and housewives.

To free them from most traditional household chores, so that they could work on the land, Rural Communes established communal canteens and laundries. In both Rural and Urban Communes, communal nurseries and kindergartens allowed them to escape child minding and return to work. Thus, in some ways, these developments helped implement Communist policies for giving women equal rights and opportunities.

However, most of these communal roles were performed by old women. Furthermore, women's work received fewer work points or wages than that of men. Although women's wages were regularised and so became an important contribution to family incomes, it was many years before equal pay for equal work was established.

Mao's revolution, 1956–61

> **QUESTION**
> To what extent did the establishment of Rural Communes result in greater equality for Chinese women?

Agricultural crisis and famine

The Great Leap had even worse unforeseen and unintended consequences for agriculture. Although the weather in 1958 was good, the harvest did not reflect this. One reason for this was that the industrial projects that Rural Communes were encouraged to undertake meant there were not enough people to harvest the crops properly – as a result, some crops were spoiled before they were harvested. In addition, local cadres sent in exaggerated accounts of how much grain had been produced.

Although the initial government claim of 375 million tonnes was revised down to 250 million tonnes, the real figure was probably even lower than the revised official claim – as suggested by Source 3.4. Yet some of the more prosperous Communes – taking the official figures at face value – increased the amount of food members could consume. This meant food stocks were significantly depleted.

SOURCE 3.4

[An] official communiqué of 26 August [1959] recognized that the figures published previously for economic achievement during the first year of the 'Great Leap' were exaggerated by 40 to 50 per cent. In particular, the grain harvest had been only 250 million tons instead of 375. (The real figure was undoubtedly still lower.) Another bad harvest in 1959, due in part to natural calamities, but also to the disorganization of the economy and the resistance of the peasantry to the extremes of collectivization and discipline practised in the communes was to lead to a lean and bitter winter. This crisis was met and surmounted by maintaining the existence of the communes as administrative units, but introducing a greater and greater degree of decentralization, by which the effective control of economic activity was handed over first to the 'production brigade', corresponding to the former cooperatives, and then to the 'production

3 The People's Republic of China (1949–2005)

> team', corresponding on the whole to mutual aid teams introduced in 1950–51. The overly heavy accent on industry in economic planning was corrected, and it was recognized that for some time to come agriculture would constitute the basis of the national economy.
>
> Schram, S. 1967. **Mao Tse-tung**. Harmondsworth. Penguin Books. pp.299–300.

This would not have mattered too much if the 1959 harvest had been a good one. However, there was the worst and most prolonged drought for a century in northern and central China, resulting in no harvest at all in some of those areas. At the same time, parts of southern China suffered from severe typhoons and floods. In addition, various pests afflicted many regions of China. In all, about 60 per cent of all farming land was affected by these natural catastrophes.

ACTIVITY

Carry out some additional research on famines in China since 1900. Then draw up a table giving the dates of famines, and the estimated number of deaths for each one.

Consequently, the 1959 harvest was only 170 million tonnes, compared to 187 million tonnes in 1957, and 200 million tons in 1958. In many areas, there were serious food shortages and some people in areas began to experience malnutrition and even starvation. However, many local officials tried to keep this secret so, at a time of serious food shortages, the government – believing that there was a vast surplus in most rural areas – actually sharply increased the grain quotas peasants had to sell to government stores at low prices.

Unfortunately, the weather in 1960 was even worse; this, combined with the disruptions and confusions associated with aspects of the Great Leap policies, resulted in an even lower harvest, of approximately 144 million tonnes. It wasn't really until then that the central government realised the extent of the famine crisis – outlined by Source 3.5 – and cut the quotas. Although there was a slight increase in grain production in 1961, output did not return to 1957 levels until 1965.

Mao's revolution, 1956–61

SOURCE 3.5

That summer [1959], the inflated reports of bumper harvests continued, as did the foolhardy new planting methods, some of which were personally espoused by Mao. The result was deepening crisis. Crops that year failed, as they did in 1960 and 1961. [The] Chinese came to refer to these as the 'Three Bitter Years' for the impact on rural China was devastating. The very young and the very old died first, but even the able-bodied weakened as a result of the severe shortages. An estimated 30 million Chinese died before the country began to recover (Becker, 1996). Peasants were forbidden to leave their communes and, as a result, millions of Chinese remained unaware of the widespread impact of the Chairman's Great Leap.

Benson, L. 2002. **China Since 1949.** Harlow. Pearson Education. p.34

Figure 3.7: The areas of China worst hit by the famine of 1959–61.

3 The People's Republic of China (1949–2005)

The result was a major famine that turned out to be one of the worst in China since the start of the century. Although the government imported grain from Australia and Canada to meet the shortfall and introduced rationing, the numbers dying in 1959 from starvation, and illnesses associated with malnutrition, was possibly as high as 9 million.

By the end of the famine in 1961, the total death toll was probably in excess of 20 million – with some later estimates of over 30 million famine and famine-related deaths (though some writers add in the number of children not born to calculate total 'deaths').

Figure 3.8: The effects of the 1959–61 famine in China.

Mao's revolution, 1956–61

> **DISCUSSION POINT**
>
> After 1976, it became increasingly frequent for some writers – both within and outside China – to portray Mao as a mass murderer comparable to Stalin or even Hitler. While, as the main architect of the GLF, he clearly bears most of the moral and historical responsibility for the famine of 1959–61, are such comparisons entirely valid? Does the fact that Mao did neither intend such awful consequences nor wilfully plan any genocide mean his moral responsibility is therefore less?

Divisions within the CCP

Though the famine was not entirely down to Mao's GLF policies, most of the chaos and waste that accompanied many aspects of the Great Leap was. As a result, divisions – over the GLF, Mao's position and control of the PLA – which had been building up in the CCP since 1956, came to a head at the Lushan Conference in the summer of 1959.

The Lushan Conference, July-August 1959

The view later expressed by Liu was that the disaster of the 'Three Bitter Years' was '70 per cent man-made, and 30 per cent due to natural causes'. It soon became clear that the centre-right of the Party placed Mao's responsibility at the centre of the 'man-made' element. In fact, just before the first Lushan meeting, Mao had accepted that his rapid push for the establishment of Rural Communes had led to 'chaos on a grand scale'.

At the two Lushan meetings, which took place in July and August 1959, Mao's decision in December 1958 to resign as Chairman of the PRC, and his replacement by Liu, were formally accepted by the Party. This meant that Mao was no longer formally involved in routine government work. By then, there was mounting evidence of serious food shortages in some regions.

However, a strong attack on Mao and his Great Leap was launched by Peng (see Sources 3.6 and 3.7) who, according to some sources, might have been involved with Gao and Rao before they were purged in 1954–5.

Peng had also expressed criticisms of Mao's GLF to Khrushchev during a visit to the Soviet bloc in the spring of 1959. In part, this was because

3 The People's Republic of China (1949–2005)

Peng believed the industrial problems were depriving the PLA of the modern equipment it needed, and that the revival of a people's militia threatened the very existence of the PLA. He also believed the GLF was undermining Sino-Soviet relations which, in view of the active hostility of the US, he believed were essential for China's security.

SOURCE 3.6

Dear Chairman:

This Lushan Meeting is important. In the discussions in the Northwest Group, I commented on other speakers' remarks several times. Now I am stating, specially for your reference, a number of my views that I have not expressed fully at the group meetings. I may be as straightforward as Zhang Fei, but I possess only his roughness without his tact…

But as we can see now, an excessive number of capital construction projects were hastily started in 1958. With part of the funds being dispersed, completion of some essential projects had to be postponed… Because we did not have a deep enough understanding, we came to be aware too late. So we continued with our Great Leap Forward in 1959 instead of putting on the brakes and slowing our pace accordingly. As a result, imbalances were not corrected in time and new temporary difficulties cropped up…

Extracts from the letter sent by Peng Dehuai, in which he criticised aspects of the Great Leap Forward. Quoted in: Ebrey, P. (ed). 1981. **Chinese Civilization: A Sourcebook.** *New York. The Free Press Education. pp.436–9.*

Although centre-right leaders such as Liu, Zhou and Deng agreed with much of what Peng said, they did not openly back him. As a result, Mao and his supporters were able to launch a counter-attack, despite growing opposition to the GLF. Despite admitting to some of the problems of the GLF, Mao continued to defend its main principles and direction.

At one point, Mao threatened that, if the Party endorsed Peng's ideas, he would go 'to the countryside' to raise a new peasant army to overthrow the government – though he believed that most of the PLA would support him rather than those who agreed with Peng. Although many Party leaders shared Peng's views, no one was prepared to risk that.

Mao's revolution, 1956–61

> **SOURCE 3.7**
>
> The mounting conflict within the CCP leadership became even more intense over the course of two meetings – of the Politburo and the Central Committee – that were held in the summer of 1959 at the hill station on Mount Lushan… The first of these meetings, the Lushan Conference, which was technically an enlarged meeting of the Political Bureau of the Chinese communist Party, lasted from 2 July to 1 August. By the end of the meeting, Mao Zedong had launched a ferocious attack against Peng Dehuai, China's defence minister and one of the ten Marshals of the People's Liberation Army, and had set in motion the procedures necessary to replace Peng with Marshal Lin Biao…
>
> Peng Dehuai's attack on Mao and on the whole approach of the Great Leap Forward was a tour de force. It was in turns emotional, sarcastic and mordant. He attacked the fanaticism of the collectivisation frenzy and the unreality of Mao's ambitions, but in particular he condemned the sycophancy and craven performance of party leaders who had encouraged the exaggeration of both targets and achievements in industrial production. The majority of those present at the conference may have sympathised with Peng's strictures but his condemnation of the Great Leap Forward was not just an argument about policy: it was a direct assault on Mao and the nature and quality of his leadership.
>
> Dillon, M. 2012. **China: A Modern History.** London. I. B. Tauris. pp.313–5

Thus there was no open support for Peng, and Mao was able to persuade the CC to agree to purge those leaders with 'right opportunist' ideas who were associated with an 'anti-Party clique' headed by Peng.

Peng was then dismissed from all his posts, including that of Minister of Defence, and Mao managed to get one of his strongest supporters, Lin Biao, to take Peng's place. Mao then pushed for a second 'Anti-Rightist' campaign within the Party to root out other 'right opportunists'. This more general purge continued until 1961 – one of its victims in 1960 was Chen Yun.

Mao and the GLF after Lushan

Nonetheless, Mao's political victory proved shortlived, as the Party leadership insisted that production targets should be revised downwards to more realistic levels. During 1960–61, the Great Leap Forward was

3 The People's Republic of China (1949–2005)

essentially abandoned. Communes were reduced in size to make them more manageable; the 'backyard' steel furnaces were run down; and more emphasis was placed on technicians and experts. In addition, bonus payments for skilled workers were re-introduced, and peasants who had flooded into towns but had not found work were directed to return to rural areas.

In rural areas, the size of communes were further reduced, with the number rising to about 70 000. Peasants were also shifted back to agricultural production, a lot of decision-making was devolved from central commune administrations to production brigades and teams. This left the communes mainly in charge of public works and security.

Payments were also more closely linked to the amount and quality of work done. As for skilled workers in urban areas, bonuses and incentives were re-introduced for peasants, to help boost production. More significantly, private plots were again allowed, with any surplus they produced being sold in markets for private profit. In some areas, peasants began to farm previously uncultivated land under a 'household responsibility' scheme which, in many ways, effectively allowed families to farm as private owners. By the end of 1961, 20 per cent of farmed land was being farmed by individual families, as opposed to that farmed by communes.

Mao's position

Although the centre-right – often referred to as 'moderates' – were now clearly in charge of policy, this did not mean that Mao and his supporters were completely sidelined. In particular, Mao still had a lot of political 'capital' as the main leader of the 1949 revolution. For the time being, however, he largely withdrew from public life; during this time, he became increasingly concerned that the policies that marked the retreat from the GLF were moving China back from the socialist path towards a possible restoration of capitalism.

Thus, in many ways, the GLF can be seen as a serious political failure for Mao. He had hoped that it would enable him to go down in China's history, not only as the main architect of the victorious revolution of 1949, but also as the leader who had created a fully socialist and prosperous society. In addition, he had failed to overcome those Party and state leaders and officials he feared were taking China down the 'capitalist road'.

Mao's revolution, 1956–61

Yet, though temporarily having little direct influence over economic policy, he soon began to take steps to put himself back at the centre of affairs and to regain control of the CCP which, he felt, had been infiltrated by 'bourgeois elements'. Some historians, however – such as Maurice Meisner – believe that Mao was sufficiently demoralised by the Lushan Conference to abandon, at least initially, any active political struggle.

KEY CONCEPTS QUESTION

Consequence: What were the most important impacts of the Great Leap Forward on developments within the CCP in the period 1959–61?

3 The People's Republic of China (1949–2005)

Paper 3 exam practice

Question

To what extent had Mao's Great Leap Forward of 1958 been successful by 1961? **[15 marks]**

Skill

Planning an essay

Examiner's tips

As discussed in Chapter 2, the first stage of planning an answer to a question is to think carefully about the wording of the question so that you know what is required and what you need to focus on. Once you have done this, you can move on to the other important considerations:

- Decide your main argument/theme/approach *before* you start to write. This will help you identify the key points you want to make. For example, this question requires you to make a decision/judgement about the degree to which Mao's Great Leap Forward had been successful in the period 1958–61. Deciding on an approach helps you produce an argument that is clear, coherent and logical.
- Plan the structure of your essay – i.e. the introduction, the main body of the essay (in which you present precise evidence to support your arguments), and your concluding paragraph.

For this question, you will first have to identify Mao's various aims regarding the Great Leap Forward. Also, whatever your overall view about the success/failure of the Great Leap Forward, you should try to write a balanced argument, by presenting arguments and evaluating evidence that show it to have been both successful and a failure.

As a rough guide for this type of question, you would need to deal with both the 'successful' and 'failure' arguments – for example on the basis of 60% for your view and 40% for opposing views or interpretations.

Whatever the question, try to link the points you make in your paragraphs, so that there is a clear thread that follows through to your conclusion. This will help to ensure that your essay is not just a series of unconnected paragraphs.

Mao's Revolution, 1956–61

You may well find that drawing up a spider diagram or mind map helps you with your essay planning. For this question, your spider diagram might look this:

- MAO'S AIMS
- ECONOMIC RESULTS
- **THE GREAT LEAP FORWARD, 1958-61**
- SOCIAL IMPACTS
- POLITICAL CONSEQUENCES

When writing your essay, include linking words or phrases to ensure that each paragraph dealing with one of the smaller 'bubbles' is linked to the 'main bubble' (the question). For example:

Although Mao's main aims for the Great Leap Forward in 1958 were to make China's economy comparable to those of more developed Western countries within 15 years, and to complete China's 'transition to socialism', the evidence strongly suggests that – despite some gains – the GLF was a failure overall.

For instance, despite the rapid construction of many infrastructure projects – such as dams – one of the biggest failures of the GLF was the 'backyard steel' campaign. Although over 500 000 such furnaces were constructed all over China, most of the steel they produced was of such poor quality that it proved unusable. The GLF also led to rapidly deteriorating relations between China and the USSR which, under Khrushchev, had warned Mao that the whole project was far too risky. When Mao ignored him, the Soviet Union withdrew all its experts working in China in 1960, ended its loans, and stopped providing spare parts. This left China with many unfinished factory and construction projects.

3 The People's Republic of China (1949–2005)

Furthermore, as regards agriculture, the overall results were even worse. By shifting so many peasants onto industrial projects in rural areas, grain production actually fell. These shortages were made worse by an exceptionally severe drought in many northern and western parts of China, and by widespread flooding in the south. In addition, the government grain tax took almost twice the amount previously taken, while the low price paid by the state for surplus grain led some peasants to cut back on their planting. As a result, the GLF was an agricultural as well as an industrial failure.

In addition, the GLF also had disastrous social results, in that it culminated in three years of famine, from 1959 to 1961. Estimates vary as to the numbers who died as a result, but most historians suggest it was between 20 and 40 million – either from starvation or from diseases linked to malnutrition....

However, many historians also point out that, from Mao's point of view, the GLF was also a political failure. He had hoped it would result in him being hailed as the CCP leader who, in addition to leading the Communists to victory in 1949, had also been responsible for China becoming a fully developed and prosperous socialist society. He had also seen the GLF as a way of overcoming signs of growing bureaucratism and conservatism within the party and the state. Instead, it led to him being edged out of real influence within the party. Furthermore, instead of combatting those political developments within the party which had worried him, centre-right Communists became more influential than they had been before 1958. Some historians, such as Maurice Meisner, in fact, speak of a 'bureaucratic restoration' after 1961...

There are clearly many aspects to consider, which will be difficult under the time constraints of the exam. Producing a plan with brief details (e.g. dates, main events/features) under each heading will help you cover the main issues in the time available. It will also give you something to use if you run out of time and can only jot down the main points of your last paragraph(s). The examiner will be able to give you some credit for this.

Common mistakes

Once the exam time has started, one common mistake is for candidates to begin writing straight away, without being sure whether they know enough about the questions they have selected. Once they have written several paragraphs, they may run out of things to say – and then panic because of the time they have wasted.

Producing plans for each of the three questions you intend to answer in Paper 3 at the start of the exam, before you start to write your first essay, will help you see if you know enough about the questions to tackle them successfully. If you don't, then you need to choose different ones!

Activity

In this chapter, the focus is on planning answers. So, using the information from this chapter and any other sources of information available to you, produce essay plans – using spider diagrams or mind maps – with all the necessary headings (and brief details) for well-focused and clearly structured responses to at least two of the following Practice Paper 3 questions.

Remember to refer to the simplified Paper 3 mark scheme in Chapter 10.

Paper 3 practice questions

1 'The Hundred Flowers campaign of 1956–57 was merely a cynical attempt to identify Mao's political opponents.' To what extent do you agree with this statement?

2 Discuss the reasons for, and the consequences of, the Anti-Rightist Campaign of 1957.

3 To what extent was the Great Leap Forward solely down to Mao's determination to transform China into a fully socialist society before the Soviet Union?

4 Examine the nature and impact of the Great Leap Forward.

5 Evaluate the significance of the Lushan Conference of 1959 on political developments within the Chinese Communist Party.

4 Power struggles and the Cultural Revolution, 1962–71

Power struggles and the Cultural Revolution, 1962–71

Introduction

As was seen in Chapter 3, in January 1958 Mao had announced his Great Leap Forward.

Figure 4.1: Commune members building the Sanmenshia Dam during the Great Leap Forward, 1958.

However, after some initial successes, things had begun to go badly wrong. Apart from a general economic failure in industry, there was a particularly severe crisis in agriculture – in part the result of bad weather – which led to food shortages and famine during the 'Three Bitter Years' from 1959–61.

This had led some leading Communists to criticise Mao's economic policies – the most outspoken critic had been Peng Dehuai. His letter to Mao during the Lushan Conference in July 1959, despite approving the general approach of Mao's Great Leap Forward to 'building socialism', had voiced very strong criticisms of the specific policies and implementation of the GLF. Although Mao had been able to get the Central Committee to repudiate this letter and to purge Peng and his supporters from their positions, the mounting problems caused by the Great Leap Forward led to the loss of some of his influence.

4 The People's Republic of China (1949–2005)

Nonetheless, despite Mao giving up his position as Chairman (president) of the PRC, and relinquishing direct supervision of government affairs, he remained as Chairman of the CCP. He thus retained considerable prestige, as well as theoretical precedence, within the Party. From 1962 onwards, he began moves to re-establish his pre-eminent leadership.

TIMELINE

1962 Sep: Socialist Education Movement launched

Dec: 'Four Cleanups' campaign announced

1963 May: First Ten Points raised by Mao

1964 Feb: Mao calls for intellectuals to 'learn from the peasants'

May: Publication of *Quotations from the Thoughts of Chairman Mao*

Jun: Mao calls for a 'rectification' campaign against intellectuals

1965 Jan: Mao warns of 'capitalist roaders' within the CCP; announcement of the Twenty-three Articles

Jul: Campaign to study Mao's thoughts begins

1966 May: PLA calls for purge of 'anti-socialist' elements; Central Cultural Revolutionary Committee set up

Jun: 'Four Olds' campaign announced

Aug: 'Sixteen Articles' call for a Cultural Revolution; mass rally in Beijing

1968 Dec: Mao and Lin start to limit actions of Red Guards; Liu and Deng dismissed from posts

1969 Apr: Cultural Revolution called off; Lin Biao emerges as Mao's successor during Ninth Congress of CCP

Sep: PLA disarm the Red Guards

Dec: Central Cultural Revolutionary Committee abolished

1970 Aug: Lin attacks Zhou Enlai's policies at the Second Plenum of 9th CC

1971 Sep: '571 Affair'; death of Lin Biao

KEY QUESTIONS

- How did Mao begin to re-establish his political leadership after 1961?
- What were the main features of the Cultural Revolution?
- Why was there another power struggle after the Cultural Revolution?

Power struggles and the Cultural Revolution, 1962–71

Overview

- The economic problems that resulted from Mao's Great Leap Forward had reduced his power and influence.
- Under Liu Shaoqi and Deng Xiaoping, economic and administrative policies were introduced that undid many of Mao's initiatives.
- Mao decided to oppose these 'Rightists' and, after launching his Socialist Education Movement in 1962, began the Cultural Revolution in 1966.
- By 1969, this had resulted in Liu and Deng being removed from power. Mao then began to curb the activities of the Red Guards.
- Mao was supported during the Cultural Revolution by Lin Biao, and by what became known as the Gang of Four.
- However, in 1971, serious differences emerged between Mao and Lin: Lin died trying to escape after his alleged plot against Mao had failed. This began another power struggle – between Rightists such as Zhou and Deng, and the Maoist Gang of Four.

4.1 How did Mao begin to re-establish his political leadership after 1961?

Liu Shaoqi – who had long been seen as Mao's likely successor – took over from Mao as chairman of the PRC. To tackle the serious problems of China's agricultural system, Liu – who saw the GLF disaster as *'seventy per cent man-made and thirty per cent due to natural causes'* – allowed peasants to have private plots, so that, after they had worked on the commune lands, they could grow extra food for their families. He also introduced bonuses and other incentives for the hardest workers on the communes, and for factory workers, in order to increase production.

At the same time, in order to ensure these new policies were implemented at all local levels, the authority of central Party and state bodies was re-established. Instead of the 'voluntarism' and relative autonomy of Party cadres in local rural communes which had marked the GLF, the authority of higher Party organs was strengthened. During

4 The People's Republic of China (1949–2005)

1961–62, for instance, the Politburo and the CC initiated a campaign that stressed the Leninist principle of 'democratic centralism' – with the emphasis very much on centralism. Yet these policy changes saw the Chinese economy slowly begin to recover from the impact of the GLF.

Although the centre-right – often referred to as 'moderates' – were now clearly in charge of economic policy, this did not mean that Mao and his supporters were completely sidelined. In particular, as Philip Short and other historians have suggested, Mao still remained an important member of the leading group of Communists, while his considerable political 'capital' as the main leader of the 1949 Revolution meant he continued to have much political influence over CCP members and ordinary Chinese people. For the time being, however, he largely withdrew from public life – he later said this gave him the opportunity to think and plan, instead of being bothered with daily administrative matters. However, other historians – such as Maurice Meisner in Source 4.1 – have suggested that, at first, Mao became pessimistic about the immediate future of the Chinese Revolution.

SOURCE 4.1

Shortly after his victory over Peng Dehuai at Lushan in August 1959, Mao removed himself from the day-to-day affairs of the Party. The withdrawal was perhaps voluntary, or at least graceful, but it was certainly motivated by Mao's awareness that Peng's criticisms of the Great Leap were widely shared by Party leaders, even if they did not share Peng's bluntness, by a recognition that he could not command a majority of the Central Committee to continue the socially radical policies of the Great Leap (even assuming that he might have been inclined to do so), and that a collapsing economy and a demoralized peasantry did not provide favourable circumstances for any attempt to override the Central Committee as he had in the past…

With the disintegration of the Great Leap and his consequent isolation from the center of political power, Mao began to suffer from an uncharacteristic loss of confidence in the future of the revolution. He no longer entertained any hope of an imminent transition from socialism to communism.

Meisner, M. 1999. **Mao's China and After: A History of the People's Republic.** New York. The Free Press. pp.253–4

Power struggles and the Cultural Revolution, 1962–71

> **QUESTION**
>
> How, according to Source 4.1, did the Great Leap Forward lead to a loss of political influence for Mao?

In fact, Meisner has seen the victory of the centre-right of the CCP as a 'Thermidorian reaction' – similar to what had happened in the French Revolution in 1794, when the radicals were overthrown by more conservative leaders – in which the centre-right succeeded in overturning the temporary halt to bureaucratisation which had been a feature of the GLF. According to him, it was the growing expansion of Party and state bureaucratic centralism after 1961 that worried Mao, as he feared this social strata was rising above society and becoming the dominant force in China – and was using its growing power to emphasise order and stability over the revolutionary goals of 1949.

> **ACTIVITY**
>
> Both Soviet and Chinese Communists often referred to key developments of the French Revolution when commenting on current issues. Try to find out what was meant by the terms 'Thermidorian reaction' and 'Bonapartism' (which appears later in this chapter). How valid do you think the use of such terms was in the context of Chinese history in the 1960s?

Historians such as Meisner see Mao's anti-bureaucratism as stemming mainly from the influence of anarchist ideas during his pre-Marxist youth, and from his attraction to the more anti-authoritarian aspects of Marxism. However, other historians see his 1960s campaign against bureaucracy merely as a way of crushing his political opponents and re-establishing his personal authority.

Mao's political views in 1961

During 1960–61, Mao became increasingly concerned that the political and economic policies that marked the retreat from the GLF were moving China back from the socialist path towards a possible restoration of capitalism. In particular, he was worried by the renewed emphasis being placed on technical 'experts'. He had always been suspicious of

4 The People's Republic of China (1949–2005)

experts, fearing they might put their interest above those of the people and the revolution.

Mao also believed that the Soviet model of industrialisation was not appropriate for a country like China. He had come to the conclusion that the Russian Revolution had been undermined by the reliance on experts and administrators. He believed this had led to a new 'class' of bureaucrats who gave themselves privileges and, under Khrushchev, had begun to restore aspects of capitalism in the Soviet Union. He believed that 'moderates' such as Liu and Deng were now trying to do the same in China.

> ### DISCUSSION POINT
> Is the emergence of a bureaucratic élite of administrators and experts – effectively beyond the control of electorates and even governments – inevitable in any large society? Or is it possible to devise democratic political controls that ensure the political wishes of ordinary people remain paramount when policies are being drawn up and implemented?

Though temporarily having little direct influence over economic policy, he soon began to take steps to put himself back at the centre of affairs and to regain control of the CCP which, he felt, had been infiltrated by 'bourgeois elements' who were using political bureaucracy to undermine the gains of the 1949 Revolution.

The Socialist Education Movement and 'rightist deviations'

Mao became increasingly worried about Liu's economic and Deng's political policies, and a serious debate soon developed within the leadership of the CCP over future economic policy. Liu and Deng argued for more incentives – including larger private plots – for peasants, and for a return to the methods of the First Five-Year Plan, which had been drawn up with the advice of Soviet experts. Mao disagreed with such ideas and, in his view, the Party was taking China off the 'revolutionary socialist road', resulting in a tendency towards 'creeping capitalism'.

Yet, according to several historians, the differences between Mao, and leaders such as Liu and Deng, were not as great as was later claimed. Maurice Meisner in Source 4.2, for instance, sees Liu's economic policies as very similar to those followed by Lenin in Soviet Russia in the early 1920s.

> **SOURCE 4.2**
>
> During the cultural revolution of 1966–1969, the economic policies of the preceding half-decade were condemned for leading China on a retreat from 'socialism' to 'capitalism,' and the Party leaders responsible for implementing those policies were purged as 'capitalist roaders' who allegedly exercised a 'bourgeois dictatorship'. This, in brief, was the Maoist judgment on the early 1960s, or at least the dramatic picture of a 'life-and-death struggle' between capitalism and socialism that Maoists presented to the world.
>
> Yet the differences between what became known as the Maoist and Liuist roads do not appear to be nearly so sharp. It is instructive to compare the economic policies pursued by Liu Shaoqi in the early 1960s with those adopted by Lenin in the Soviet Union forty years earlier… The economic policies adopted by the Chinese leaders… were in some respects similar to Lenin's NEP… Yet, as an alleged 'retreat to capitalism', the Chinese program was but a pale reflection of its earlier Soviet counterpart.
>
> Meisner, M., 1999, **Mao's China and After: A History of the People's Republic**, New York, The Free Press, pp.260–1

In order to correct this bureaucratic 'Rightist deviation', Mao – and the other radicals who supported him – decided that what was needed was a mass revolutionary campaign among Chinese youth: Mao called this the 'Socialist Education Movement' (SEM). It was based on three 'isms': collectivism, patriotism and socialism, and involved workers and peasants studying his works, and attending rallies and meetings. He paid particular attention to stressing the importance of school and college students, believing they should be encouraged to take action in a 'new' revolution. Mao saw this as important because most had been born after 1949, and so had no real idea of what China had been like before. If they saw nothing wrong with the economic policies currently being advocated by the centre-right of the Party, Mao believed that capitalism would soon re-emerge in China.

4 The People's Republic of China (1949–2005)

> **QUESTION**
> Why did Mao stress the importance of the younger generation?

In September 1962, he made a speech at a Central Committee meeting, warning it was still possible for China to move backwards to a 'restoration of the reactionary classes'. He persuaded the Central Committee that the period of transition to communism would be marked by a continuing class struggle between the proletariat and the bourgeoisie, so that it was necessary to condemn 'revisionist tendencies' in the Party, and to strengthen socialist principles – especially in the countryside. In Mao's view, Liu and Deng's policies were taking China along a 'capitalist road', and he attacked those administrators and peasants who, he believed, showed signs of becoming 'capitalists'.

Although the SEM was initially intended as a campaign to restore collectivisation in rural areas, it soon widened out to tackle the growing problem of corruption – in the countryside and elsewhere. In December 1962, the 'Four Cleanups' campaign was launched initially in two provinces, but was soon extended to the rest of China. The focus was on four main aspects: the administration of collective accounts, communal granaries, public property and work points. As part of this, the role of middle and poor peasants in agricultural management was to be enhanced, and more 'experienced' (politically reliable) cadres from urban areas were sent to assist in the campaign.

In May 1963, the Central Committee issued a resolution, known as the 'First Ten Points', which set down the campaign's objectives and methods (see Source 4.3). Work teams were sent to rural areas to monitor the campaign. However, these soon faced considerable opposition from many peasants. As a result, two revised versions – by Deng Xiaoping and Liu Shaoqi – came out in September 1963 and September 1964 respectively. These tried to limit the scope of the campaign – in particular, they called for greater support for private plots, and for a market economy in rural collectives.

Power struggles and the Cultural Revolution, 1962–71

> **SOURCE 4.3**
>
> This is a struggle that calls for the re-education of man. This is a struggle for reorganizing the revolutionary class army for a confrontation with the forces of feudalism and capitalism which are now feverishly attacking us. We must nip their counterrevolution in the bud… With cadres and masses joining hand in hand in production labor and scientific experiments, our Party will take another stride forward in becoming a more glorious, greater, and more correct Party…
>
> Extracts from the 'First Ten Points', translated in Baum, R. & Teiwes, F. C., 1968, **Ssu-Ch'ing: The Socialist Education Movement of 1962–1966**, Berkeley, University of California Press, pp.62–71.

Consequently, Mao – increasingly dissatisfied with political developments in the early 1960s – became concerned that the campaign was no longer being carried out in a truly revolutionary way, and that such leaders were de-railing the revolution. At first, Mao's ideas had little support but, during 1964–65, the support of **Lin Biao**, the Minister of Defence responsible for the People's Liberation Army (PLA), became increasingly important. As a first step towards greater equality, Lin Biao had abolished all ranks and insignia in the PLA; and, during the early 1960s, the PLA and its values – especially simplicity, self-sacrifice and devotion to duty – had increasingly come to be held up as a model for the whole of Chinese society.

> **Lin Biao (1907–71):**
>
> Lin's real name was Lin Yurong, and he had been an important Red Army leader during the Civil War. He moved increasingly to the left after replacing Peng as Minister of Defence in 1959, and rose to prominence during the Cultural Revolution. After Liu had been purged, he was named at a Party conference as Mao's second-in-command, and described as '*closest comrade-in-arms and successor to Mao Zedong*'. As early as 1960, he had pushed for the 'concentrated study' in the PLA of Mao's writings. However, in 1971, he died under mysterious circumstances, following what became known as the '571 Affair'.

4 The People's Republic of China (1949–2005)

In May 1964, Lin – with the help of **Chen Boda** – got the Political Department of the People's Liberation Army (PLA) to publish the pocket-sized book, *Quotations from the Thoughts of Chairman Mao Zedong* – later known as the 'Little Red Book'. This was made required reading for all 4 million PLA soldiers, who were expected to be able to memorise at least some of the quotations. As a result, the PLA soon became a stronghold of Maoist thought – this support gave Mao a significant power base which enabled him to push his ideas forward; it was also the starting point for the creation of a cult of personality around Mao.

Chen Boda (1904–89):

Chen joined the CCP in 1927 and, in 1937, became Mao's researcher and secretary. After 1949, he became one of the most important interpreters of Mao's thoughts; in 1958, he became editor of *The Red Flag,* the CCP's journal. At the Lushan Conference in July 1959, he put forward Mao's criticisms of Peng Dehuai. In May 1966, he joined the Politburo and became the head of the newly formed Central Cultural Revolutionary Committee, working closely with Jiang Qing. After 1972, when centre-right 'moderates' increasingly returned to power, his radicalism put him at odds with the new leadership: in 1973, he was expelled from the CCP and, once the Gang of Four had been overthrown, was briefly imprisoned in 1981.

QUESTION

What is the message of the photograph in Figure 4.2? How does it get the message across?

Power struggles and the Cultural Revolution, 1962–71

Figure 4.2: Mao and Lin Biao together. Lin is holding a copy of the Little Red Book.

In all, nearly a billion copies of Mao's book were printed, along with 150 million copies of the fourth edition of *Mao's Selected Works*, which had been published in 1960. In July 1965, the press mounted a formal campaign to encourage the study of Mao's works. By then, the 'Mao cult' had spread across China – and he became known as 'the Great Helmsman'.

Mao had previously said that personality cults had valuable political uses – he attributed Khrushchev's overthrow in the Soviet Union in 1964 to the fact that he had not developed a cult of personality. When Edgar Snow, an American journalist partly sympathetic to Communist China, visited China in the winter of 1964–65, he was puzzled by the 'immoderate glorification' of Mao – and, as Source 4.4 shows, compared it to Stalin's personality cult in the Soviet Union.

The People's Republic of China (1949–2005)

> **SOURCE 4.4**
>
> Giant portraits of him now hung in the streets, busts were in every chamber, his books and photographs were everywhere on display to the exclusion of all others… It gave me … [an] uneasy recollection of similar extravaganzas of worship of Joseph Stalin seen during wartime years in Russia… The one-man cult was not yet universal, but the trend was unmistakable.
>
> Snow, E., 1971, *The Long Revolution*, New York, Random House, pp.68–9.

> **QUESTION**
>
> Why did Mao allow a 'personality cult' of himself to develop during the early stages of his campaign to regain power?

Intellectuals and 'revolutionary successors'

In February 1964, Mao called for intellectuals to be sent from the cities to the countryside, to 'learn from the peasants'. Mao had long distrusted intellectuals, and the cities they resided in – cities were seen by Mao as breeding grounds of ideological corruption and revisionism. In June 1964, he called for a 'rectification' campaign, similar to the anti-rightist one of late 1957, conducted against intellectuals.

By then, Mao and his supporters were becoming increasingly concerned about the need to train 'revolutionary successors' among the youth of China. He therefore proposed that the period of formal education be reduced and that, instead, education should be combined with productive labour – in order to stop the 'corruption' of China's youth.

This led to growing unease among intellectuals in the Party. However, those in the Party who opposed Mao's statements, and who wanted a more flexible interpretation of Marxism, looked for an opportunity to undermine Mao. An earlier veiled criticism had been made by allowing publication of a play, in 1960, by Wu Han (a professor of history, a playwright and deputy mayor of Beijing). Although set in the Ming period, its main theme – the wrongful dismissal of an official for telling

Power struggles and the Cultural Revolution, 1962–71

the emperor the truth – had clear parallels with the dismissal of the PLA general Peng Dehuai in 1959, which Mao had pushed for. This play was just one of several anti-Maoist satires written during the 'Bitter Years' that followed the collapse of the GLF. Although the number of such satires rapidly declined once the Socialist Education Movement had begun in September 1962, these writers and intellectuals had been supported by both Liu and Deng.

This led Mao to take more serious action: in January 1965, at a Politburo meeting, he identified as the principal enemy of socialism 'those people in authority within the Party who are taking the capitalist road'. Mao's concerns about the existence of 'capitalist roaders' within the CCP leadership were then published in the 'Twenty-three Articles', which explicitly warned that the struggle between socialism and capitalism was also taking place within the Party at its highest levels, and that socialism was being threatened by these 'capitalist roaders'.

He then demanded that Wu Han's play be criticised by the Party, as part of a 'cultural revolution'. But this was delayed repeatedly so, urged on by his wife, **Jiang Qing**, Mao had a critical review published in a magazine in Shanghai in November 1965 – most of Mao's supporters later saw this as the start of the Cultural Revolution.

> ### Jiang Qing (1914–91):
> Jiang was an actress, and had married Mao in 1938 as his fourth wife (or third, if Mao's first arranged marriage – which he refused to consummate – is ignored). During the 1950s, she worked with the Ministry of Culture, where she supported and promoted plays and operas that reflected revolutionary sentiments. In the 1960s, she increasingly took control of the national media to ensure it followed a 'correct' cultural line. This control allowed her to become increasingly politically important, and she was able to gather a group of radical supporters – mainly from Shanghai – around her. Several leading communists became worried about her influence – especially during the Cultural Revolution. Later, she and her main Shanghai supporters became known as the 'Gang of Four' (see Chapter 6).

4 The People's Republic of China (1949–2005)

Liuists versus Maoists

By the spring of 1966, differences within the Party leadership had resulted in the emergence of two clear factions: the 'Liuists' who dominated the Party and state apparatus; and the minority 'Maoists', supported by the PLA. In fact, this division had first become apparent during the Lushan meetings of 1959, at which the political consensus of the Communist leadership, established in the years before 1949, had first begun to disintegrate.

These two distinct political responses to the failures of the Great Leap Forward, which emerged at Lushan, sowed the seeds for the deep political polarisation which culminated in the Cultural Revolution just seven years later.

In early May 1966, the PLA's *Liberation Army Daily* began to call for a purge of anti-socialist elements in cultural circles – and also of 'anti-socialist elements' in the Party itself. As a first step, the heads of newspapers, and cultural and propaganda departments in Beijing were purged. In particular, Mao moved against the 'Group of Five', an informal group – headed by the mayor of Beijing – which had been set up by the CC in January 1965, to initiate a revolution in China's culture. However, four of the five tended to support Liu and Deng, and the committee had done little – so Mao abolished it, and replaced it with a new 'Central Cultural Revolutionary Committee'.

This was headed by Chen Boda, and was packed with his supporters, including Jiang Qing. With her support – and that of other leftists associated with her – Mao began what turned out to be his last mass political campaign.

> ### KEY CONCEPTS ACTIVITY
>
> **Significance:** Using the information in this section, and any other sources available to you, draw up a table to summarise the main political and economic differences between the 'Liuist' centre-right and the 'Maoist' left within the CCP by the end of 1965. Then write a paragraph to explain which difference you think was the most important one.

4.2 What were the main features of the Cultural Revolution?

From May 1966, as a way to restore his power, Mao launched the Cultural Revolution – its official name was the 'Great Proletarian Cultural Revolution' – which is generally taken as lasting from May 1966 to April 1969. However, those who took power after his death – many of whom were its victims – state that it lasted till October 1976, when the Gang of Four were overthrown and arrested.

It has thus been described as a decade-long 'catastrophe', which resulted in the 'heaviest losses' suffered by the Party, state and the people of China since 1949. Other commentators have seen it as continuing as late as 1980, only ending with the final victory of the 'moderates'. Although the Cultural Revolution was based in part on the *Quotations from Chairman Mao*, the destructive aspects of the Cultural Revolution were not apparently anticipated by Mao.

Reasons for the Cultural Revolution

The Cultural Revolution was, on one level, Mao's attempt to eradicate old anti-revolutionary ideas, especially 'capitalist' and 'bourgeois' ideas. It was also directed against those holding such ideas – especially the political and administrative élite which he saw as taking control of the revolution. Thus he hoped that, by removing them, and remoulding Chinese society and culture, he could ensure that there would be no more attempts to take China off the 'revolutionary path' – and that China would avoid the 'revisionist' errors which, in his view, had overtaken the Soviet Union. Finally, on another, more simple, level, it was also part of Mao's bid to restore his own personal power and influence, which had been reduced as a result of the Great Leap Forward.

4 The People's Republic of China (1949–2005)

To carry it out, Mao relied on the PLA and the radical youth of China – seen by him as the 'revolutionary successors' who would carry his ideas forward and so secure the revolutionary future. Thus, the Cultural Revolution was a deliberate attempt to turn the young against the old.

SOURCE 4.5

These cataclysmic plunges [the Great Leap Forward and the Cultural Revolution] were, it is generally agreed, due largely to Mao himself, whose policies were often received with reluctance in the party leadership, and sometimes – most notably in the case of the Great Leap Forward – with frank opposition, which he overcame only by launching the 'Cultural Revolution'. Yet they cannot be understood without a sense of the peculiarities of Chinese communism, of which Mao made himself the spokesman. Unlike Russian communism, Chinese communism had virtually no direct relations with Marx and Marxism. It was a post-October [1917] movement which came to Marx via Lenin, or more precisely Stalin's 'Marxism-Leninism'. Mao's own knowledge of Marxist theory seems to have been almost entirely derived from the Stalinist *History of the CPSU [b]: Short Course* of 1939. And yet below the Marxist-Leninist top-dressing, there was – and this is very evident in the case of Mao, who never travelled outside China until he had become head of state, and whose intellectual formation was entirely home-grown – a very Chinese utopianism.

Hobsbawm, E. 1994. Age of Extremes: The Short Twentieth Century, 1914–1991. London. Michael Joseph. p.467

QUESTION

How far do Sources 4.5 and 4.6 agree on 'Maoism' and the Cultural Revolution having limited connections to Marxism and earlier developments in the Soviet Union? Do you agree with these interpretations?

> **SOURCE 4.6**
>
> The forms taken by the Mao cult today [1966–7] appear even stranger against the background of this iconoclasm [in the Cultural Revolution]. Without assuming that they represent simply a new metamorphosis of the imperial tradition, it is clear that they owe a great deal more to certain patterns from the Chinese past than to Marxism. Ironically, the Great Proletarian Cultural Revolution, which presents itself as an attack on the 'bourgeois' and 'feudal' values of the past in the name of universal proletarian truth, is accompanied by developments which contradict both the universalist and the rationalist elements in Marxism…
>
> This time, of course, the whole process takes place in Marxist terms: it is not an encounter among diverse schools of thought, but reflects a debate within the [party] élite about the correct interpretation of Marxism-Leninism today.
>
> *Schram, S. 1966.* **Mao Tse-tung.** *Harmondsworth. Penguin Books Ltd. pp.344–5*

Although the Cultural Revolution had much to do with political rivalries among the leadership, it was also based on real ideological differences. These included dealing with aspects such as growing social inequalities, the fading of socialist idealism and commitment, and the emergence of new bureaucratic élites divorced from the people. These problems were seen by the Maoists as having increased as a result of the political and economic policies adopted by the Liuists.

Mao used the Cultural Revolution to purge the Party of his opponents and rivals, and as an attempt to get the youth of China – who only knew from books how bad things had been under the emperors, the warlords and the Nationalists – to favour the continuation of a 'revolutionary road' for China in the future. It became increasingly violent and destructive – it also split the Party, and turned young against old. Mao and Jiang Qing – who had established a power base in Shanghai – moulded the young so they could be the vanguard of this revolutionary campaign and become the 'revolutionary successors' of the pre-1949 generation.

4 The People's Republic of China (1949–2005)

The course of the Cultural Revolution

In June 1966, Mao called for the 'Four Olds' – bourgeois (capitalist) tendencies still existing in old ideas, old culture, old customs, and old habits – to be destroyed. His call was then published in the *People's Daily*, edited by Chen Boda. Mao's call was taken up enthusiastically by many of the younger generation. These young people were instructed to form revolutionary groups known as Red Guards – named after the armed workers and soldiers who, in 1917, had secured the victory of Lenin's Bolshevik Revolution.

The first to respond to Mao's calls to rebel against established authority were university and middle school students in Beijing, who began to put up large posters that criticised 'capitalist roaders' and those displaying 'bourgeois tendencies'. By early June, there was much turmoil in universities across China. Schools and colleges were then closed down for six months while new curricula were drawn up that would place more emphasis on Communist education and values.

This long holiday enabled students to concentrate on the political campaign in support of Mao and his ideas. Mao also gave students free travel so that they could extend the campaign to the rest of China. In addition, the PLA provided transport and support – between 1966 and 1969, over 450 million copies of Mao's Little Red Book were printed and distributed.

On 8 August 1966, Mao returned to active politics in public, and got the Central Committee to issue a directive – based on his 'Sixteen Articles' (sometimes known as the 'Sixteen Points') – calling for a great 'cultural revolution' to attack all remnants of the old society so that a new truly revolutionary one could be built. Extracts from this document are provided in Source 4.7. In order to get this directive through, many non-Maoist Party leaders were excluded from the meeting, and their places taken by more radical supporters of Mao.

Power struggles and the Cultural Revolution, 1962–71

SOURCE 4.7

The Great Proletarian Cultural Revolution now unfolding is a great revolution that touches people to their very souls and constitutes a new stage in the development of the socialist revolution in our country… Although the bourgeoisie has been overthrown, it is still trying to use the old ideas, culture, customs and habits of the exploiting classes to corrupt the masses, capture their minds and endeavour to stage a comeback…

Since the Cultural Revolution is a revolution, it inevitably meets with resistance. This resistance comes chiefly from those persons in power taking the capitalist road who have wormed their way into the Party… Don't be afraid of disturbances. Chairman Mao has often told us that revolution cannot always be so very refined, so gentle… Make the fullest use of big-character posters and great debates to… criticize the wrong views and… draw a clear line between ourselves and the enemy.

Extracts from The 16-Point Directive on the Cultural Revolution, 8 August 1966. From Miton, D., et al., 1974, **The China Reader: People's China,** *New York, Random House, pp.272–83.*

QUESTION

What is meant by the phrase 'taking the capitalist road' in Source 4.7? Which members of the Communist leadership do you think were being referred to?

Mao then got a new Standing Committee of the Politburo appointed, made up entirely of those who supported him. This new body then elected Lin as vice-chairman of the Party, which in effect marked him out as Mao's successor. Finally, on 18 August 1966, the Cultural Revolution was officially launched at a mass rally of a million young people in Tiananmen Square in Beijing. The choice of location was significant, as Mao's political opponents were essentially based in Beijing.

4 The People's Republic of China (1949–2005)

Figure 4.3: The mass rally in Beijing, August 1966, at the start of the Cultural Revolution.

In an attempt to turn the attentions of the Red Guards away from Communist Party bodies and leaders, Liu and Deng sent official party 'work teams' to get students to attack 'bourgeois authorities' instead – i.e. individual intellectuals, teachers and professors. It was thus not the Maoists but official Party-organised groups sent by the Liuists who first began the violent persecution of individual intellectuals. Soon, however, Maoist Red Guard units began to oppose these more 'moderate' work teams, which were under instructions to divert criticisms away from Party officials and organisations.

The Red Guards – with full equality between male and female members – then went back to their areas to carry out attacks on traditional Chinese culture. Soon, they began to publicly criticise Party leaders, teachers and professors they thought were 'Rightists' who were not sufficiently carrying out Mao's ideas. 'Counter-revolutionary' teachers and university principals – and later state officials – were often paraded through the streets wearing dunces' caps. Sometimes, they were

Power struggles and the Cultural Revolution, 1962–71

forced to do manual work, such as cleaning toilets or working in the fields. During this early stage, the police were instructed not to intervene.

Figure 4.4: Red Guards in Beijing, parading a government official wearing a dunce's cap, during the Cultural Revolution in 1967, to show that he was a 'counter-revolutionary'.

QUESTION

What does the photograph in Figure 4.4 tell us about the nature of some aspects of the Cultural Revolution?

As the Red Guards carried out their campaigns across China, Mao moved against his political opponents in Beijing. This group included Liu Shaoqi, who was accused of being a 'Rightist' and dismissed from his Party post in July 1966, though he remained as president until 1968. He was then sent to prison, where he died in 1969. Another of those purged in the period 1966–68 was Deng Xiaoping – accused in 1967 of being the 'number one capitalist roader', and of trying to destroy the revolution from within by keeping Mao out of power after 1958.

4 The People's Republic of China (1949–2005)

In 1969, Deng was 'sent down to the countryside', to be 're-educated' by learning from the peasants and commune industrial workers. Deng was forced to work in a tractor factory in Jiangxi; conditions were quite hard, but it seems that Zhou Enlai used his influence to lessen the effects of the punishment.

During 1967–68, the Cultural Revolution became increasingly violent. Factories, offices and homes were broken into. Books, jewellery, works of art – and even technology and machinery – which were considered 'bourgeois', were destroyed. Thousands of innocent people were accused of being 'capitalist roaders', and many were beaten, imprisoned and even killed. It is calculated that up to 3 million people were dismissed or imprisoned during the Cultural Revolution, of whom about 400 000 died as a result of torture, beatings and forced suicides. Thousands more were brutalised by the physical punishments, while many suffered psychological damage from the public self-criticisms and humiliations (such as being forced to wear dunces' caps).

The situation began to get increasingly out of hand, and even local Communist Party headquarters were taken over by more radical groups. In Shanghai, the radicals around Jiang Qing actually overthrew the official administration, and instead set up a revolutionary commune committee. By 1967, some parts of China were in a state of virtual civil war, with different groups of Red Guards – sometimes armed by sympathetic members of the PLA – fighting each other for not being sufficiently supportive of Mao's ideas. Initially, Mao ignored this, and a 'cult of Mao' was deliberately encouraged – in 1969, 'Mao Zedong Thought' was even written into the constitution.

However, as early as September 1967, Mao and Lin had felt the excesses needed to be curbed. In December 1968, Mao began to curb the activities of the Red Guards and, in April 1969, he decided that the Cultural Revolution had achieved its main objectives. On 5 September, the PLA was ordered to disarm Red Guard units and restore order and young people were then ordered to return home and go back to school. There was then a harsh crackdown on those wanting to continue their revolutionary campaign: many of the main leaders were arrested, while others were sent to work on the communes or in industry.

Power struggles and the Cultural Revolution, 1962–71

Gradually, order returned to China – although the political campaigning continued, this was done by propaganda rather than by demonstrations. However, Lin and Jiang Qing then used the PLA to carry out a repressive campaign against 'counter-revolutionaries'. Some historians suggest that, during this new purge, large numbers were killed.

> **ACTIVITY**
>
> Find out what life was like during the Cultural Revolution for:
>
> a the Red Guards
>
> b their victims.

The impact of the Cultural Revolution

Mao judged the Cultural Revolution to be a success – in part, as he was once again the most powerful person in China, while in the provinces and regions, many 'Rightist' leaders had been purged, and replaced by those loyal to Mao's more radical plans. To prevent any future return to bureaucratic rule, and the taking of 'the capitalist road', he called for a shake-up of government structures. 'Revolutionary Committees' – which included workers, Party members, and members of the PLA – were set up to run the government, communes and industries.

> **QUESTION**
>
> Why did Mao think the Cultural Revolution had been a success?

However, China had suffered economically during this upheaval – the majority of the campaigns were in urban areas, so industrial production suffered as workers were involved in political campaigns and meetings. Agricultural production also declined. After Zhou Enlai expressed concerns about the disruption to production and education – even government statistics showed an increase in illiteracy among the under-30 age group – schools and colleges were re-opened. Thus, Mao's hopes for an economically and militarily strong China suffered another serious setback as a direct result of his campaign during 1966–69. At the same time, many had become used to repeating politically 'correct'

4 The People's Republic of China (1949–2005)

slogans, rather than saying what they really felt. This resulted in growing cynicism about Mao and the CCP.

> **Theory of Knowledge**
>
> History and bias:
>
> History is often seen as being more prone to bias than the natural sciences – especially when this involves consideration of political and economic theories, systems and actions. Is it possible, for instance, for Western historians to make objective judgements about Mao's opposition to the 'capitalist road' in China? Or are they just likely to reflect the cultural, economic and political values which dominate their own societies?

With power firmly in his hands, Mao began to introduce relatively egalitarian socio-economic policies (such as more equal wages) during the late 1960s and early 1970s, in an attempt to reverse the 'Liuist' economic policies. But the violence of the years 1966–69 left considerable animosity and bitterness, which later formed the backdrop to what happened after Mao died.

> **KEY CONCEPTS QUESTION**
>
> **Causation and consequence:** Why did the Cultural Revolution become so violent, and what were the main results of the Cultural Revolution by the end of 1969?

4.3 Why was there another power struggle after the Cultural Revolution?

Mao's position in 1969 seemed politically very secure. Most of the centre-right 'moderates' had been expelled from the Party and the government, and his supporters held all the top positions. Although this proved not to be quite the case, in April 1969, the Ninth Congress of the CCP hailed the GPCR a success and termed itself a congress of 'unity and victory'. In addition, Lin Biao was named as Mao's 'successor' and 'close comrade in arms'.

Soon, however, new struggles broke out. Although these were partly connected to foreign policy (see Chapter 5), they were also connected to Mao's increasing ill-health. His heavy smoking led to serious lung and heart problems in his later years – this led political rivals to begin manoeuvring for position after his death. In particular, concerns about Mao's health contributed to a rift that began to develop between Lin and Mao.

The first indication of such a rift emerged over the decision to restore Party control which, during the Cultural Revolution, had passed largely to the army. Mao accepted Zhou's conclusion that restoration of Party authority was essential – and that to do this, many of those purged during the Cultural Revolution should be allowed to return to office. However, it was clear that the return of these leaders would seriously undermine Lin's influence once Mao was dead. Consequently, Lin proposed that the Central Cultural Revolutionary Committee should continue – even though he disagreed with it on many issues. Nonetheless, it was abolished in December 1969.

In addition, although Lin had supported Mao's Cultural Revolution, as early as 1968 he had begun to have doubts about Mao's increasing attempts to limit the more radical activities of the Red Guards. From 1970, Lin seemed to think that Mao was power-mad and would never step aside to let him become the new leader. However, Mao and other Communist leaders saw the re-establishment of Communist Party authority as a check to any 'Bonapartist' ambitions possibly arising from Lin and other PLA commanders – Mao even began to criticise the Lin as 'arrogant'.

In August 1970, at the Second Plenum of the Ninth CC in Lushan, the rift between the two widened when Lin launched an attack (with no prior notification to Mao) on Zhou's domestic and foreign policies. Lin was criticised, and this increased his doubts about the directions Mao was favouring. By then, both men had come to distrust each other. In particular, Mao (now 77 years old) felt Lin might not wait until he had died to become the next leader of the CCP, while Lin believed Mao had become power-hungry and would not share power.

4 The People's Republic of China (1949–2005)

Figure 4.5: The main rivals in the power struggle in 1976 – from left to right: Zhou Enlai, Lin Biao, Mao and Jiang Qing.

> **QUESTION**
> Why did a rift develop between Mao and Lin after 1970?

The 'Project 571' affair

Aware of Lin's power as head of the army, Mao began to remove political and military leaders loyal to Lin, and ordered Lin's troops from Beijing to Manchuria. These actions were seen as moves to prepare Lin's removal from power. Meanwhile, Mao pushed ahead with domestic and foreign policies which Lin opposed. During September 1971, in what later became known as the 'Project 571' affair, Lin vanished from the public scene, and there was a wholesale purge of the upper reaches of military and civilian administrations, including 21 from the Politburo.

The official Chinese account – not given until July 1972 – was that Lin had plotted, with the approval of the Soviet Union, to blow up Mao (apparently referred to as 'B-52') as part of a coup, codenamed 'Project 571'. When the plot was discovered, Lin had tried to flee China to the USSR by plane, but had been killed – along with several co-conspirators – when his plane had crashed (a later version said it had been shot down) somewhere over Mongolia.

Figure 4.6: An official government photograph of the wreckage of the plane in which Lin Biao was said to have tried escaping to the USSR in September 1971.

However, several historians – such as Maurice Meisner – wonder if the sequence was that Mao had determined to remove Lin from his positions of power, rather than the other way round – and that it was this that led Lin to draw up plans for a counter-coup.

SOURCE 4.8

It may well be that Mao was actively planning to exclude Lin from power and that Lin had got wind of this. It is not impossible that Lin Biao was actively plotting to overthrow Mao, although it is more likely that he realised that Mao was a sick man and was trying to ensure that after the chairman's death it would be Lin, and not Jiang Qing, who succeeded to the highest office of the state and party… Whatever the case, the facts, and then the exact circumstances of Lin's death remain confusing and ambiguous.

Dillon, M., 2012. **China: A Modern History.** London, I. B. Tauris, p.347

Other historians argue that tensions between Mao and Lin were deliberately created by the centre-right in order to prevent Lin from taking over when Mao eventually died. Certainly, as early as 1972, new divisions over policy began to emerge between the centre-right and the left, and these became increasingly significant in the period leading up to Mao's death in 1976. After his death in 1976, the struggle for power became much more open.

4 The People's Republic of China (1949–2005)

Paper 3 exam practice

Question

Examine Mao's reasons for launching the Cultural Revolution in 1966.
[15 marks]

Skill

Writing an introductory paragraph

Examiner's tips

Once you've planned your answer to a question (as covered by Chapters 2 and 3), you should be able to begin writing a clear introductory paragraph. This needs to set out your main line of argument and to outline briefly the key points you intend to make (and support with relevant and precise own knowledge) in the main body of your essay. Remember: 'Examine…', 'Discuss…', or 'Evaluate…' questions (just like 'To what extent…?' questions) clearly require analysis of opposing arguments, interpretations or explanations – not simply description. If, after doing your plan, you think you will be able to make a clear overall or final judgement, you might find it a good idea to flag up in your introductory paragraph what overall line of argument/judgement you intend to make.

Depending on the wording of the question, you may also find it useful to define in your introductory paragraph what you understand any 'key terms' to mean – in this case, some definition of 'Cultural Revolution' is required. Other possible terms for this question might be: 'bourgeois', 'capitalist roader', or 'revolutionary successors'.

For this question, you should:

- establish Mao's political position in 1966
- set out the possible reasons for launching the Cultural Revolution
- write a concluding paragraph that explicitly gives your judgement about the most important reason(s).

You will need to:

- outline relevant political and economic developments in the decade or so before 1966
- examine a range of reasons for Mao's decision to launch the Cultural Revolution
- provide a judgement about which reason/reasons was/were most important.

Setting out this approach in your introductory paragraph will help you keep the demands of the question in mind. Remember to refer back to your introduction after every couple of paragraphs in your main answer.

Common mistakes

A common mistake – one that might suggest to an examiner a candidate who hasn't thought deeply about what's required – is to fail to write an introductory paragraph at all. This is often done by candidates who rush into writing before analysing the question and doing a plan. The result may well be that they focus entirely on the words 'Cultural Revolution', an approach that may simply result in a narrative of the main events of the Cultural Revolution. Even if the answer is full of detailed and accurate own knowledge, this will not answer the question, and so will not score highly.

Sample student introductory paragraph

This is a good introduction, as it shows a good grasp of the topic, and sets out a clear and logical plan, clearly focused on the demands of the question. It shows a sound appreciation of the fact that to discuss and assess why Mao launched the Cultural Revolution, it is necessary to identify a range of different reasons, and it explicitly demonstrates to the examiner what aspects the candidate intends to address. This indicates that the answer – if it remains analytical, and is well-supported – is likely to be a high-scoring one.

When Mao launched the Cultural Revolution in 1966, his position and power within the CCP seemed considerably less than they had been in 1949, immediately after the Revolution of which he was acknowledged main leader.

Many historians have thus explained the Cultural Revolution as essentially his attempt to re-establish his paramount position within the party and the state.

4 The People's Republic of China (1949–2005)

While it is true that, after the great problems resulting from his Great Leap Forward, he had felt obliged to give up the day-to-day supervision of government policy, it seems fair to argue that Mao's reasons for launching the Cultural Revolution were more complicated than simply wanting to be regain his former power. In many ways, the Cultural Revolution – directed against the 'four olds' of pre-revolutionary Chinese culture – can be explained by concerns that Mao – and other CCP leaders – had that, during the early 1960s, the Chinese government was pursuing 'capitalist' economic policies. It is also possible to argue that Mao was particularly concerned about how increasing bureaucracy risked creating a void between the party and the people, and even abandoning the aim of creating a communist society. Finally, Mao was also conscious of the fact that young people born after the 1949 Revolution – seen by him as the 'revolutionary successors' – needed to experience revolutionary activity in order not to take the gains of 1949 for granted.

Thus it is probably fair to conclude – as have several historians – that there were many different reasons behind the Cultural Revolution. Overall, the need to change economic and political policies away from the 'capitalist road', and back to revolutionary socialism, was probably the most important reason.

Activity

In this chapter, the focus is on writing a useful introductory paragraph. So, using the information from this chapter and any other sources of information available to you, write introductory paragraphs for at least two of the following Practice Paper 3 questions.

Remember to refer to the simplified Paper 3 mark scheme in Chapter 10.

Practice Paper 3 questions

1 Examine the reasons why, in 1959, Mao gave up his position as chairman of the PRC.

2 Evaluate the importance of Lin Biao, in the years 1960–65, to Mao's attempts to overturn the policies being pursued by Liu Shaoqi and Deng Xiaoping.

3 Discuss the degree to which the Cultural Revolution had achieved Mao's aims.

4 To what extent were young people merely used by Mao in the Cultural Revolution to remove his political opponents?

5 'By 1971, the "rightists" and "capitalist roaders" within the CCP leadership had been decisively defeated.' To what extent do you agree with this statement?

5 | Foreign policy, 1949–76

Foreign policy, 1949–76

Introduction

China's – and Mao's – foreign policy during the period 1949–76, at least during the early years, was mainly influenced by four closely-related factors:

- making China independent and strong
- modernising and greatly developing China's industry and agriculture
- moving rapidly towards the goal of creating a socialist economy and society
- helping bring about worldwide revolution.

During the 19th century and the early years of the 20th. century, China's military weakness in the face of stronger and more economically developed countries had been made painfully clear. The massively destructive Japanese invasion of 1937 had just been the latest example of China's vulnerability. By 1945, many Chinese people had come to see Mao and the CCP, rather than Jiang and the GMD, as China's best bet for establishing a strong and independent nation.

Mao, as well as being a communist, was also a nationalist and thus wanted China to be strong: for him, only a modernised and developed China could maintain its independence in the modern Cold War world. Mao was also attracted by the idea that a strong and independent China could replace the Soviet Union as the leader of the world communist movement – and might even be accepted as an important world power.

Yet, despite resoundingly winning the Civil War in 1949, the Communist government of the newly proclaimed People's Republic of China was faced with the fact that Jiang still claimed to be the real leader of China. Having retreated to Taiwan, Jiang established the 'Republic of China', and threatened to invade and overthrow the Communists in the near future.

This threat was made more serious by the fact that Jiang was backed by the might of the USA, which used its veto in the UN Security Council to block recognition of the PRC and, instead, to back Jiang's regime as the true representative of China.

While the primary concern of the new Communist government was to restore China's industry and agriculture after the tremendous disruption

5 The People's Republic of China (1949–2005)

of the Civil War and the destruction during the Japanese invasion, the early years were always marked by the fear that Jiang might invade the mainland with US support.

Thus it was not surprising that Mao 'leaned to one side' during the Cold War, or that China's new leaders quickly turned to the Soviet Union for support – especially when the Korean War broke out in 1950. However, tensions soon emerged between these two Communist states and, in just over ten years, a deep division had erupted.

During the 1970s, Communist China established diplomatic relations with the US which, up to then, had been attacked by China as an evil warmongering 'reactionary imperialist' power.

These shifts in foreign policy were often closely related to political and economic developments within China, with foreign and domestic policies reflecting genuine ideological and policy differences and divisions within the leadership of the CCP.

TIMELINE

1950 Jan: US Defensive Perimeter speech
Feb: Sino-Soviet Treaty signed
Jun: Start of Korean War
Oct: China sends troops to help North Korea
1951 May: 17-Point Agreement between China and Tibet
1953 Mar: Death of Stalin
Jul: Armistice ends Korean War
1954 Sep: US forms SEATO; First Taiwan Strait Crisis begins
1956 Feb: Khrushchev's 'secret speech'
1957 Nov: Conference of Communist Parties, Moscow
1958 Jul: Khrushchev visits China
Aug: Start of the Second Taiwan Strait Crisis
1959 Mar: Dalai Lama flees to India; Tibetan uprising begins
1960 Jun: Conference of Communist and Workers' Parties, Romania
Jul: Soviet Union withdraws technicians from China
1964 Oct: China explodes its first atomic bomb
1967 Jun: China explodes its first hydrogen bomb
1969 Mar: Start of Sino-Soviet border clashes
Apr: Clashes between Mao and Lin Biao over foreign policy

Foreign policy, 1949–76

1970 Nov: Majority support in UN for China to join Security Council
1971 Oct: US allows China to join UN Security Council
1972 Feb: Nixon visits China
       Sep: Japan's prime minister visits China
1973 Aug: Congress of CCP approves new foreign policy

KEY QUESTIONS

- What were the main features of Communist China's early foreign policy?
- Why did a serious rift develop between China and the Soviet Union in the 1960s?
- What was the significance of Communist China's rapprochement with the USA in the 1970s?

Overview

- Despite various differences with the Soviet Union, Mao decided that Communist China should 'lean to one side' in the Cold War. In February 1950, the two countries signed the Sino-Soviet Treaty.
- In June 1950, with China still in the throws of land reform and re-establishing central control, the Korean War began.
- In October 1950, after US troops crossed into North Korea and approached the Chinese border, Mao sent in Chinese troops to push them back. In July 1953, an armistice ended the fighting.
- China had been unhappy about the amount of aid the Soviet Union had supplied during the war and, after Stalin died, began to have serious differences with the Soviet Union's foreign policy of 'peaceful coexistence'. China particularly resented the fact that the Soviet Union did not support it during the two Taiwan Crises in the 1950s.
- In 1960, these differences led the Soviet Union to withdraw its technicians from China, and the Sino-Soviet split in 1961 divided the world communist movement into pro-Moscow and pro-Beijing parties.

161

5 The People's Republic of China (1949–2005)

- In 1969, following several clashes along the Sino–Soviet border, China decided the USSR was the main enemy, and began to change its attitude to the US. In 1971, the US allowed China to join the UN's Security Council and, in 1972, US president Nixon visited China.
- After 1972, diplomatic and trade relations were established with the US and Japan, and Chinese foreign policy followed a strongly anti-Soviet direction.

5.1 What were the main features of Communist China's early foreign policy?

Mao and the CCP – and most Chinese people – wanted China to become a strong and independent nation, able to withstand interference from any foreign powers. As well as trying to achieve this by modernising and developing China's economy, a speech made by Mao in June 1949 made it clear that foreign policy was also clearly going to be important (see Source 5.1).

SOURCE 5.1

Only thus can our great motherland free herself from a semi-colonial and semi-feudal fate and take the road of independence, freedom, peace, unity, wealth and power… We are willing to discuss with any foreign government the establishment of diplomatic relations on the basis of the principles of equality, mutual benefit, and mutual respect for territorial integrity and sovereignty, providing it is willing to sever relations with the Chinese reactionaries, stops conspiring with them or helping them, and adopts an attitude of genuine, and not hypocritical, friendship towards People's China. The Chinese people wish to have friendly cooperation with the people of all countries and to resume and expand international trade in order to develop production and promote economic prosperity.

Extracts from a speech made by Mao in June 1949. Quoted in: Schram, S. 1966. **Mao Tse-tung.** *Harmondsworth. Penguin Books. pp.249–50*

Foreign policy, 1949–76

'Leaning to one side'

In the context of the Cold War, the Soviet Union seemed the natural ally of Communist China and, at first, these two countries tried to construct a solid united front towards the capitalist West. Yet the relations between Mao and Stalin – who disliked each other from their very first meeting – were already quite cool. After Stalin's death in 1953, deep ideological differences over both economic and foreign policies began to emerge between these two Communist countries.

> **QUESTION**
> What, in the context of the Cold War, is meant by the phrase 'leaning to one side'?

Early relations with the Soviet Union

Before Lenin's death in 1924, Communist Russia had given help to both the GMD and the small Chinese Communist Party. This aid continued under Stalin, even though he believed China was too backward – economically and culturally – to have its own socialist revolution for decades to come. Even after the GMD had massacred their former Chinese Communist allies in 1927, Stalin had continued to give aid to Jiang Jieshi.

These tensions between the Soviet Union and China's Communist leaders were further increased after 1945 by Stalin's view of what should happen in China following the end of the Second World War. Although Stalin did hand over to the PLA the weapons surrendered by Japanese forces in China after August 1945, he was initially opposed to the CCP taking power. Instead, fearful that a Communist victory in China would result in the US withdrawing its approval of a Soviet 'sphere of influence' in Eastern Europe, he put pressure on the Communists not to renew the civil war after 1945 and, instead, to enter a coalition government with the GMD. Mao, however, had rejected this advice and, following the Communists' victory in the Civil War, the PRC had been proclaimed in October 1949.

5 The People's Republic of China (1949–2005)

The Sino-Soviet Treaty 1950

As it was obvious that Communist China would not receive financial or technical help from the West, Stalin – seeing China as a potential useful ally in the Cold War – decided to assist the new PRC government. At first, in 1948, Liu Shaoqi had discussions with Anastas Mikoyan of the Soviet Union who, in January 1949, visited China and had further meetings with Mao. Then, during July–August 1949, Liu Shaoqi headed a delegation to Moscow to prepare the way for Mao, who stayed in Moscow during the winter of 1949–50.

Mao met Stalin for the first time on 16 December 1949. However, the face-to-face meetings were difficult – in large part because Stalin made it clear that he felt all Communists states should subordinate their own interests to those of the Soviet Union. Mao also resented what he felt was Soviet arrogance, especially the assumption that Communist China would naturally look to the Soviet Union for advice and guidance. As there appeared to be deadlock, Zhou Enlai came to Moscow on 20 January 1950 to help move the discussions along. Mao later claimed Stalin had not wanted to sign the Treaty because he feared that China might become too independent of the USSR.

Eventually, on 14 February 1950, China signed the Sino-Soviet Treaty of Friendship, Alliance and Mutual Assistance with the Soviet Union, which agreed to provide China with Soviet financial and technical assistance over the next fifteen years. This mainly consisted of a $300 million loan (repayable, at a 1% rate of interest), the provision of over 20 000 Soviet and East European engineers and experts (whose upkeep was to be paid by China), and sending machinery for 300 modern industrial plants. At the same time, over 80 000 Chinese went to the USSR to study science and technology.

Although the Treaty effectively ended all the USSR's special privileges in China, Stalin insisted on being given the rights to explore and develop natural resources in the Xinjiang region, directly across the Soviet Union's far-eastern border, and to maintain the use of Dairen and Lüshun (Port Arthur) on China's Liaodong peninsula. Finally, most of China's bullion reserves were handed over to the Soviet Union.

Mao and the Chinese delegation finally returned to Beijing in March 1950. Mao in particular felt that the aid provided by the Soviet Union in the 1950 Treaty was insufficient – though, given the Soviet Union's mammoth task of rebuilding after the destruction of World War II, this

Foreign policy, 1949–76

was a rather harsh judgement. However, Mao was also angry that the USSR refused to help China develop its own atomic bomb.

> **QUESTION**
>
> In what ways did the Sino-Soviet Treaty of 1950 disappoint Communist China?

Further Sino-Soviet agreements were made in 1953, 1954 and 1956. It was advice from Soviet experts that led the PRC to set up a State Planning Commission to design a Five-Year Plan to expand and modernise China's economy. However, as has been seen in Chapters 2 and 3 – especially in relation to the Great Leap Forward – Mao's growing suspicion of the political impact of experts led, eventually, to conflict with those CCP leaders who wished to continue to follow the Soviet model of economic development.

The Korean War

Within six months of the signing of the Treaty with the Soviet Union, the PRC faced what it saw as a serious threat to its existence; this was the Korean War, which broke out in June 1950. With Korea on China's northeast borders, and US troops being quickly deployed there, this war created a sense of great tension and isolation in China – and, as has been seen, increased the tendency to purge 'hidden traitors' within the Party and the country at large. It also prevented an attempt to invade Taiwan and thus end the Civil War, as the US took the opportunity to send the Seventh Fleet to 'neutralise' the Taiwan Strait – and so protect Jiang's rule of Taiwan – even though, at this early stage, China was not involved in the war. This US policy in the Taiwan Strait continued even after the Korean War ended in 1953.

Korea before 1950

Korea had been controlled by Japan since its annexation in 1910. At the end of the Second World War, the Allies had agreed that Korea should be temporarily divided along the 38th parallel (or northern line of latitude), into North and South Korea, with the intention of creating a unified and independent state. However, this agreement broke down as a result of the developing Cold War. Instead, the US established an authoritarian capitalist regime in the South, under the leadership of

5 The People's Republic of China (1949–2005)

Syngman Rhee, which was recognised by the UN; in the North, the USSR established an authoritarian Communist regime, led by **Kim Il-Sung**.

Syngman Rhee (1875–1965):

Rhee was a nationalist – but his politics were right-wing and strongly anti-communist. He was opposed to Japanese rule of Korea but, unlike Kim Il-Sung, spent the 1930s and 1940s in exile – mostly in the US or in the US territory of Hawaii. After 1945, he campaigned for the reunification of Korea, and at times used violent methods to secure his domination of South Korea. His rule was, like Kim Il-Sung's, authoritarian and, towards the end of the Korean War, he tried unsuccessfully to sabotage the peace negotiations as he hoped the US would then bring about reunification of Korea and put him in charge of the whole country.

Kim Il-Sung (1912–94):

Kim Il-Sung's real name was Kim Song-Ju, and he had grown up in Manchuria, where his parents had fled to avoid Japanese rule in Korea. He was both left-wing and a nationalist, and joined a communist youth movement in Manchuria. In 1930, he returned to Korea to join the communist-led guerrilla resistance to Japanese occupation. He later also fought the Japanese in north China and then, once the Soviet Union had been invaded by Nazi Germany, he led a Korean contingent in the Soviet Union's Red Army. Once he took control of North Korea after 1945, he campaigned for reunification of the country. His government was authoritarian, and a big personality cult grew up around him, which referred to him as 'The Great Leader'. When he died in 1994, he was succeeded by his son, Kim Jong-Il.

Both Korean leaders were intensely nationalistic, and both wanted to reunite their country – but each wanted to be the sole ruler of a reunified Korea. As a result, there had been various military clashes between the two states after 1945; these had increased after 1948–49 when the Soviet Union and the US withdrew their troops from North and South Korea respectively. With most Koreans wanting reunification, and both countries threatening each other, it seemed a nationalist civil war might break out in the near future – which it did, in June 1953.

Foreign policy, 1949–76

In fact, several historians – in opposition to explanations for the war that claim Stalin had instigated it – have argued that the 1950 invasion was in many ways a continuation of a much longer civil war between North and South Korea.

US historian Bruce Cummings, for example, has suggested that the North Korean invasion was the result of Kim's strong nationalist and revolutionary ideals, and had very little to do with Soviet wishes. Since the collapse of the Soviet Union and the end of the Cold War, access to previously restricted Soviet documents has revealed that it was Kim – not Stalin or Mao – who was the main driving force behind the North's decision to invade the South in order to reunite the country.

In January 1950, US Secretary of State Dean Acheson made a speech in which he outlined US Cold War strategy in the Pacific area. In particular, he referred to a Defensive Perimeter: all countries to the east of that line were seen as countries that the US would, in the context of the Cold War, 'defend' from any communist aggression.

This Defensive Perimeter did not include South Korea – nor, for that matter, either Taiwan or Vietnam. This led Kim Il-Sung to assume he could invade South Korea without fear of any US military intervention.

> **KEY CONCEPTS QUESTION**
>
> **Causation:** How did the US announcement of its 'Defensive Perimeter' in Asia contribute to the outbreak of the Korean War in 1950?

5 The People's Republic of China (1949–2005)

Figure 5.1: The US Defensive Perimeter of 1950 in the Pacific region.

China's involvement

Consequently, encouraged by the recent Communist victory in China, and believing that the US would not get involved, North Korea invaded the South on 25 June 1950. At first, China's reaction was muted. However, this began to change when South Korea appealed to the United Nations (UN) for help. Taking advantage of the Soviet Union's boycott of the Security Council (as a protest against the USA's refusal to recognise Communist China), the US persuaded the UN to intervene. Although fifteen nations eventually provided troops, the vast bulk were US troops, and US General Douglas MacArthur – who was answerable to the US president, not the UN – was in overall command.

Communist China had not been involved with the post-1945 developments in Korea and, after their victory in 1949, the CCP had concentrated on consolidating its rule, land reform and an alliance with the Soviet Union. The evidence would suggest that the timing of this war came largely as a surprise to Communist China, as it appears that Stalin – who did know something about North Korea's plans – did not

Foreign policy, 1949–76

share this information with Mao. However, during May 1950, Kim Il-Sung did visit China to ask for general approval of any future invasion of South Korea. Mao apparently offered to supply several Chinese units, but this was rejected.

As far as Mao and the CCP were concerned, a war – coming so soon after the establishment of their regime in 1949 – was something to be avoided. This was because funds vital for China's modernisation programmes would have to be diverted into military expenditure. In addition, with the US backing Jiang in Taiwan, there was the fear that Jiang might launch an invasion while Communist China was distracted by the Korean War. Thus, even after fighting began, China seemed more concerned with the US decision to deploy its Seventh Fleet in the Taiwan Strait.

However, from September 1950, US/UN forces began to push the North Korean forces back over the 38th parallel. Then, on the first anniversary of the foundation of the PRC, US forces – in defiance of the UN mandate – crossed into North Korea and began to move towards the Yalu River, which was the border between North Korea and China. This – and General MacArthur's hints about the possibility of using nuclear bombs – made the PRC feel particularly threatened. Given US support for Jiang, Mao and other CCP leaders felt that the PRC was now particularly vulnerable. In addition, Stalin began pressing China to help North Korea.

During the first two weeks of October, the CCP leadership debated what to do, finally deciding to set up the Chinese People's Volunteers (CPV), under the command of General Peng Dehuai, who took charge of several units of the PLA. In fact, as Source 5.2 suggests, Peng may have played a decisive role in helping Mao get the support of those CCP leaders who were at first doubtful of the wisdom in getting involved in a war so soon after gaining power. For China, the Korean War now became the 'War to Resist America and Aid Korea'. On 18 October, Peng's forces crossed the Yalu River, and were soon involved in battles against US forces – inflicting on MacArthur's forces the greatest defeat in US military history.

5 The People's Republic of China (1949–2005)

SOURCE 5.2

Peng Dehuai was later to claim that a majority of the CCP leadership had been opposed to involvement in Korea but that Mao had overruled them and that he, Peng, had supported Mao or at the very least had not opposed him. Mao was concerned that the very existence of the PRC would be endangered if North Korea was defeated, and he realised that his support for Kim was important in the power play within the Communist bloc.

Dillon, M. 2012. **China: A Modern History,** *London, I. B. Tauris. pp.277–8.*

KEY CONCEPTS ACTIVITY

Perspectives: Consider the events leading up to China's involvement in the Korean War. In pairs, discuss how and why perspectives on the causes and importance of the war would have differed in China and the USA in 1950. How has hindsight and the end of the Cold War affected our understanding of the causes of the Korean War?

Despite heavy losses, Peng's 400 000-strong CPV army, in five major campaigns between October 1950 and July 1951, pushed the invaders out of North Korea. MacArthur, who wanted to escalate the war, was dismissed by President Truman, and the war soon became a stalemate. However, China's heavy losses had a big impact on China's troops, and Mao and Zhou informed Kim Il-Sung of their desire to withdraw their forces. Hence both North Korea and China welcomed the UN's attempt in July 1951 to bring about an armistice. However, it was not until July 1953 that an armistice was agreed that ended the fighting and confirmed the 38th parallel as the border between the two parts of Korea.

Foreign policy, 1949–76

Figure 5.2: Some of the CPV troops who were sent to help North Korea and to keep US/UN troops from the Chinese border.

Political impact of the war

During the fighting, China lost approximately 1 million men who were killed or wounded, including Mao's oldest son. China also lost massive amounts of resources – as well as having to repay the Soviet Union over $1 billion for the military aid it had received during the war. There was also some Chinese resentment that the Soviet Union decided not to get involved in the fighting, leaving it to China to bear the heavy costs. There was only limited cooperation between Communist China and the Soviet Union during the war, and Mao also felt that Soviet military aid was not sufficiently extensive or prompt.

ACTIVITY

Make a list of the main ways in which the start and the course of the Korean War impacted on China's relations with the Soviet Union.

5 The People's Republic of China (1949–2005)

In addition to resentments over the Soviet Union's limited help during the war, China's leaders were concerned by the increased support the US now gave to Jiang. This merely confirmed CCP leaders in their belief that the US was determined to overthrow Mao and the PRC at the first opportunity. As a result, the government – and the people – of China saw the US as the main enemy threatening their independence. However, the success of the PLA in pushing the US/UN troops from North Korea, and then fighting them to a standstill, increased Mao's prestige within China, along with China's international reputation.

As seen in Chapter 2, the outbreak of war in 1950 impacted on political developments within China. The war enabled the government of the newly established PRC to use the potential threat from Jiang and the US to unite the Chinese people against foreign interference. As part of this, Mao and the CCP launched a series of 'Rectification Campaigns' during 1951–52 against 'reactionaries' and 'counter-revolutionaries' (see Section 2.1). The war gave these campaigns – especially the 'Five-Anti' campaign, launched in January 1952 when a stalemate had developed in Korea – a very bitter aspect, as there were increased fears of an imminent US invasion. The fears arising from this situation thus allowed Mao to eliminate potential opponents and to strengthen the Party's central control. The war also led to the intensification of the Campaign for the Suppression of Counter-Revolutionaries.

The 'Resist America' campaign

In 1950, one mass mobilisation campaign that was clearly linked to the Korean War was the 'Resist America and Aid Korea' campaign. Rallies were held to increase Chinese suspicion of foreigners, particularly those from the West. People from the US were singled out because of their involvement in Korea. Many foreigners, including missionaries, were arrested. Christian churches were closed and priests and nuns were expelled. By the end of 1950, China was closed to all foreigners, except Russians, and institutions with links to the West were monitored or closed down. However, once the war developed into a stalemate, the internal terror against opponents declined.

Because of its involvement in the war, China remained excluded from the UN, and generally isolated from the wider international community. This sense of isolation contributed to an atmosphere of distrust and fear within China that lasted into the 1960s, and also increased ideological divisions within the CCP which, eventually, culminated in the Cultural Revolution.

Tibet

Despite the Korean War, the PRC pushed ahead with the re-incorporation of Tibet, which was seen by the Chinese government and Chinese nationalists as part of China. In May 1951, the Tibetan authorities signed the Seventeen Point Agreement with the PRC, which gave Tibet limited autonomy within China – including the continuation of its traditional government and politico-religious feudal structures. Thus the feudal landowners and the monasteries retained their landholdings within central Tibet. The Agreement also re-drew the borders of Tibet, with the result that many Tibetans now became residents of the Chinese provinces of Sichuan, Gansu and Qinghai.

> **ACTIVITY**
>
> Try to find out more about the landholding system that existed in Tibet before 1949. Then draw a table with two columns, headed 'Preserve' and 'Reform', and write down the main arguments for and against changing the socio-economic structures in Tibet.

When government authorities then began to implement land reform programmes (which they'd agree not to implement within the new Tibetan borders) in these areas, there was strong resistance and fighting broke out in 1955, which took six months to suppress. Afterwards, Tibetan language and culture were targeted, and many Tibetans were moved to other areas of China, while Han Chinese were brought in to replace them.

Tensions continued as the central government in Beijing began to press ahead with radical land reform and, in 1957, some Tibetan factions, armed by the US – as Source 5.3 states – planned a rebellion. In March 1959, the Dalai Lama fled to India (where he was granted asylum), and a bloody uprising broke out against Communist rule. This was quickly suppressed by the PLA – in part because the CIA did not keep its promises of providing further military aid. Beijing – following the earlier lead of the Dalai Lama – then announced that the Seventeen Point Agreement no longer applied, and the lands of the theocratic and landed élites were re-distributed to Tibet's peasants. In 1965, Tibet officially became an Autonomous Region of the PRC.

5 The People's Republic of China (1949–2005)

SOURCE 5.3

The situation [in Tibet] remained tense, continuing into 1957. Mao himself assured the Dalai Lama that he would delay land reform in China for another six years and possibly longer. Unimpressed with Chinese assurances, however, factions within Tibet began arming themselves, some with assistance from the United States (Goldstein, 1997). The situation was brought to a head in March 1959 when Tibetan leaders decided that the Dalai Lama would only be safe outside Tibet. He and his top advisers fled to India under cover of darkness. A bloody uprising against Chinese rule erupted but was quickly suppressed. From exile in India, the Dalai Lama declared the 17-point Agreement invalid, as did the Chinese government.

Benson, L. 2002. **China Since 1949.** Harlow, Longman. pp.35–6.

China and the Non-Aligned Movement

After the Korean War, Communist China was briefly involved in the Non-Aligned Movement – partly as a result of the role played by Nehru, India's prime minister, in ending that war. This Non-Aligned Movement was an international organisation of developing countries – mainly Asian and African – which, in the context of the Cold War, tried to avoid formally allying with either the US or the Soviet Union. This was despite Mao's assertion in 1950 that there was no 'Third Way', and despite the Treaty of Friendship between China and the Soviet Union that had been signed that year.

However, for a brief time during the early 1950s, the foreign policy of the PRC seemed to moderate, and began evolving towards the Soviet line of 'peaceful coexistence'. Thus, in 1955, China was represented at the Bandung Conference (in Indonesia) – which brought together 29 developing states – by Zhou Enlai. There was at first close cooperation between India and China, with the CCP arguing (like the Soviet Union) that the national bourgeoisies of developing countries – provided they remained neutral in the Cold War – could bring about genuine independence and progressive economic and social changes in their respective countries.

Foreign policy, 1949–76

Thus, for a time, Communist China was seen by many developing states as representing a way of achieving independent economic growth and political independence. Yet, from 1957, when China's foreign (as well as domestic) policy took a more radical direction, China's role within the Non-Aligned Movement rapidly declined.

The Taiwan Strait Crises

In early 1950, Mao had been planning to invade Taiwan and so end the Civil War by taking the one-remaining Nationalist stronghold. However, these plans had to be postponed at the end of 1950 because of the Korean War. Apart from Taiwan, China was also pre-occupied with taking control of various smaller Chinese offshore islands that had remained in the hands of the GMD after 1949. These concerns increased in September 1954, when the US created the South East Asia Treaty Organisation (SEATO) – a NATO-type organisation intended to 'contain' the spread of communism in Asia. Mao was convinced that this meant the US was determined to separate Taiwan permanently from mainland China.

In September 1954, the First Taiwan Strait Crisis broke out, when China began shelling the offshore islands of Jinmen (Quemoy) and Mazu (Matsu), in order to force the GMD to withdraw. These islands were very close to mainland China – and Jiang, after announcing an imminent attack on China as part of a new 'holy war' against communism, had increased the number of GMD troops placed on them. The Chinese government thus tried to repossess them; in addition, in 1955, the PRC began shelling the Tachen islands, which were also occupied by GMD troops.

With both sides carrying out artillery attacks, the US (after eventually deciding against using nuclear weapons) backed Taiwan. It signed a firm mutual defence pact with Taiwan, and threatened to invade China. Without any corresponding help from the Soviet Union, the PRC – after seizing the Tachen islands, was forced to back down and promise not to use force to re-take Taiwan.

Tensions over these islands flared up again into a Second Taiwan Strait Crisis. In 1957, the US had agreed to supply Taiwan with missiles capable of carrying nuclear warheads. This worried Communist China, which asked the Soviet Union for its support in re-taking the islands. But, despite clear US threats against Communist China, the USSR

175

5 The People's Republic of China (1949–2005)

initially refused, saying it would only provide assistance if the US invaded mainland China. Khrushchev even accused Mao and the CCP of 'dangerous adventurism', and of being 'Trotskyists', because of their confrontational foreign policy. Both sides began shelling each other in August 1958 – and the US then supplied Taiwan with air-to-air missiles, which enabled it to establish air superiority over the Taiwan Strait. With the US, once again, threatening Communist China with a nuclear strike, Mao was eventually forced to back down and abandon the plan in January 1959.

Internally, the crisis over these islands in August 1958 became linked to the revival of the people's militias and the arming of the peasantry, which was part of the move towards Communes. In the event of any US-backed invasion by the GMD, these militias could conduct guerrilla warfare across the country. Thus the internal 'war against nature' in Mao's Great Leap Forward became linked to the threat of external aggression.

5.2 Why did a serious rift develop between China and the Soviet Union in the 1960s?

Mao did not see Marxism simply as a political theory and movement – it was also the way that China could be modernised and developed. He and his supporters often had a very 'Sino-centric' view of Marxism – this argued that China needed to adapt it to the specific circumstances that existed in post-war China. In particular, this meant that the Soviet Union – despite its revolutionary prestige as the world's first workers' state – was not necessarily able to tell Communist China what policies it should follow. This soon resulted in political differences between these two post-capitalist states, both of which came to see themselves as representing 'true' Communism.

China and the Soviet Union

As noted earlier, Stalin had believed that Mao's peasant-based movement could not possibly result in a socialist revolution, and had advised Mao

Foreign policy, 1949–76

not to push ahead for an all-out victory after 1945. Such differences had been increased by the Korean War, which had severely tested the relationship between the PRC and the Soviet Union. Especially as Mao believed he had not been properly consulted in relation to North Korea's decision to invade the South.

Thus, after Stalin's death in 1953, it seemed that relations between China and the Soviet Union might improve. The new Soviet leadership, for instance, was more willing to supply aid and technicians to Communist China, and later admitted that the 1950 Treaty was an 'insult to the Chinese people'. However, the relationship between the USSR and Communist China began to cool after Khrushchev emerged as the dominant Soviet leader in 1956.

Khrushchev's 'secret speech', 1956

From 1953, Mao had become increasingly concerned by developments within the Soviet Union and its satellites in Eastern Europe. The first worrying sign was an uprising in East Germany in 1953; then came Khrushchev's 'secret speech' attacking Stalin in February 1956. Among other things, Khrushchev's speech attacked the 'cult of personality' that had grown up around Stalin.

Many Communist parties – including the Chinese – resented the fact that they'd not been consulted about the speech in advance. For the CCP, the speech raised the problem of how to tell the Party and the Chinese people why, for decades, they had praised Stalin as a great 'Marxist-Leninist' revolutionary leader. In particular, this speech could be seen as a specific criticism of Mao's own style of leadership, as Mao had consciously modelled his political style on Stalin's, and a 'cult of Mao' was already beginning to emerge in China. Consequently, the speech was at first not published in China. Instead, in April 1956, China's *People's Daily* newspaper published an editorial that stressed the importance of the role of leaders in helping to bring about fundamental changes.

QUESTION
Why did Khrushchev's 'secret speech' of 1956 disturb Mao and other CCP leaders?

5 The People's Republic of China (1949–2005)

Then, in June 1956 came serious protests in Poland and then, in October, the Hungarian Uprising. Although Mao had had several significant criticisms of the way Stalin had treated Communist China, he saw these East European protests as evidence that Khrushchev's more liberal 'de-Stalinisation' policies were dangerous. He also feared the new economic policies being pursued by Khrushchev were likely to lead to the restoration of capitalism in the Soviet Union. This made China feel increasingly vulnerable as regards US hostility.

World revolution

Mao thus began to suspect that Khrushchev was moving the Soviet Union away from communist ideology and a truly revolutionary foreign policy. At the same time, Mao resented the fact that the Soviet Union did not support his increasingly radical policies – in particular, his Great Leap Forward (see below and Section 3.2). All this confirmed Mao and his supporters in their growing belief that the Soviet model was not necessarily the best one for China's future development. Finally, the role of intellectuals in these East European protests led the CCP to try to keep China's intellectuals on the side of communist transformation – one result was the Hundred Flowers campaign.

China and 'peaceful coexistence'

In particular, Mao strongly opposed Khrushchev's new foreign policy of 'peaceful coexistence' with the USA and its Western bloc. Mao saw this as a revisionist 'heresy' that was abandoning communist commitment to help bring about world revolution as soon as possible. For Mao, this 'reactionary' foreign policy explained the refusal of the Soviet Union to support China's attempts to take possession of the off shore islands that were still under GMD control. Mao believed that 'peaceful coexistence' with a hostile capitalism was impossible – especially given the USA's determination to 'roll back' communism and to establish what Mao saw as a global US capitalist empire.

As Khrushchev persisted with attempts to reduce Cold War tensions between the Soviet Union and the US, Mao became increasingly suspicious of Khrushchev's motives. In November 1957, Khrushchev convened a Conference of Communist Parties in Moscow, in order to heal the growing rift. The range of issues that were increasingly causing conflict between Khrushchev and Mao are set out in Source 5.4.

However, Deng Xiaoping attacked the Soviet Union over its attempt to achieve better relations (known as *détente*) with the US and the West. In opposition to Khrushchev's views, China's Communist leaders argued that the proletarian world revolution could only be achieved by armed struggle. Mao tried to get Khrushchev to abandon his 'revisionist' foreign policy, but was ignored. For Mao, the USSR should be supporting liberation movements around the world – not making overtures to imperialist Western nations that were 'class enemies'. Although the Chinese delegation failed to change Soviet policy, their speeches won some limited support from other delegations, such as the Albanians – this acutely embarrassed the Soviet leaders.

SOURCE 5.4

The issues and arguments [within the international communist movement] are clear enough. The Left [represented by Mao] sticks to what it regards as the orthodox Leninist view about imperialism and communism. It does not believe in the possibility of any genuine détente and considers all talk about ending the Cold War as a 'dangerous illusion'. It suspects Khrushchev of taking his disarmament proposals quite seriously and endangering thereby the security of the communist bloc. It sees the chances of new communist revolutions, especially in the underdeveloped countries, as being far greater than Khrushchev cares to admit; and it thinks that Khrushchev compromises these chances in the interest of his diplomacy. Mao holds that there is 'too much diplomacy and too little communism' in all Khrushchev does. Finally, there are the differences over domestic policies, the Chinese communes, the treatment of consumer interests, and political 'liberalization'. On the other hand, the right-wing communists or revisionists discarded the Leninist view on imperialism as obsolete long before Khrushchev did so; and they reproach Khrushchev with not being consistent and persistent enough in striving for détente and disarmament.

Deutscher, I., (ed. Halliday, F.), 1970. **Russia, China and the West 1953–1966.** *Harmondsworth. Penguin Books. p.206*

Although relations between the two non-capitalist states seemed fine during Khrushchev's official visit to Beijing during July and August 1958, there were growing problems behind the scenes, and tensions between the states remained high. Once again, Deng attacked the Soviet

5 The People's Republic of China (1949–2005)

Union – this time for its 'great nation, great party chauvinism' – and accused it of betraying the international communist movement.

Figure 5.3: Mao and Khrushchev during Khrushchev's visit to China in August 1958.

The Great Leap Forward

Sino-Soviet relations deteriorated further when the Soviet Union began to criticise Mao's Great Leap Forward – in July 1959, Khrushchev made a speech in Poland attacking the very idea of the communes. In fact, Mao believed Peng Dehuai's criticisms of the Great Leap Forward (see Section 3.2) had been encouraged by the Soviet Union. In addition, Khrushchev began to ask for concessions from China, such as guaranteeing facilities for the re-fuelling of Soviet ships, and the granting right to build a radio station in China.

The Sino-Soviet split, 1960–61

The growing tensions between these two Communist countries finally came into the open at the Conference of Communist and Workers' Parties held in Romania in June 1960. The Soviet delegation began to criticise aspects of Mao's domestic policies; in reply, the Chinese delegate bitterly attacked Soviet policy. Shortly after that, in July, Khrushchev abruptly ended all Soviet aid to China and ordered the Soviet technicians back to the USSR. As we have seen (see Section 3.2),

Foreign policy, 1949–76

this came at the time of internal criticisms of Mao's Great Leap Forward and its failures, and when China needed such help more than ever.

Figure 5.4: A cartoon, published in the *Washington Post*, 24 June 1960, commenting on the growing Sino-Soviet split within the world Communist movement.

QUESTION

What is the message of the cartoon in Figure 5.4?

In November 1960, at the Conference of Communist and Workers' Parties in Moscow, the focus shifted to the Soviet Union's policy of 'peaceful coexistence' with the capitalist world. This was bitterly attacked by the Chinese delegation – headed by Liu and Deng – which, in part, saw this policy as an attack on Mao's position. Although these disagreements were not made public, the press in the respective countries turned on minor countries associated with the two big players: China's press attacked Yugoslavia, while the Soviet press turned on Albania, which was defying Moscow.

The worldwide communist movement soon split into pro-Moscow and pro-Beijing parties – with, from 1961, Albania siding with China which had stepped in after the USSR had ended its aid. At the Congress of the CPSU in Moscow in October 1961, which China attended as an observer, Khrushchev attacked both Stalin and Albania, and Zhou Enlai, the Chinese representative, walked out of the meeting. The Sino-Soviet split was now clear.

Developments, 1961–64

After the public split in 1961, Sino-Soviet relations continued to worsen. The Soviet Union's apparent climb-down over the Cuban Missile Crisis in 1962, and the nuclear Test Ban Treaty that followed in 1963, were both seen by China as evidence of Soviet 'revisionism'. A bitter Sino-Soviet propaganda war ensued over the correct revolutionary path to socialism – made worse by China's anger over the USSR's refusal to support it when a short-lived war broke out with India (which had granted sanctuary to the Dalai Lama) in 1962, along the border with Tibet. For China, there should be no peaceful coexistence between oppressed and oppressor nations. In 1963, the Soviet Union responded by accusing Communist China of following the Trotskyist policy of 'permanent revolution', which it condemned as a 'deviation' from Marxism – and even of being prepared to risk a nuclear war.

The Third Front

Chinese fears about the loss of its Soviet ally, and the international situation in general, led to a secret attempt to construct, between 1964 and 1971, a self-reliant economy in China's remote interior. This military-industrial complex – known as the Third Front (or the Third Line) – was first mooted by Lin Biao in early 1962, as a way of negating any US-backed attack by Jiang and the GMD on the PRC.

The project was to a large extent supervised by Deng who, in particular, ensured an adequate communications network was established that would allow the Chinese government to continue to function, economically and militarily, in the case of war with the US or any of its neighbours. The idea was that, in the event of war, the people and industries of the vulnerable eastern and southern provinces could be moved to the remoter regions of central China. Some observers have

Foreign policy, 1949–76

claimed that the Cultural Revolution was, in part, an attempt to conceal this massive investment and construction programme.

This 'bunker mentality' was in large part the result of China's growing sense of isolation. Ever since the Korean War, Mao had seemed convinced that the US was planning to invade China at some point. Support for this Third Front policy was increased by the escalating US intervention in Vietnam – its long-range bombers, which began attacking North Vietnam in 1964, were within easy striking distance of China.

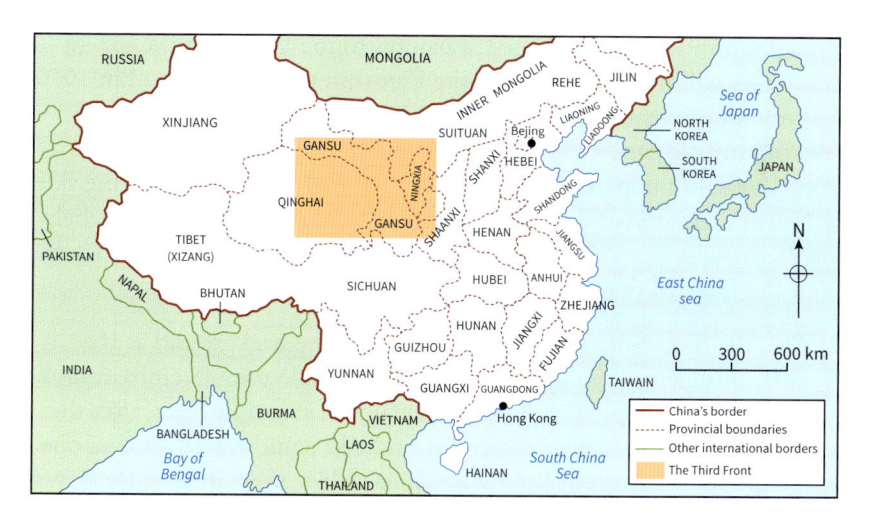

Figure 5.5: Map of China showing the Third Front.

China and nuclear weapons

In addition, growing tensions with the USSR also added to Chinese anxieties about impending war. In 1957, during the Second Taiwan Strait Crisis, the Soviet Union eventually made an agreement to provide China with modern military technology, including blueprints and a sample atomic device. However, the Soviet Union had insisted that this be under joint-control. This was unacceptable to Mao and, in June 1959, shortly after Peng had returned from a military mission in the Soviet Union, Khrushchev had ended the agreement and withdrawn its nuclear physicists from China. Tensions between the two countries increased in October 1964, when China – without Soviet help – was able to explode its first atomic bomb, codenamed '59/6'. In June 1967, China exploded its first hydrogen bomb.

5 The People's Republic of China (1949–2005)

Foreign policy and the Cultural Revolution

Although Khrushchev fell from power in 1964, relations between the USSR and China did not improve, as the collective leadership – increasingly dominated by Brezhnev – which replaced him continued to support détente. During the early years of the Cultural Revolution, the PRC – preoccupied with internal problems – seemed to lose interest in foreign policy. At the time, the US was massively escalating the war in Vietnam, it was dropping bombs very near the Chinese border, but Mao and his supporters saw their internal struggle as more important to the world revolution than helping North Vietnam. In fact, it was Liu Shaoqi who issued the strongest warnings to the US about the extent of China's willingness to support the Vietnamese. Mao later said in 1970 that one of the reasons he had purged Liu was because he favoured reviving the old Sino-Soviet alliance, which had broken down in the early 1960s. Liu hoped the prospect of Chinese intervention on the side of North Vietnam would limit US aggression in Vietnam, and thus help the Vietnamese. For Mao, however, this would have distracted the Party from the internal political struggle of the Cultural Revolution.

At first, the Sino-Soviet dispute simmered in the background as Red Guard contingents regularly demonstrated outside the US embassy and those of its main capitalist allies – especially Britain. However, after the main aspects of the Cultural Revolution had begun to settle down, one of the questions that remained was China's place in an international arena dominated by two hostile powers: the US and the USSR. Soon, the greatest political attacks began to be directed against the 'revisionist' and 'social imperialist' USSR.

The invasion of Czechoslovakia by Soviet-led Warsaw Pact troops in 1968 had worried the Chinese Communists as it – and the later Brezhnev Doctrine issued to justify it – clearly showed that the USSR was prepared to override the national sovereignty of states in the 'Communist camp'. The invasion weakened Soviet prestige, with the result that when Brezhnev convened a Communist Conference in Moscow in June 1969, with the aim of getting it to condemn China, the Conference did not unanimously condemn China.

Foreign policy, 1949–76

Border disputes

Sino-Soviet relations worsened in 1969 as a result of clashes along the Sino-Soviet border, which covered several thousand miles. Disagreements over disputed land had led to increased tensions, with both states increasing the number of troops deployed along it. Then, between March and August 1969, there were a series of border clashes: along the Ussuri River, which ran along the border between Manchuria and the Soviet Union; along the Amur River; along the Xinjiang-Soviet border; and in Yumin County.

Several of these border incidents led to deaths on both sides and, during September-October, Zhou Enlai, China's foreign minister, began to have talks with Alexei Kosygin, the Soviet prime minister. This resulted in an agreement to replace aspects of earlier 'unequal treaties', and tensions lessened. However, normal relations between the two countries were not fully restored, and both sides maintained large numbers of divisions along the border – this remained the case for the rest of the existence of the Soviet Union.

5.3 What was the significance of Communist China's rapprochement with the USA in the 1970s?

Since 1949, the USA – unlike several European countries – had refused to allow Communist China representation at the UN. Instead, the US insisted that the true representative of China was Jiang's tiny state of Taiwan. In addition, as has been seen, the US deliberately took a hard line with Communist China over the offshore islands – partly in the hope that, if they could discourage the Soviet Union from helping the PRC in this dispute, the lack of Soviet support would anger Mao and so cause a split between the USSR and China – and thus destroy the alliance established by the 1950 Treaty.

5 The People's Republic of China (1949–2005)

Thus, it was not surprising that, in China, the US was for decades portrayed as 'the number one enemy nation', and the great enemy of China and socialism. US 'imperialists' were attacked as 'paper tigers', and 'Death to the American imperialists and all their running dogs' was a chant frequently heard in China during the 1950s and 1960s. The various anti-US campaigns reached a peak during the Vietnam War: although China was not officially involved in the war, it gave limited support to North Vietnam in its struggle against the US-backed South. As the massive US presence in Vietnam – on China's southern borders – recalled the Korean War of ten years before, fear of a possible US invasion of China helped consolidate support for Mao and the CCP.

Figure 5.6: A Chinese poster of 1965 – the text reads: 'Imperialism and all reactionaries are all paper tigers!'

QUESTION

What, according to the cartoon in Figure 5.6, were the three main 'imperialist' and 'reactionary states'?

Foreign policy, 1949–76

Changing views of the USA

By 1969, China was increasingly concerned about tensions on its borders with the Soviet Union, and by the fact that both North Vietnam and North Korea, each with borders with China, were Soviet allies. The decision by the USSR to use Warsaw Pact troops to invade Czechoslovakia in 1968 had been taken by China's leaders as evidence of the Soviet Union's preparedness to act outside its borders in defence of its interests. Finally, relations with India – which also had a border with China – remained strained.

Consequently, Mao commissioned four of the most senior Marshals of the PLA to write a report on China's foreign policy priorities. The report concluded that China should abandon its ties with the Soviet Union, and its ideological claim to lead the world communist movement. Instead, it should adopt a more pragmatic approach which placed China's interests and national security at the top, and should thus deal with other states on this basis.

These suggestions particularly angered Lin Biao whose stance was essentially 'neither Moscow nor Washington' and who thus was opposed to any alliance with either of these two Cold War nations. Thus, he was angered by Mao's acceptance of these suggestions – and especially by his surprising decision that Communist China should ally itself with the US in order to counter the perceived threat from the Soviet Union. Mao, on the other hand, saw an improvement in relations with the US as a way of undermining the Soviet Union and so limiting Soviet opportunities.

> **QUESTION**
>
> How did China's foreign policy towards the US after 1969 cause tensions between Mao and Lin Biao?

The US and China

By 1969, the US – realising that it was losing the Vietnam War – was also reappraising its foreign policy, including towards the PRC. In part, this was because as more and more member states of the UN supported China's admittance to the Security Council, it was clear that the US would soon lose this vote. In November 1970, for the first time, there was a simple majority vote in the UN in favour of the PRC taking the

5 The People's Republic of China (1949–2005)

Chinese seat – although a two-thirds majority was necessary to bring this about. The US also saw closer relations with China as a way of putting pressure on the Soviet Union. In particular, the US thought this might persuade the USSR to push North Vietnam into signing an agreement.

The turn to the US

Within China, Mao came to see an agreement with the US as a way to undermine the Soviet Union's position as a powerful nation. Consequently, negotiations – spear-headed by Zhou, who had become aware of the shift in US attitudes – began between China and the US. In December 1970, the world – and the Chinese people – were staggered by Mao's decision to invite the US president to China. In March 1971, the US lifted restrictions on US citizens travelling to Communist China – these had been in place ever since the Korean War. The US then relaxed the embargo on Sino-US trade and the use of US dollars by the PRC. The US also agreed to give China access to top secret satellite intelligence regarding Soviet troop and nuclear weapons deployments.

The US – which had been portrayed for years as China's main imperialist enemy – was now spoken of as a friend of China. In July 1971, Henry Kissinger, who was US president Nixon's National Security Adviser, visited China, and held discussions with Zhou Enlai, preparing the ground for this volte-face. The agreement over the visit was preceded by a series of table-tennis tournaments and what became known as 'ping pong diplomacy'. These developments – given Lin Biao's strong opposition to any deal with the US – undoubtedly played a part in what became known as 'Project 571', which resulted in the death of Lin Biao in September 1971, two months after Kissinger's visit to China (see Section 4.3).

In October 1971, the US – backed by its ally, Japan – finally allowed Communist China to join the UN, and agreed to exclude Jiang's Taiwan. In February 1972, Nixon became the first US president to visit Communist China. After the meetings between Mao and Nixon, the 'Shanghai Communiqué' mainly endorsed the positions the Chinese had been setting forth since 1949: it called for the progressive withdrawal of US military forces from Taiwan, and accepted that the future of Taiwan was an internal Chinese matter. The 'Shanghai Communiqué' also called for continued talks and the complete normalisation of Sino-American

Foreign policy, 1949–76

relations – though the latter didn't happen until 1979, three years after Mao's death, with the establishment of full diplomatic relations.

Figure 5.7: The historic meeting between Mao and Nixon in Beijing, during Nixon's visit to China in February 1972.

QUESTION

What is the value and limitations of Figure 5.7 for historians studying Communist China's foreign policy in the early 1970s?

The anti-Soviet aspects of the new foreign policy were later underlined in a speech by Ronald Reagan in 1972. Reagan (a Republican and staunch anti-communist, who became president in 1981) stated that one aim of this new foreign policy was to ensure that the Soviet Union would have to permanently keep 40 divisions of troops on the Chinese border.

5 The People's Republic of China (1949–2005)

China and the world after 1972

One dramatic result of China's accommodation with the US was to change the nature of the Cold War – before 1972, the Cold War had led to an essentially bi-polar world, in which most states often aligned with one of the two Cold War antagonists. After 1972, the Cold War became a tri-polar affair. With the Soviet Union seeming now to face two major opponents, it arguably prevented the USSR from shifting spending from military to civilian spending, and so contributed to the eventual collapse of the Soviet Union in 1991.

The US decision to allow China to take up its position in the UN Security Council also led to improved relations with Japan. In September 1972, **Kakuei Tanaka**, the prime minister of Japan visited China and began the first attempts at the normalisation of Sino-Japanese relations since the end of the Second World War. This process continued and, in 1978, two years after Mao's death, a friendship and trading treaty was signed between the two countries. This was to prove vitally important to the Chinese economic reforms of the 1980s. As a result, by 1976, China was recognised as a powerful state in the world, and the way was paved for China to become increasingly important within the global capitalist market.

Kakuei Tanaka (1918–93):

Kakuei was conscripted into the Japanese army in 1939, but invalided out in 1941. He then went into the construction industry, eventually marrying into a family which ran a large civil engineering company. His early involvement in politics was marked by corruption scandals; nonetheless, in 1957, he became Minister of Posts and Telecommunications in the Liberal Democratic Party's newly elected government.

In 1971, as a result of important political connections and public popularity, he became prime minister. Apart from normalising relations with China, he also improved Japan's welfare system. However, fresh corruption scandals led to his resignation in 1974; in 1976, he was arrested for taking bribes from the US aviation firm, Lockheed. He was found guilty in 1983 and, despite appealing against the verdict, it was confirmed in 1987. He appealed again, but died in 1993, while the court case was still taking place.

Foreign policy, 1949–76

Proletarian internationalism

Although the new foreign policy designed by Zhou began to pay great nationalist dividends, it did so at an enormous cost to China's previously proclaimed principles of 'proletarian internationalism.' The new Chinese policy of *'peaceful coexistence between countries with different social systems'* was then gradually put into operation. Thus China, maintained entirely peaceful relations with both Pakistan and Sri Lanka, even as they crushed popular rebellions in their respective countries. Various feudal monarchs and military dictators – previously denounced as 'fascists' – were welcomed in Beijing. This included establishing diplomatic and trade relations with the Francoist dictatorship in Spain, and the military junta in Greece.

The justification for all these foreign policy U-turns was that they were in the interests of 'socialist' China as they weakened the Soviet Union which was a 'social imperialist' threat to China. These foreign policies were endorsed at the Tenth National Congress of the CCP in August 1973. China then emerged as a great friend of the US-dominated NATO, and even maintained formal diplomatic and trade relations with Pinochet's military dictatorship in Chile after its brutal overthrow of Allende's government in September 1973.

Theory of Knowledge

Politics and ethics:

Did China's political, economic and military support of repressive and 'reactionary' governments and movements – provided they were hostile to the Soviet Union – mean the CCP had abandoned all its earlier commitments to world revolution? How similar was China's new foreign policy to that of the US which, during the Cold War, often claimed to be 'defending the free world' and upholding 'democratic values' – but supported brutal dictatorships and terrorist organisations because they were anti-communist?

In the spring of 1974, Deng headed the Chinese delegation to a special session of the UN, where he announced that the post-war 'socialist bloc' no longer existed, and that China should now be seen as part of the Third World. In early 1976 – the year in which both Zhou and Mao died – China participated in the Angolan civil war on the same side as the US and apartheid South Africa.

5 The People's Republic of China (1949–2005)

The impact on CCP

This new Chinese foreign policy of 'peaceful coexistence', endorsed by the CC of the CCP, was precisely the policy for which Mao, in the early 1960s, had condemned Khrushchev and the Soviet Union as being 'revisionist' – i.e. attempting to move away from orthodox Marxism and proletarian solidarity by advocating the possibility of peace between countries with different social systems. Not surprisingly, such a major foreign policy shift had repercussions within the CCP – in particular, as Source 5.5 states, it was one of the factors behind the growing rift between Mao and Lin Biao.

SOURCE 5.5

Zhou, undoubtedly with the strong support of Mao, was advocating a new global diplomatic strategy.... It was a strategy which defined the Soviet Union as the principal enemy, and correspondingly, dictated a tactical accommodation with the United States.... This new diplomacy was of course wholly inconsistent with the proclaimed principle of 'proletarian internationalism'... that briefly had held sway. To Lin Biao [the new diplomacy] seemed, if not necessarily so much a betrayal of principle, then certainly a politically damaging repudiation of the vision of a worldwide 'people's war' with which he had been so intimately identified. On the question of China's foreign policy, particularly the policy of rapprochement with the United States, one of the battle lines between Mao and his designated 'successor' was drawn.

Meisner, M., 1999, **Mao's China and After: A History of the People's Republic.** New York, The Free Press, p.379.

During the April 1969 Congress, Lin Biao's main report had equally attacked Soviet and US imperialisms. However, Zhou – with the support of Mao – had argued that the USSR was the main threat, and that therefore it was necessary to come to some understanding with the US to counter this. Nonetheless, Lin still saw the US as the *'most ferocious enemy of the people's of the world'*, and saw this suggested accommodation with US imperialism as a betrayal of 'proletarian internationalism' This issue led to a clear division within the leadership of the CCP – and played a large part in the increasingly strained relations between Mao and Lin.

Foreign policy, 1949–76

> **DISCUSSION POINT**
>
> How important do you think ideals and principles should be in politics? Should Lin Biao have taken the pragmatic approach over foreign policy in the period 1969–71? Or is it sometimes necessary to defend certain values, regardless of the consequences for you or other people?

However, from the mid 1970s – with Mao's health continuing to deteriorate – Party leaders increasingly turned their attention away from foreign policy towards other, more pressing, domestic concerns. As the following chapters will show, these were about the leadership of the Party after Mao's death, and the economic policies China should pursue in the future. In the decades that followed, China's foreign policy moved increasingly away from alliances towards obtaining trade and investment agreements with the West.

5 The People's Republic of China (1949–2005)

Paper 3 exam practice

Question

'The Sino-Soviet split of the 1960s was largely the fault of Mao's obstinance and refusal to compromise.' To what extent do you agree with this statement? **[15 marks]**

Skill

Avoiding irrelevance

Examiner's tips

Do not waste valuable writing time on irrelevant material – by definition, if it's irrelevant, it won't gain you any marks. Writing irrelevant information can happen because

- the candidate does not look carefully enough at the wording of the question (see Skill at end of Chapter 2).
- the candidate ignores the fact that the questions require selection of facts, an analytical approach and a final judgement; instead the candidate just writes down all that she or he knows about a topic (relevant or not), and hopes that the examiner will do the analysis and make the judgement.
- the candidate has unwisely restricted his or her revision. So, for example, if a question crops up on China's role in the Korean War, rather than the expected one on Mao's foreign policy towards the US – the candidate tries to turn it into the question he or she wanted! Whatever the reason, such responses rarely address any of the demands of the question asked.

For this question, you will need to:

- cover the events during the 1960s that led to the split
- outline the actions and policy decisions of both the Soviet Union and Communist China
- provide a judgement about the extent to which you agree with the statement – for instance, were both countries equally to blame, or was one country more responsible than the other?

Foreign Policy, 1949–76

Common mistakes

One common error with questions like this is for candidates to write about material they know well, rather than material directly related to the question.

Another mistake is to present too much general information, instead of material specific to the person, period and command terms.

Finally, candidates often elaborate too much on events outside the dates given in the question (see the guidance in Chapter 3).

Sample paragraphs of irrelevant focus/material

Before trying to decide whether Mao was mainly responsible for the Sino-Soviet split, it will be necessary to explain the Soviet Union's foreign policy towards China in the period before 1949. In particular, the ways in which Stalin belittled and ignored Mao and the CCP is relevant to answering this question.

Before the Communist victory in China in 1949, earlier Soviet foreign policy towards the Chinese Communists played a big part in the eventual Sino-Soviet split of the 1960s. One aspect which particularly annoyed the CCP was Stalin's insistence, from the late 1920s right through to the end of the Second World War, that China was not ready for a socialist revolution. As a result, he insisted that the CCP join in a coalition with the Nationalist GMD. Even after Jiang had launched a massacre of Chinese Communists in Shanghai and elsewhere in 1927, Stalin still continued to send aid to the GMD.

[There then follow several more-detailed paragraphs about Stalin's advice and instructions to the CCP during the 1930s.]

In 1945, with Japan defeated and Jiang's forces demoralised, Mao and the CCP believed they were close to bringing the civil war to a victorious end. Yet, once again, Stalin decided to put Soviet interests above those of the Chinese Communists.

In fact, Stalin did nothing to stop the US from organising a massive airlift to fly 80 000 GMD troops to areas which they could seize before the Communists' Red Army could get there. Stalin did this because he had obtained US approval of a Soviet 'sphere of influence' in Eastern Europe. As China had been agreed to be a US 'sphere', he did not want a Communist victory putting this agreement at risk. He also urged the CCP to accept the US proposal for a GMD-CCP coalition government in 1945. However, most of the time – even when making

5 The People's Republic of China (1949–2005)

formal agreements with Stalin – Mao and the other CCP leaders generally ignored what they were told to do and, instead, carried out their own policies.

[There then follow several detailed paragraphs about the renewal of the civil war in 1946, and the limited aid sent by Stalin to the Communists.]

Thus, by the time the Communists were able to proclaim the birth of the new People's Republic of China in October 1949, Stalin and the Soviet Union had done much to create suspicion and anger among the leaders of the CCP. While it is true that Mao's ego meant he was often over-sensitive to what he saw as Soviet arrogance, the main responsibility for the Sino-Soviet split was not his – the blame rests almost entirely with Stalin and the Soviet Union. This was because they put Soviet interests first, and often treated their Chinese allies with typical Western arrogance.

> **EXAMINER COMMENTS**
>
> This is an example of a weak answer. Although a brief comment on the state of Sino-Soviet relations before 1949 would be relevant and helpful, there is certainly no need to go into detail about the period 1927–49. Thus the material marked in blue is irrelevant, and will not score any marks. In addition, the candidate is using up valuable writing time, which should have been spent on providing *relevant* points and supporting knowledge.

Activity

In this chapter, the focus is on avoiding writing answers that contain irrelevant material. So, using the information from this chapter, and any other sources of information available to you, write an answer to one of the following Practice Paper 3 questions, keeping your answer fully focused on the question asked. Remember – doing a plan *first* can help you maintain this focus.

Remember to refer to the simplified Paper 3 mark scheme in Chapter 10.

Paper 3 Practice questions

1 Examine the reasons for China's alliance with the Soviet Union during the 1950s.

2 Discuss the reasons for, and the consequences for China of, the Sino-Soviet split in the period, 1956–62.

3 'If Peng Dehuai had been in charge of Chinese foreign policy, the Sino-Soviet split could have been avoided.' To what extent do you agree with this statement?

4 To what extent were the agreements with the US in the 1970s an abandonment of all of Mao's earlier principles.

5 Evaluate the success of Mao's foreign policy during the period 1962–76.

6 The struggle for power, 1972–82

The struggle for power, 1972–82

Introduction

In September 1976, Mao Zedong – who had been in charge of China for most of the time since the Communist Revolution of 1949 – died. By then, the Chinese economy was beginning to show signs of stagnation: the main problem seemed to be how to achieve economic growth and modernisation without weakening the political power and control of the Party bureaucracy. Eventually – and unlike the communist rulers of the Soviet Union – the Chinese Communists proved able to achieve rapid economic growth with the maintenance – so far – of their one-party rule.

Almost immediately, Mao's death in 1976 triggered off a struggle for power over what direction China was to take. In many ways, this struggle for power had been going on since the early 1970s, and many of the issues involved were linked to the debates and policies of the previous two decades. Eventually, after the fall of Jiang Qing and her three main supporters (who became known as the Gang of Four), China witnessed the re-emergence of Deng Xiaoping and his eventual achievement of political dominance.

TIMELINE

1973 Feb: Zhou allows Deng to return to Beijing

Mar: Deng becomes deputy premier of the State Council

Aug: 10th Congress of CCP confirms return of 'Rightists'; Deng elected to CC and Politburo

1975 Jan: Zhou announces the Four Modernisations

Feb: 'Leftists' campaign against 'bourgeois' ideas; Deng's influence reduced

1976 Jan: Zhou dies; replaced as premier by Hua Guofeng

Apr: Qingming Festival protests; Deng dismissed

Sep: Mao dies

Oct: Gang of Four arrested

1977 Jul: Third Plenum of 10th CC; Hua confirmed as Chairman of CCP; Deng restored to former positions

1978 Dec: Third Plenum of 11th CC; Deng attacks Hua and the 'Whateverists'

1980 Sep: Hua forced to resign as premier; replaced by Zhao Ziyang

6 The People's Republic of China (1949–2005)

Nov: Trial of Gang of Four begins

1981 Jan: Gang of Four found guilty

Apr: Hu Yaobang becomes Chairman of CCP

Jun: Official reappraisal of Mao; Hua resigns as Party chairman and chair of the Military Commission; then removed from Politburo

1982 Sep: 12th Congress of CCP confirm the leadership changes; Deng now seen as 'paramount leader'

KEY QUESTIONS
- Why were there tensions within the CCP from 1972 to 1975?
- What was Mao's legacy?
- What were the main stages of the power struggle, 1976–82?

Overview

- After Lin Biao's death in 1971, another power struggle – between Rightists such as Zhou Enlai and Deng Xiaoping, and the Leftist Gang of Four – emerged.
- During 1973–74, Zhou helped Deng and other 'Rightists' to return to political posts
- In January 1975, Zhou announced the Four Modernisations, but the Leftists began a campaign against 'bourgeois' ideas – this began to reduce the influence of Deng and other Rightists.
- In January 1976, Zhou died; after protests during the Qingming Festival, leading Rightists were again dismissed.
- In September 1976, Mao died, and the struggle for power intensified. At first, Mao's position was taken by Hua Guofeng, a more moderate Maoist. He then arrested the Gang of Four.
- In 1977, Deng and the Rightists were once again restored to their positions. Slowly, Deng and his supporters sidelined Hua. During 1980 and 1981, Hua was forced to resign from most of his posts, leaving Deng the 'paramount leader' by 1982.

The struggle for power, 1972–82

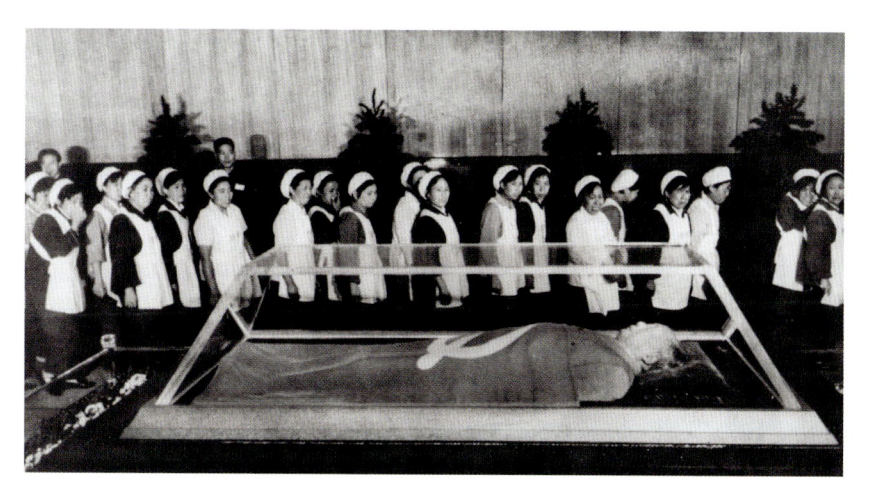

Figure 6.1: Mao's body lying in state after his death in 1976; note that several of the mourners are crying.

6.1 Why were there tensions within the CCP from 1972 to 1975?

Immediately after Lin Biao's plot and death in 1971, Liuists and Maoists in the CCP had remained briefly united. However, during 1972, members of these two factions soon began taking different positions, and another political clash between Rightists and Leftists was clearly imminent. In many ways, this was a struggle between the older leaders who had been attacked during the Cultural Revolution, and the younger ones who had risen during it. From 1973, differences over economic and foreign policy, and over revolutionary political ideology, saw the Rightists, now led by Zhou Enlai, frequently disagreeing with the Leftists.

Rightists versus Leftists

The 'discovery' of Lin's plot had undermined faith in Mao – as he had clearly made a mistake in favouring Lin. In February 1973, again with

201

6 The People's Republic of China (1949–2005)

help from Zhou Enlai, Deng was allowed to return to Beijing from the political exile that had been imposed on him during the Cultural Revolution. By that time, Mao's health was rapidly worsening, and the struggle for power between Rightists and Leftists intensified. Several Rightists who had been demoted or expelled during the Cultural Revolution were quietly re-habilitated and restored to power.

The Rightists were initially led by Zhou Enlai, the prime minister, and Deng Xiaoping. Zhou wanted to focus on economic development and saw Deng, who was appointed a Vice-Premier of the Council of State in March 1973, as a useful ally, as he was prepared to consider things from a pragmatic (practical) point of view rather than ensuring revolutionary ideology was maintained at all costs.

The Leftists were led by Mao's wife, Jiang Qing and three radical Party members from Shanghai – these later became known as the 'Gang of Four'. They were supported by the trades unions, by the Communist Youth League and by the militias of the big cities.

The new economic and foreign policy initiatives taken since 1970 were endorsed by the Tenth National Congress of the CCP in August 1973 and, in elections to the Politburo, the return of the old pre-Cultural Revolution 'capitalist roaders' was confirmed, with Deng re-elected to the CC and the Politburo. In this clear split between right-wing 'moderates' and left-wing radicals, the Rightists increasingly had a greater say than the younger leaders who'd been promoted during the years 1966–69. At this time, however, it was assumed that Mao still favoured the Leftist emphasis on correct ideology as the way to achieve economic development.

The Gang of Four

During the Cultural Revolution, in November 1966, a 17-strong Central Cultural Revolutionary Committee had been headed up by Jiang as first vice-chairwoman. This Committee included several of her closest Shanghai political associates: **Zhang Chunqiao** (deputy secretary of Shanghai's Municipal Committee); **Yao Wenyuan** (Mao's chief propagandist); and **Wang Hongwen** (a trade union leader).

Zhang Chunqiao (1917–2005):

Zhang joined the CCP in 1938, and later became an important journalist and political theorist in Shanghai. From the late 1950s and early 1960s, he emerged as a firm supporter of Mao in the struggle against Liu Shaoqi. He rose to prominence during the Cultural Revolution as a radical Maoist in Shanghai, where he met Jiang Qing. In 1967, along with Wang and Yao, he organised the Shanghai Commune, which essentially overthrew the local Party and government organisations; he then became the chairman of Shanghai's Revolutionary Committee. He also acted as one of the leaders of the Cultural Revolution Group and, in 1969, was made a member of the CCP's Politburo. In 1975, when Deng was first vice-premier, he became the second vice-premier – in 1976, Deng was removed from his post.

Yao Wenyuan (1931–2005):

Yao joined the CCP in 1948, and was a radical leftist; during the Hundred Flowers campaign, he wrote an article attacking those 'rightist' intellectuals opposed to the Party. This led to him being promoted to a senior position in the CCP's propaganda department in Shanghai, where he worked closely with Zhang Chunqiao in the 'anti-rightist' campaign. He rose to real prominence during the Cultural Revolution – in fact, an article he wrote in 1965 (which attacked the play, *Hai Rui Dismissed from Office*, as an implied criticism of Mao's dismissal of Peng Dehuai in 1959), is seen as providing an opportunity for Mao to launch the Cultural Revolution in 1966. In 1969, Yao was promoted to the Politburo of the CCP, and became the editor of *Liberation Daily*, Shanghai's main newspaper.

6 The People's Republic of China (1949–2005)

> **Wang Hongwen (1935–92):**
>
> Wang was the youngest member of the radical communist group known as the Gang of Four, and rose from the ranks of the working class via his trade union activism to become the vice-chairman of the CCP. He fought in the Korean War and joined the CCP in 1953. He was sent to Shanghai, where he came into contact with Zhang. In 1967, he helped organise the Shanghai Commune, and was elected to the Central Committee of the CCP in 1969; in 1973, he became vice-chairman of the Central Committee, and was elected to the Politburo. By 1973, he was the third-highest ranking member of the CCP and, for a time, was seen as Mao's possible successor. However, when Zhou died in January 1976, he did not become premier, losing out to Hua Guofeng.

They had been Mao's strongest supporters during the Cultural Revolution – though whether they were controlled by him, or they were increasingly imposing their views on him remains unclear.

During the Cultural Revolution, the members of this Committee had tried to promote the 'Thoughts of Chairman Mao', and to eliminate all traces of the 'Four Olds'. They had been very active in campaigns against the Rightists, such as Liu and Deng; and had encouraged the Red Guards to hold mass protest rallies. They had used quotations from Mao's Little Red Book to support their accusations and actions, making it difficult for people to oppose them – unless they wanted to be seen as disagreeing with Mao himself.

These four leading members of this Committee later became known as the Gang of Four – the term was allegedly first coined by Mao. The 'Gang of Four' favoured an even more revolutionary approach to politics and the economy, and were among the highest leaders of the CCP – all four were members of the Politburo, and two of them (Zhang and Wang), were members of its Standing Committee. Both these bodies were more or less equally divided between 'Rightists' and 'Leftists'.

However, although Jiang's position gave them an advantage over their opponents, they were not that strong, as their power base was mainly within the cultural and media organisations. They had little support in the Party as a whole, or in the People's Liberation Army (PLA). Nonetheless, although the excesses of their supporters during the

Cultural Revolution had been eventually quelled by the PLA in 1969, Jiang retained her influence.

> **SOURCE 6.1**
>
> What the [Gang of] Four did represent was a sector of the post-Cultural Revolution bureaucracy, especially the millions of younger and lower-level cadres who had been admitted to the Party or had risen in rank by virtue of the Cultural Revolution. These were not the genuine radicals of the Cultural Revolution era, all of whom had now vanished in the continuing purge of the ultra-left that had begun in 1967, but rather more the careerists and the opportunists who (like the Four to whom they looked for leadership) had wound their way upward in the political hierarchy by faithfully following all the twists and turns of the Maoist line.
>
> Meisner, M., 1999, *Mao's China and After: A History of the People's Republic.* New York, The Free Press, p.399.

> **ACTIVITY**
>
> With a partner, make notes on how other historians view (or have viewed) the supporters of the Gang of Four, and produce a mind map that summarises these views. Then make a short presentation to the class to explain how typical Maurice Meisner's view is.

The role of foreign policy changes

As has been seen (see Chapter 5), political tensions within the CCP were increased by the developing relationship with the USA – which, since 1949, had always been depicted as an evil imperialist power. However, apart from the wider issues of foreign policy, the arguments centred on whether political principles were more or less important than practical economic considerations. Shortly after Nixon's visit and the controversial Shanghai Communique of February 1972, Mao had become increasingly ill, and both factions began to position themselves for the struggle that was bound to emerge after his death.

6 The People's Republic of China (1949–2005)

These two factions disagreed about almost everything. However, the fundamental differences were over whether politics or the economy was more important, and whether to use capitalist techniques to modernise the economy. The Rightists wanted an end to the political arguments and upheaval that had dominated China since the start of the Cultural Revolution in 1966. Instead, they wanted to build a strong and wealthy China.

The Leftists, on the other hand, wanted to continue the political struggle to ensure that China followed a 'correct' revolutionary line. This meant, in particular, removing from power all those 'moderates' – or 'reactionaries' – who favoured introducing capitalist mechanisms. Instead, they wanted to involve the mass of the Chinese people in decision-making. In particular, they believed that decisions should be based on what was good for the revolution – even if they did not make the greatest economic sense. They also believed that everyone should do some manual labour, so they could keep in touch with the people.

The Four Modernisations

Between 1974 and 1976, this political and ideological split was particularly focused on a plan known as the Four Modernisations. This plan – which was favoured by the Rightists, and was put forward by a dying Zhou in January 1975, at the Fourth National People's Congress – sought to modernise China's agriculture, industry, science and technology, and national defence.

It had first been proposed by Zhou at the Third National People's Congress in 1964. In 1973, Deng had made similar proposals; and the plan was eventually presented at the Eleventh Congress of the CCP in 1977.

Afterwards, Deng – who was appointed as Chief of Staff of the Armed Forces – often stood in for Zhou at State Council meetings. Once restored to some influence, Deng began attempts to move the CCP away from the more revolutionary – and disruptive – influences of the Gang of Four. Deng, who favoured the use of capitalist methods, continued to be supported by Zhou, who had disliked the disorder of the Cultural Revolution.

The struggle for power, 1972–82

> **QUESTION**
> What were the 'Four Modernisations'?

Jiang and her group, however, persisted in arguing in favour of continuing the Cultural Revolution, and to criticise those in the Party who they saw as promoting Western thoughts and values. At first, Mao seemed to support her but then began to distance himself from her, and to criticise some of the activities of her supporters – though he also used them to keep control of other members of the Politburo.

In February 1975, the Leftists stepped up their campaigns against 'bourgeois' and outdated ideas in the arts and in education. Although also attacking Zhou's ideas, their campaign was really directed at Deng. Though Deng fell from favour again in 1975, Zhou continued to back him.

However, as he became weaker, Mao came increasingly to rely on his nephew, Mao Yuanxin (sympathetic to the Leftists) who, from 1975, was his main liaison with the Politburo. While this gave the Gang of Four an advantage over their rivals, Mao's bodyguard, led by **General Wang Dongxing**, was opposed to them, and worked with some members of the Politburo against them.

> ### General Wang Dongxing (1916–2015):
> Wang joined the youth wing of the CCP in 1932, and became commander of Mao's bodyguard. After being dismissed, he was later reinstated and, in that role, played an important part in the coup against the Gang of Four in October 1976. Although becoming vice-chairman of the CCP and a member of the Politburo under Hua in 1977, he was increasingly sidelined by Deng (whose ideas Wang generally opposed) and, by 1982, had lost all important positions of power. In 2011, he was reported as saying that, because of Deng's economic reforms, Chinese socialism was 'in retreat' before capitalism.

6 The People's Republic of China (1949–2005)

> **KEY CONCEPTS ACTIVITY**
>
> **Significance:** Draw up a table to summarise the main political and economic differences between the Leftists and the Rightists during the period 1971–75. Then write a couple of lines to explain which one you think was the most important one.

6.2 What was Mao's legacy?

By the end of 1975, it was thus clear that, once Mao died, a major power struggle would break out within the CCP. Essentially, this power struggle – which broke out in 1976 – was over Mao's legacy and the direction China was to take economically and politically after his death.

Mao's economic and political legacy

Since Mao's death, there have been various assessments made of his legacy. While many in China still see him as China's greatest 20th-century leader, Western historians have a much more negative view: even the kindest ones (such as Jonathan Spence or Ross Terrill) tend to dismiss most of what he did after 1949. Yet others – such as Linda Benson in Source 6.2 – while noting the millions of deaths resulting from some of his economic policies, point to the fact that much was still achieved: for example, the increase of life expectancy from 36 in 1949 to 65 by 1976.

Both industry and agriculture increased under Mao from very low bases; and, as a result of new laws, equality for women in education and employment was achieved. Education and literacy – despite the upheavals resulting from political campaigns such as the Cultural Revolution – also greatly improved.

The struggle for power, 1972–82

> **SOURCE 6.2**
>
> Mao's impact on China also must be assessed in terms of economic and social changes in China after 1949. Despite the setbacks of the Great Leap Forward and the Cultural Revolution, overall China's economy made decided advances during the Maoist period. China's industrial sector grew rapidly and agricultural output was once again showing increases by the time of Mao's death. China's infrastructure expanded with the addition of new railways and improved roads. Electricity became available in all but the most remote villages. Life expectancy reached 65 years by the time of Mao's death, a remarkable increase over the 1949 figure [of 36]. Under the new laws of the PRC, women held equal status with men and, as a result of the commune movement, worked outside the home. Although efforts to expand education stumbled repeatedly due to political campaigns, the number of literate men and women climbed as schools and colleges grew in number throughout the period. These accomplishments are part of the legacy of the first generation of revolutionary leadership.
>
> Benson, L. 2002. **China Since 1949.** London. Longman. p.45

Aside from these material changes, though, there was also Mao's political legacy. Since 1949, he and the Chinese Communists had set themselves two tasks: to carry through and complete a bourgeois revolution to modernise China and then, once this was achieved, to move to the creation of a socialist society.

By 1976, the Rightists essentially believed more modernisation of the economy was the priority. On the other hand, the Leftists believed that the battle over ideas and direction was paramount – and that, if the socialist aims were not prioritised, China risked taking the road back to capitalism instead of forward to socialism. That there was clearly a close connection between politics and economics is highlighted by Source 6.3.

The People's Republic of China (1949–2005)

> **SOURCE 6.3**
>
> Among the distinguishing features of the Mao period, many observers once believed, was a unique attempt to reconcile the means of modern industrialism with the ends of socialism. That, no doubt, was Mao's aim, and it certainly was the Maoist claim. But, in the end, Mao Zedong was far more successful as an economic modernizer than as a builder of socialism. This judgment, of course, does not accord with the conventional wisdom of the day, which tells us that Mao sacrificed 'modernization' to 'ideological purity' and that economic development was neglected as the late Chairman embarked on a fruitless quest for a socialist spiritual utopia. The actual historical record conveys a rather different story, and it is essentially a story of rapid industrialization. The post-Mao critiques of the Maoist economic legacy, which dwell less on the accomplishments than on the deficiencies of the era, nonetheless reveal that the value of gross industrial output grew thirty-eight fold, and that of heavy industry ninety-fold, albeit starting from a tiny modern industrial base whose output had been halved by the ravages of foreign invasion and civil war. But between 1952 (when industrial production was restored to its highest pre-war levels) and 1977, the output of Chinese industry increased at an average annual rate of 11.3 per cent, as rapid a pace of industrialization as has ever been achieved by any country during a comparable period in modern world history.
>
> *Meisner, M. 1999.* **Mao's China and After: A History of the People's Republic.** *New York, The Free Press. pp.414–5*

Mao had often stressed that technological and industrial development needed to be accompanied by a 'permanent' process of radical social and political transformations. Therefore, he had argued that socialist institutions and communist values had to be given equal priority by the Party. In his view, progress to socialism would be achieved by ensuring economic development would simultaneously be accompanied by reductions of the 'three great differences'. By this, he meant the elimination of the distinctions between intellectual and manual labour, between industrial workers and peasants, and between town and country.

However, as pointed out by historians such as Maurice Meisner, by the time of Mao's death in 1976, the attempt to construct a socialist society in an economically undeveloped country had had limited success as regards creating a new 'socialist' people. The successful creation of a modern industrial base – by capitalist development – had been seen by Marx as the necessary prerequisite on which to build a socialist society. Yet Mao's programme of industrialisation had led to significant contradictions: economic resources from rural areas had been successfully diverted to cities in order to create a modern industrial base. One result of this, however, had been to generate new forms of social inequality – both relatively and absolutely – which were at odds with socialist values. For instance, from 1952 to 1975, annual per capita consumption among the rural population increased from 62 to 124 yuan (in current prices); however, for urban populations, the increase was from 148 to 324 yuan. Thus it was clear that, instead of reducing the 'three great differences', in many ways these had actually increased.

Economic rationality and the emergence a professional bureaucracy – even under Mao – had thus tended to blunt socialist aims and goals. While it is true that the Maoist regime had tried to lessen these new inequalities – especially if compared to similar developments in the Soviet Union – this fundamental problem still remained. It was contradictions such as these that had, in large part, led to the launching of the Cultural Revolution. Although by 1969, the main upheavals of this political campaign were over, the problems it was intended to rectify still existed in 1976. It was the continuing debate over these contradictions that mainly lay behind the frequent struggles for power – both before and after 1976.

An additional political legacy Mao left to his successors was to do with the state. According to classical Marxism – which had some aspects in common with anarchism – a workers' revolution would result, for the first time, in the majority of the population being the new ruling class. Consequently, it would be accompanied by the 'withering away' of the central state and its massive bureaucratic apparatus. This would allow the whole working population to control both the conditions and the products of their labour and life.

Yet, as with the attempt, at the same time, to modernise the economy and move towards the creation of socialist relations and norms, Mao's China resulted in the state becoming even more dominant – just as had happened in the Soviet Union under Stalin. In some ways, the development of the cult of Mao Zedong was an attempt to close the gap between its bureaucratic state and the people, by trying to establish a closer link between the ruler and the ruled. However, this political

6 The People's Republic of China (1949–2005)

dilemma of the relationship between Communist China's rulers and the Chinese people had led to problems as regards popular influence over policies and the exercise of individual rights while Mao's power was secure.

His Hundred Flowers campaign – which he himself had seen as an attempt to deal with the contradiction between 'the leadership' and 'the led' by allowing people to comment on and make suggestions about government policies had led to demands for political democracy and intellectual freedom which had been suppressed in the 'Anti-Rightist' crackdown that had followed. Thus the contradictions between rulers and ruled, as regards popular influence and control, remained unresolved. His attempt during the Cultural Revolution to reduce the power of both Party and state bureaucracies, in order to achieve a much more democratic reorganisation of political power – by removing Party and state officials who had become too remote from the people (and from the goal of socialism) – had eventually been ended. Instead, the authority of the Party and state apparatuses – and his own power – had eventually been restored.

China as a transitional society

Thus, ultimately, on both economic and political fronts, Mao's legacy to his successors was ambiguous and contradictory. While it was clear that his regime had brought about considerable socio-economic advances since 1949, the political achievements – as regards 'socialist democracy' – were extremely limited. By 1976, China was clearly not a capitalist society, as Mao and the CCP had abolished private ownership of the means of production. However, it was not socialist either – despite the tremendous expansion of industry – as real power had not been devolved to the masses. Such states have been variously described as being 'post-revolutionary' or 'post-capitalist'. Another term is the one coined by Leon Trotsky in the late 1930s about the Soviet Union: a 'transitional society'. By this, he meant that, in the end, such a society – as explained in Source 6.4 – would either have to move forwards to socialism or it would eventually slide back to capitalism. While such a transitional society could exist for many decades, it could not remain in such a transitional stage indefinitely. The analogy he used to explain this was of a person half-way across a bridge: they couldn't remain there indefinitely, but would have to decide to go forward to the other side – or go back to where they had come from.

The struggle for power, 1972–82

SOURCE 6.4

It would be truer, therefore, to name the present Soviet regime [1937] in all its contradictoriness, not as a socialist regime, but a preparatory regime transitional from capitalism to socialism…To define the Soviet regime as transitional, or intermediate, means to abandon such finished categories as capitalism (and therewith 'state capitalism') and also socialism. But besides being totally inadequate, in itself, such a definition is capable of producing the mistaken idea that from the present Soviet regime only a transition to socialism is possible. In reality a backslide to capitalism is wholly possible…. Without a planned economy the Soviet Union would be thrown back for decades. In that sense, the [Soviet] bureaucracy continues to fulfil a necessary function. But it fulfils it in such a way as to prepare an explosion of the whole system which may completely sweep out the results of the [1917] revolution.

L. Trotsky, 1972, **The Revolution Betrayed: What is the Soviet Union and Where is it Going?**, *New York, Pathfinder Press, pp. 47, 254 & 285–6.*

After Mao's death in 1976, all these economic and political contradictions and tensions within Mao's legacy would explode in a power struggle within the CCP over how best to resolve them – and over what road China should take for the future.

6.3 What were the main stages of the power struggle, 1976–82?

The death of Zhou Enlai

In January 1976, Zhou died; this was a big setback for the Rightists. In July, Zhu De (Mao's long-time military commander) also died. Meanwhile Mao himself had increasing health problems (he too was to die in September). Mao and Zhou had dominated China's communist

6 The People's Republic of China (1949–2005)

state for almost 30 years: thus Zhou's death, and Mao's illness and impending death, created a power vacuum and a struggle for power, as shown by Source 6.5. Although the Cultural Revolution had, in many respects, ended in 1969, the Gang of Four still seemed powerful, and it remained difficult to criticise them. However, once Mao's health took a serious turn for the worse, the struggle for power became more intense.

SOURCE 6.5

For China, and for Deng Xiaoping, 1976 was a year of destiny. A succession of high-profile political deaths cleared the way for modest changes in the political system, and structural changes in the economy became possible for the first time in decades. This was not a straightforward process. For insiders, dispirited after the 'ten catastrophic years' of the Cultural revolution, the two years that followed – 1976–78 – were dominated by a life-and-death struggle during which the very existence of the Chinese Communist Party and its state hung in the balance. This conflict is often represented as a struggle between two political slogans: 'seek truth from facts' and the 'two whatevers'…. The 'seekers of truth from facts' were Deng and his supporters, determined to do what was practically necessary for China irrespective of ideological considerations – and for which they had been ferociously criticised as 'empiricists'. The 'two whatevers' were whatever Mao Zedong had said and whatever Mao Zedong had done; these indicated Mao's revolutionary line and that was what China must follow. The 'two whatevers' were the touchstones for the supporters of Jaing Qing.

*Dillon, M. 2015. **Deng Xiaoping: The Man Who Made Modern China**. New York. I. B. Tauris. pp.217–18*

As with the power struggle in the Soviet Union that began following Lenin's first stroke in 1921, this contest was essentially an ideological one rather than simply a case of individuals wanting to obtain power for the sake of it. It demonstrated a fundamental split between the two main factions of the Chinese Communist Party (CCP): the 'Leftist' radical 'Gang of Four' and the 'Rightist' more 'reformist' elements of the CCP. The latter term is a bit confusing as in the context of Chinese politics in 1976, this meant those who seemed to favour almost outright capitalism. Under Mao, such people had been termed 'revisionists' (i.e. wanting to 'revise' Marxism almost out of existence), and even 'capitalist roaders'.

The struggle for power, 1972–82

The nature of the struggle

Essentially, the Gang of Four were Maoist revolutionaries who felt that since the late 1950s, Chinese Communism had lost its way – their response was to push for the re-introduction of greater radicalism. Their leader, Jiang, was growing increasingly influential during Mao's illness and decline. Opposed to them were those – led by Deng – who argued that China needed to adopt aspects of market capitalism and Western technology in order to improve and modernise the Chinese economy.

Thus the struggle was between economic 'modernisers' – portrayed by the Leftists as the 'bourgeois right' – and those who wanted to reduce social and economic inequalities more than just focusing on increased production and efficiency. In addition, while the Left favoured more authoritarian control, to prevent capitalist restoration, the Right seemed prepared to loosen controls to an extent. Again – as in the USSR in the 1920s – there were those in the middle of these two factions who favoured a compromise between these two positions. This more moderate 'Maoist' centrist group was led by **Hua Guofeng**, who had been named as a possible successor to Mao after Lin's death in 1971.

Hua Guofeng (1921–2008):

Hua's real name was Su Zhu, and he had been a relatively unknown top security official from Hunan, Mao's home province. His rapid rise to prominence in the Party led to his nickname, the 'helicopter.' While he was a moderate Leftist, he did not particularly like the Gang. He actively tried to broaden his support base and had some backing from Deng's supporters. It was rumoured that he was Mao's son – he certainly tried to look like him as regards hair style and mannerisms.

The rise of Hua Guofeng

After Zhou's death in January 1976, many waited to see who Mao would favour as successor – his choice would be likely to determine what future direction China would take. The Gang tried to get Zhang appointed as premier, in order to ensure a more leftwing and radical set of policies. However, Zhou had favoured Deng, who wanted to introduce market mechanisms into China's centrally planned economy.

6 The People's Republic of China (1949–2005)

In the end, Mao surprised many by opting for Hua – a virtual unknown – who became the new premier.

As he had a centrist position, there were no serious objections from either of the two opposed factions. Mao seemed to trust him more than Deng, and is supposed to have said in 1976 – in what some sources claim were Mao's last coherent words – 'With you in charge, I am at ease.'

Figure 6.2: A painting of Hua (on the left) talking to Mao. Immediately after the Gang of Four had been overthrown, this painting was frequently published – and it was hinted that Mao had just written the words 'With you in charge, I am at ease' on the paper shown resting on the table.

QUESTION

What is the message of the painting shown in Figure 6.2? How does the artist try to get their message across? Do sources like this have any value for historians trying to find out about this power struggle?

The Qingming Festival, 1976

This annual festival was an important traditional Chinese festival, in which people visited the graves of their ancestors to pay their respects. It was seen by the CCP as 'superstitious', 'bourgeois' and an outmoded feudal hangover, and they had tried to stamp it out.

During early April 1976, crowds of people in Beijing decided to use the festival as a way of showing their respect for Zhou, who had been a popular leader. Thousands went to Tiananmen Square over a four-day period to lay wreaths and white paper chrysanthemums in his memory. The Gang, who did not want the funeral of a Rightist to last too long, decided to cut short the mourning period for Zhou.

Figure 6.3: The wreaths for Zhou Enlai in Tiananmen Square, Beijing, April 1976, photographed shortly before they were removed by police, triggering serious rioting.

Particularly worrying for the Gang was that some of the crowd wrote poems on the ground around the Monument to the People's Heroes, which showed support for Zhou, and for Deng and the Rightists – and even criticised Mao himself, not just Jiang and the Gang of Four.

This apparently spontaneous protest worried the Party leadership. Hua advised Mao to have the wreaths quietly removed by the police at the end of the festival, hoping this would end the criticisms. However,

6 The People's Republic of China (1949–2005)

when news spread about their removal on 5 April, masses of protestors marched to the square in protest, and over 10 000 placed more wreaths in the Square, and wrote even stronger criticisms of Mao.

As indicated by Source 6.6, this protest – which later became known as the April 5th Movement – was an important development in popular protest and resistance against the authoritarian Chinese government, and became a powerful political symbol over the following years.

Hua asked for Mao's opinion on what to do: Mao, and the Politburo, decided this was counter-revolution, and the Beijing authorities used force to disperse the protestors. Riots broke out and many were beaten and arrested.

SOURCE 6.6

On 4 April, the eve of Qingming, the police arrived in force without warning and took away all the tokens of grief and respect. Tian'anmen Square was cordoned off by police barricades and the crowds of people who were still attempting to leave their tributes were held back. In the face of these clumsy and boorish tactics, the commemoration of Zhou rapidly turned into a political demonstration… The events of 5 April 1976 became known as the Tian'anmen Incident but also as the April Fifth Movement…

As the demonstrations grew in number and intensity, the nature of the poems and eulogies changed radically from simple praise of Zhou Enlai to political diatribes against Jiang Qing. They revealed a deep revulsion towards the policies of the ultra-Maoists and they marked the beginning of a new period of dissent that was to erupt again in the democracy movement of the late 1980s.

Dillon, M. **China: A Modern History.** *New York, I. B. Tauris, pp.350–51*

Meanwhile, there were accusations (mainly from Jiang Qing and her radical Left supporters) that Deng had encouraged and even organised these demonstrations, in order to strengthen his position by weakening the Gang of Four.

Consequently, he was once again removed from his Party and government positions of power – though not from the Party – and was told he would be investigated for 'political mistakes'. However, he immediately fled to Canton, where he sought the protection of

The struggle for power, 1972–82

General Ye Jianying (who later played an important part in the overthrow of the Gang of Four), remaining there until Mao's death.

> ### General Ye Jianying (1897–1986):
>
> Ye was a Marshal of the PLA and, from 1978 to 1983, the chairman of the Standing Committee of the National People's Congress. At first, he had been a member of Sun Yat-sen's GMD but, in 1927, had joined the CCP. In 1932, he became one of the leaders of the CCP's Fourth Front Army. He helped plan the Long March, and helped Mao become the recognised leader of the CCP in 1935. However, he disagreed with aspects of Mao's post-1949 land reforms and, while he kept his military roles, he was dismissed from his political posts. He used his influence to protect some of those purged during the Cultural Revolution and, after Lin Biao's death, became a vice-chairman of the Central Committee of the CCP in 1973, and then Defence Minister in 1975. He supported Hua Guofeng and so played a leading role in the coup against the Gang of Four in 1976. In general, he was opposed to Deng's economic policies after 1981.

QUESTION
Why were the Gang of Four angered by the events of the Qingming festival?

On 7 April, it was announced that Hua Guofeng would replace Deng as first vice-chairman of the Central Committee of the CCP, second only to Chairman Mao.

Mao's death

As Mao's health deteriorated during 1976, Hua took greater control of affairs. However, when Mao died on 9 September 1976, the two main factions tried to secure their power. No longer having Mao as a supporter, the Gang made a bid for power, using their influence over the media, the urban militia and the universities. However, they miscalculated Hua's determination – and the support he had among Deng's supporters in the Politburo and the military.

6 The People's Republic of China (1949–2005)

Jiang's first steps were to try to make it seem as if she was Mao's choice as successor – even, as was later 'discovered', by altering some of Mao's writings. She certainly did order that all his personal papers be given to her, and had the media publish articles that showed the successful rule of women in China. In fact, as Mao had been incapacitated by ill-health for several months, and had not been in control of state affairs for a considerable time, many of his pronouncements in the final years had gone through the office of Jiang Qing.

In order to secure their position, Wang Hongwen – the youngest of the Shanghai radical Left leaders – attempted to get all local CCP organisations to report directly to him. On 4 October, a newspaper article then accused Hua of being a 'revisionist', and appeared to suggest that authority had been given to Jiang and her group.

However, Hua fought back – in his eulogy at Mao's memorial ceremony, he praised Mao, and then referred to one of Mao's speeches in which he had attacked the Gang of Four for factionalism. In the Politburo, Jiang then accused Hua of incompetence, and proposed that she become the Chair of the Central Committee. Hua, backed by Deng's supporters – who included the Defence Minister, Ye Jianying – insisted that the procedures should be stuck to – the vice-chair should take over until the next session of the Central Committee.

The Gang – surprised at Hua's determination, and realising their power was slipping – allegedly tried to organise a coup, which was to take place on 6 October. Mao's nephew, Mao Yuanxin, who was political commissar of the Shenyang Military Region, was later said to be the one who would have provided the military support for the coup, by marching on Beijing. The Gang apparently also had plans for the assassination of several Politburo members – including Hua and Ye.

As their military support was not that strong, it was rumoured that Jiang attempted to gain more supporters within the Politburo. Those she apparently approached included Generals Chen Xilian and Su Zhenua – but they immediately informed Hua. However, it is unlikely that the Gang did this, as they had little support among either Party officials or the PLA. More likely is that Hua and the Rightists decided that the best way to deal with the potential threat from the Gang was to strike first, and to use the allegations about the Gang as a justification for their own actions.

The struggle for power, 1972–82

The defeat of the Gang of Four

Hua than held a meeting in the PLA's headquarters with several political and military supporters of Deng – and they agreed to launch a 'pre-emptive' coup by protecting Beijing and arresting the Gang. On 5 October, Hua called an emergency meeting of the Politburo for midnight that day. When Zhang and Wang arrived on 6 October, they were immediately arrested – Yao and Jiang, who had not arrived for the meeting, were arrested later. What support the Gang had melted away, and the leaders were expelled from the Party, while plans for their trial were made.

The next day, on 7 October, Hua was appointed as Chairman of the Central Committee of the CCP and of the Central Military Committee – these were the two key posts that Mao had held before his death. The entire Chinese media then carried what were claimed to be the last words Mao had spoken to Hua: 'With you in charge, I can set my mind at rest'. In July 1977, Deng was reinstated as the first vice-chairman of the CCP – but Hua was confirmed as Chairman. However, from the start, there was an uneasy alliance between the two – mainly because Deng clearly wished to go further with economic 'modernisation' than did Hua.

Hua and his supporters, deliberately downplaying any ideological motives, then began to portray Jiang – now called 'Madame Mao' – and the Gang (now officially referred to as the 'Lin Biao and Jiang Qing counter-revolutionary clique') as mere power-hungry plotters. In particular, Jiang was presented as someone who had manipulated Mao when he was ill and dying, and who tried to use his death to secure her 'lust for power'. The press, the radio and wall posters also portrayed her as a 'luxury-loving pornographer'.

Photographs and posters, where she appeared with Mao, were 'doctored' in very obvious ways, to show the public that she had fallen from power. For instance, posters appeared, contained calls such as: 'Cut Jiang Qing in Ten Thousand Pieces' and 'Deep-Fry the Gang of Four in Oil'.

6 The People's Republic of China (1949–2005)

Figure 6.4: Translation reads, 'Decisively overthrow the anti-Party clique of Wang (top left), Zhang, Jiang and Yao', 1976.

DISCUSSION POINT

Jiang Qing, of all the four members of the Gang of Four, came in for the harshest criticisms in the Chinese media. Do you think this merely reflected her role in the period 1966–76? Or was it because, in essentially male-dominated societies, strong female leaders are seen as more of a threat to the *status quo* than male leaders?

While Jiang was increasingly vilified by the regime, Mao's reputation and image remained untarnished. When news that the Gang had been arrested reached Chinese citizens, there were celebrations across China – though not necessarily spontaneous, as some seem to have been organised by the authorities. Nonetheless, their actions during the Cultural Revolution had made them deeply unpopular in many quarters, and many were pleased at this change in the Party leadership.

The struggle for power, 1972–82

> **KEY CONCEPTS QUESTION**
>
> **Causes and consequences**: Why did Hua and Deng decide to carry out a coup against the Gang of Four in October 1976? What were the most immediate results of this coup?

Though they had been arrested in October 1976, their trials were delayed until November 1980, and did not finish until January 1981 – this gave time for the Rightists to consolidate their hold on power, and for the public to forget the Gang. When the trials began, Jiang and the other three – along with six others associated with them – were charged with 48 offences, mainly connected (as shown by Source 6.7) to violence during the Cultural Revolution; but also including plotting to assassinate Mao. The trials were highly publicised and televised – however, the actual records of the trials have not been released.

Figure 6.5: Jiang, in handcuffs and flanked by prison guards, during her trial.

6 The People's Republic of China (1949–2005)

Jiang – unlike the others – defended herself by arguing throughout that she had simply been following Mao's instructions. One statement she made was: 'I was Chairman Mao's dog. Whomever he told me to bite, I bit.' However, her outspoken defence (as shown in Source 6.8), and her refusal to admit she had made mistakes or to confess her guilt, angered many people, and made her even more unpopular.

SOURCE 6.7

In November 1980, over four years after their arrest, the Gang of Four were at last put on trial. The aim was to use them as scapegoats to explain why China had gone wrong. The general accusation was that they had betrayed Mao and the Chinese Revolution. Among the specific charges against them were that during the course of the Cultural Revolution they had been individually and collectively responsible for the deaths of 35 000 people and that they had 'framed and persecuted' a further three-quarters of a million.

Jiang Qing, the principal defendant, remained totally defiant.... Jiang's spirited resistance throughout her three-month trial embarrassed the court, but it did not save her. The trials ended in January 1981 with guilty verdicts on all those charged. Jiang was sentenced to death. Subsequently, the sentence was commuted to life imprisonment in order to give her 'time to repent'. But she was not the repenting kind; at the time of Jiang's death 10 years later in 1991 she was still angrily proclaiming her innocence.

Lynch, M. 2008. **The People's Republic of China 1949–76.** London. Hodder. pp.157–8

ACTIVITY

With a partner, carry out some additional research on the arrest and trial of the Gang of Four, and write a short newspaper article summarising their main weaknesses – and the strengths of their political opponents. Then produce a chart to illustrate these points.

The struggle for power, 1972–82

SOURCE 6.8

She argued that she had done everything during the Cultural Revolution 'on behalf of Chairman Mao Zedong' or 'according to his instructions'. Again and again, she repeated these assertions of hers: 'Arresting me and bringing me to trial is a defamation of Chairman Mao Zedong.' 'Defaming Mao through defaming me.' 'I have implemented and defended Chairman Mao's proletarian revolutionary line.' She shrilled, 'During the war I was the only woman comrade who stayed beside Chairman Mao at the front: where were you hiding yourselves then?'

Extracts from an official court summary of the statement given by Jiang Qing at her trial in 1980, from 1981, **A Great Trial in Chinese History,** *Beijing, New World Press.*

QUESTION

What are the limitations and value of Source 6.8 for a historian trying to discover what happened at the trials of the Gang of Four?

Theory of Knowledge

History, bias and ways of knowing:

Since Mao's death and the overthrow of the Gang of Four, those people in post-Maoist China who have been free to talk about the impact of the Cultural Revolution have largely been its victims. Harry Harding therefore says that it is necessary to be sceptical to a degree about their accounts of what happened – otherwise we would repeat the mistakes some observers made in the late 1960s, when the official statements of what the Cultural Revolution was about were taken at face value. Maurice Meisner says it will be decades before the full history of the Gang of Four can be written with any reasonable degree of accuracy; while Pieter Geyl said '*History is an argument without end*'. Is it therefore almost impossible for historians to establish what happened in the past?

6 The People's Republic of China (1949–2005)

Jiang was found guilty and sentenced to death, although this was later commuted to life imprisonment. When Jiang was diagnosed with throat cancer, she was transferred to a hospital; in 1991, she committed suicide. Zhang also had a death sentence commuted to life imprisonment: in 2002 he became ill, and he died of cancer in 2005. The other members of the Gang suffered similar fates. Wang was sentenced to life imprisonment, and died in hospital in 1992; Yao received a sentence of 20 years – released in 1996, he died in 2005. Others associated with the Gang or with Lin Biao were sentenced to long terms of imprisonment.

The rise of Deng Xiaoping

Although the trials of the Gang did not take place until 1980–81, the purge of the Gang and their supporters in the Party was carried out quickly, and was completed by the end of 1976. Hua was appointed as Chairman of the Party to replace Mao. Several members of the Politburo thought this was unconstitutional, as the Party had not initially chosen him; however, in the interests of unity, he was confirmed in that position. The Politburo gave Hua three tasks – to replace Mao, rehabilitate Deng, and carry out modernisation. Soon, wall posters began to appear, saying 'Bring Back Deng'. Deng was supported by the army, and he also had strong support in the Party, which cleared him of responsibility for the Tiananmen Square events of 1976. So, Deng – once he admitted to some political mistakes – was quickly re-appointed to the Politburo.

At the Third Plenum of the Tenth Central Committee in July 1977, three important decisions were made that were to shape the Politburo: the Gang were condemned for their views and actions; Hua was made Chairman of the Party and Military Commission, as well as continuing as premier (prime minister); and Deng was restored to the Standing Committee of the Politburo, and to his positions as Vice-Chairperson of the Central Committee, Vice-Premier of the State Council, Vice-Chairman of the Military Commission, and Chief of the General Staff of the People's Liberation Army.

Hua then decided that China had to once again focus its efforts on industrialisation – but this time, using very different methods from those used in the past. Deng, significantly, was put in charge of the Four Modernisations: this gave him considerable – and growing – economic and political power in the two years before he eventually became China's overall leader.

The struggle for power, 1972–82

At the same time, the Politburo was reorganized, and three factions emerged – nine members supported Hua, nine supported Deng and three supported Ye. Ye held the balance of power – thus, where decision-making was unclear, he was often the one who helped make the final decision. Nonetheless, the 11th Congress of the CCP in August 1977, which confirmed the earlier CC decisions, called for 'unity, stability and cooperation' in Party affairs.

De-mystifying Mao

Hua also had the problem of how to preserve links to Mao yet also 'remould' some of Mao's statements and policies in order to prepare the way for the significant changes in economic policy wanted by the Rightists. This 'demystification of Mao' was a delicate issue, as too much criticism would risk undermining the whole legacy of the Communist Revolution in China. In particular, this was because Mao represented all that had happened in China since 1949.

Hua began this process by making an official declaration announcing the end of the Cultural Revolution. The next step was completed by January 1981, when the trial of the Gang of Four ended. By 1981, Mao's reputation was being examined critically. The official judgement came in June 1981, when at the Sixth Plenum of the 11th CC, a Resolution – drafted by Deng – was passed, which judged that Mao had made 'gross mistakes' during the Cultural Revolution. Overall, though, it stated his mistakes were outweighed by his positive contributions: he was thus judged as being '70% right, and 30% wrong'.

Hua and the 'Whateverists'

Despite these demystification moves, in 1977, Hua and his supporters, in response to previous Gang of Four statements at their trial, had adopted a policy known as the 'Two Whatevers': to uphold whatever policy decisions Mao had made; and to follow whatever instructions he had given. This was a tactical mistake, as many in the Party now believed that it was necessary to move on from Maoist-type policies, and instead adopt more Western-style approaches. At the same time, as Hua had been in power during some of the worst excesses of the Gang, he was increasingly implicated in their activities as their trials took place. All of this was used by Deng and his supporters to undermine Hua's position. In fact, Hua's position was not that strong, as he only had limited firm support – his rise had been mainly because, as well as being Mao's

6 The People's Republic of China (1949–2005)

preferred successor, he did not represent either of the two main factions, and so did not at first engender much strong opposition.

> **QUESTION**
> Why were Hua and his supporters known as the 'Whateverists'?

Deng and the Rightists then began their moves. From 1977, with Deng restored to all his former Party positions, Hua was quietly pushed into the background. Deng then got his own supporters elected to the CC and the Politburo. Although Hua retained his posts, his real power was increasingly being reduced.

In December 1978, at the Third Plenum of the 11th Central Committee, Deng challenged the 'Whateverist' approach by making a speech which said that although revolutionary ideology was important in theory, evidence from practice was more important in deciding policies, if China was to improve living standards for both peasants and industrial workers, find extra resources for improving agriculture and consumer goods, and achieve economic progress.

Deng then criticised both Lin Biao and the Gang for trying to establish ideological taboos – and the meeting decided to reappraise Mao and his revolutionary principles. Because this was based on Mao's idea that *'practice is the sole criterion for judging truth'*, it was an easy step to move on to criticise and challenge those who followed the 'Two Whatevers'.

In September 1980, Hua was pressured into resigning as premier, in favour of **Zhao Ziyang** (who Deng had got into the Politburo in January). In April 1981, **Hu Yaobang** – another of Deng's close supporters – became General-Secretary of the CCP.

The struggle for power, 1972–82

> ### Zhao Ziyang (1919–2005):
> Zhao was one of the younger generation of communists, joining the Party during the Second World War. He rose rapidly and was appointed to the province of Sichuan which had suffered badly during the Cultural Revolution. In 1975, he began to implement successful reforms aimed at increasing food supplies. These reforms were known as the 'contract responsibility system', based on leasing commune land to individual families. He came to favour privatising state enterprises. Later on, his support for the students protesting in Tiananmen Square in 1989 led to his dismissal; he was then effectively placed under house arrest.

> ### Hu Yaobang (1915–89):
> Hu had joined the Red Army in 1930, when he was only 15, and was a Long March veteran. During this time, he served under Deng in his Second Field Army. After 1949, his fortunes had fluctuated along with Deng's; in 1980, as Hua Guofeng was forced relinquish his positions, Hu had become General-Secretary of the CCP. He was on the libertarian wing of Marxism and the CCP, favouring democratic procedures, and had supported Deng's desire to 'rehabilitate' those purged in the period before 1976.

In June 1981, Hua resigned as Party Chairman and chair of the Military Commission, and was later removed from the Politburo. After admitting he had made mistakes, he was allowed to remain as Vice-Chairman until the post was abolished in 1982. Hua's treatment after his fall indicated a desire to move away from the usual brutal treatment of those who had lost power struggles in the 1960s. In fact, he remained a member of the CC until 2002 – when he was 10 years older than the stated retirement age of 70.

The Twelfth Congress of the CCP, in September 1982, confirmed these changes – Deng was now clearly China's 'paramount leader', though he mainly operated through his protégés. These developments marked the close of the Maoist era. Almost all of the veteran Chinese Communist revolutionaries, who had begun their political struggles with the May Fourth Movement in 1919, were now dead. Despite their various differences – sometimes very bitter – they had all wanted to make

6 The People's Republic of China (1949–2005)

China both modern and socialist. The younger generation of bureaucrats were certainly committed to making China modern in both economics and political structures – but whether they remained committed to the Marxist ideals of socialism leading to Communism was a matter of speculation. This will be discussed in the following two chapters.

> ### ACTIVITY
> Using the information in this chapter, and any other resources available to you, carry out some research on Deng Xiaoping's political 'ups and downs' during the period 1971–82. Then make a chart listing the main moves in his political career, and giving brief reasons for these different moves.

The Struggle for Power, 1972–82

Paper 3 exam practice

Question
Evaluate the reasons why a power struggle broke out within the Chinese Communist Party after Mao's death in 1976. **[15 marks]**

Skill
Avoiding a narrative-based answer

Examiner's tips

Even once you've read the question carefully (and so avoided the temptation of giving irrelevant material), produced your plan and written your introductory paragraph, it is still possible to go wrong.

By 'writing a narrative answer', history examiners mean providing supporting knowledge that is relevant (and may well be very precise and accurate) but which is not clearly linked to the question. Instead of answering the question, it merely describes what happened.

The main body of your essay/argument needs to be analytical. It must not simply be an 'answer' in which you just 'tell the story'. Your essay must address the demands/key words of the question – ideally, this should be done consistently throughout your essay, by linking each paragraph to the previous one, in order to produce a clear 'joined up' answer.

You are especially likely to lapse into a narrative answer when answering your final question – and even more so if you are getting short of time. The 'error' here is that, despite all your good work at the start of the exam, you will lose sight of question, and just produce an *account*, as opposed to an analysis. So, even if you are short of time, try to write several analytical paragraphs.

Note that such a question that asks you to evaluate the different reasons why something happened expects you to come to judgements about the relative significance of those various reasons. Very often, such a question gives you the opportunity to refer to different historians' views (see Chapter 10 for more on this).

231

6 The People's Republic of China (1949–2005)

A good way of avoiding a narrative approach is continually to refer back to the question and even to mention it now and again in your answer. That should help you to produce an answer focused on the specific aspects of the question – rather than just giving information about the broad topic or period.

For this question, you will need to:

- supply a *brief* explanation of the historical context (i.e. the power struggles that had marked the 1960s)
- outline the divisions that existed in the CCP in 1976
- provide a consistently analytical examination of the reasons for the main developments in the power struggle in the period 1976–81.

Common mistakes

Every year, even candidates who have clearly revised well, and therefore have a good knowledge of the topic and of any historical debate surrounding it, still end up producing a mainly narrative-based or descriptive answer. Very often, this is the result of not having drawn up a proper plan.

The extracts of the student's answer below show an approach that essentially just describes developments in China just before and just after 1976, without any analysis or evaluation of the different *reasons* why a power struggle broke out.

Sample paragraphs of narrative-based approach

This example shows what examiners mean by a narrative answer – it is something you should not copy!

Before 1976, there had been a series of power struggles. As early as the late 1950s, following the Great Leap Forward, a power struggle had broken out which resulted in Mao being deprived of several of his posts. In particular, in 1959, although Mao remained as Chairman of the CCP, he had been replaced as president by Liu Shaoqi. The economic policies Liu had then introduced were seen by Mao as running the risk of allowing the restoration of capitalism. However, in 1962, Mao had launched his Socialist Education Movement – this had involved getting workers and peasants to study his works and attend political rallies. These attempts had been opposed by Liu and Deng Xiaoping.

The Struggle for Power, 1972–82

Then, in 1964, Mao had succeeded in getting the support of Lin Biao, the Minister of Defence. With the support of Lin and the PLA, Mao had launched the Cultural Revolution in 1966. By 1969, Mao had been able to return to power, and to dismiss those – such as Liu and Deng – who opposed his political and economic ideas. However, the deep political divisions between the left and right in the CCP had continued into the early 1970s. In 1973, Zhou Enlai helped Deng, a rightist, to return to government.

Mao's death in September 1976 was followed by another serious power struggle. In fact, 1976 was an important year, as Zhou had died in the January of that year – these two had been the main leaders of the CCP since before 1949. Zhou had tended to support the right – and, in 1975, had supported the Four Modernisations. These policies for economic modernisation were opposed by the left, which was increasingly led by Mao's wife, Jiang Qing. She headed a small but quite influential group which became known as the Gang of Four.

Although the Gang of Four tried to take power after Mao's death, power initially went to Hua Guofeng who headed a more moderate centrist group of Maoists. He had been chosen by Mao to be premier after Zhou's death in January 1976. After Mao's death, Hua was able to resist the efforts of the Gang of Four, as he was supported by Deng's supporters in the main bodies of the CCP, and by most of the leaders of the PLA. Then, in October 1976, the Gang of Four were arrested – the official line was that this was because they had tried to organise a coup against Hua…

[There then follows several more paragraphs with precise and accurate own knowledge about the main political developments in the power struggle between 1976 and 1981, and Deng's rise to pre-eminence within the CCP and the government. However, these paragraphs just *describe* the various stages and developments in the power struggle – without any explicit evaluation or analysis of the various reasons for them. Merely giving the correct details of events, and leaving it up to the examiner to work out the reasons will not score high marks.]

6 The People's Republic of China (1949–2005)

Activity

In this chapter, the focus is on avoiding writing narrative-based answers. So, using the information from this chapter, and any other sources of information available to you, try to answer one of the following Practice Paper 3 questions in a way that avoids simply describing what happened.

Remember to refer to the simplified Paper 3 mark scheme in Chapter 10.

Practice Paper 3 questions

1 Discuss the main political and economic divisions within the Chinese Communist Party in the five years before 1976.

2 Examine the significance of the role played by Zhou Enlai in the emerging power struggle during the period 1971–75.

3 Compare and contrast the political and economic policies associated with Hua Guofeng and Deng Xiaoping in the years 1976–81.

4 Evaluate the reasons for the defeat of the Gang of Four in the period 1976–81.

5 'By 1981, the revolutionary ideas of Maoism had been thoroughly rejected by the Chinese Communist Party.' To what extent do you agree with this statement?

Deng's economic revolution, 1976–89

7

7 The People's Republic of China (1949–2005)

Introduction

Within two years of Mao's death, Deng was re-established in the leadership of the CCP, and quickly became the dominant force in both Party and government for the next ten years. As his economic policies were rolled out, it became increasingly clear that many – if not most – of the aspects known as 'Maoism' were being replaced by what had previously been condemned as the 'capitalist road'. By the time of his death, in 1997, Deng had overseen a tremendous restructuring of the Chinese economy, in both agriculture and industry, and had laid the foundations for China becoming a modern country able to successfully compete with advanced Western economies in the world market.

However, there remains the question of the exact nature of the state that resulted from his policies: was it still 'communist' (some would argue it had never even been socialist). Various historians and political commentators have used a variety of terms to describe Deng's China: 'authoritarian capitalist', 'state capitalist', or 'bureaucratic capitalist'. In fact, the debate about what kind of China Deng was creating begs the question of just how socialist Maoist China was by 1976.

Private ownership of the economy – both industrial and agricultural – had been effectively ended by as early as 1956. Unlike Stalin, Mao believed that more than industrial development was needed to create a socialist and then communist society. This explains his attempts to create the right attitudes among the people, to ready them for socialism.

Yet, contradictions between modernisation and socialism emerged. In particular, there was a contrast between a powerful bureaucratised central state, and the workers' self-rule which Marxists thought would result from the 'withering away of the state'. This lack of 'socialist democracy' in Mao's China (though it nevertheless kept alive a socialist vision of the future) indicated that the political pre-conditions for socialism had not *been* created. Thus many historians have preferred to describe China under Mao as 'post-capitalist', rather than as socialist. Some have argued that, as China had not become socialist under Mao, Deng was not so much moving China from socialism as moving it even further away – arguably back to capitalism.

Deng's economic revolution, 1976–89

TIMELINE

1977 **Aug:** Deng's speech for the 'Four Modernisations'

Oct: 28th anniversary of the Chinese Communist Revolution; Hua Guofeng's first economic reforms

1978 **Feb:** Hua's Ten Year Plan

Aug: Principles of the Ten Year Plan and the Four Modernisations incorporated into Party constitution

Dec: Third Plenum of CC; 'Open Door' policy announced

1979 **Jun:** Ten Year Plan 'modified'

1980 **Jun:** CC accept the Household Responsibility System for agriculture

Aug: National People's Congress accept establishment of first Special Economic Zones

Sept Hua replaced by Zhao Ziyang as premier; official start of 'one child' policy

1981 **Apr:** Hu Yaobang appointed General-Secretary of CCP

Jun: Sixth Plenum of 11th CC sees start of critical review of Mao's record; Hua resigns as CCP Chairman

1982 **Sep:** 12th Congress of CCP approves Deng's economic plans for Phase 2

1984 **Jun:** Deng's 'Socialism with Chinese Characteristics' speech

Oct: Start of Phase 2 economic reforms

1986 **Mar:** Official announcement of Seventh Five-Year Plan

1989 **Nov:** Deng resigns as chairman of the Central Military Committee

KEY QUESTIONS

- What economic policies were followed by Hua in the period 1976–78?
- What were the main features of Deng's 'Revolution', 1979–89?
- How successful were Deng's economic reforms?

7 The People's Republic of China (1949–2005)

Overview

- Although for most of 1977 and 1978, it seemed that Hua was in control, Deng was in fact rapidly re-establishing his authority. Most of the economic policies announced by Hua during this period were heavily influenced by Deng and his support for the Four Modernisations.
- In early 1978, Hua announced an ambitious Ten-Year Plan to massively increase both agricultural and industrial production.
- In December, the Third Plenum of the CC saw Deng become dominant; the plenum also approved the 'Open Door' policy on trade with capitalist states. Problems with aspects of Hua's Ten-Year Plan led to it being officially dropped in 1979.
- In 1980, Hua and his main supporters were replaced by those close to Deng. In that year, Deng pushed forward economic reforms such as the Household Responsibility System in agriculture, and the establishment of Special Economic Zones.
- In 1982, Deng's policies were approved by the 12th Congress of the CCP. He then began planning for Phase 2, and this began officially in 1984.
- In 1986, a new Five-Year Plan was officially launched by Deng.
- Deng's reforms in agriculture and industry during the period 1978–89 led to significant increases in production, and to increased trade. However, they also led to national indebtedness and to poverty for many in rural and especially urban areas.

7.1 What economic policies were followed by Hua in the period 1976–78?

According to historians such as Maurice Meisner, the Maoist economic record, though flawed, compared favourably with comparable stages in the industrialisation of Germany, Japan and Russia, which had previously been seen as the most successful examples of late modernisation. This was an especially notable achievement as it was largely the result of China's own efforts, with little or no outside assistance – not even from the Soviet Union, with which Communist China had fallen out in the early 1960s (see Chapter 6).

The Four Modernisations

After the overthrow of the Gang of Four, Deng – in theory under Hua's direction – began to put into effect the economic policies associated with the Four Modernisations. In fact, similar policies had been first put forward by Deng in the 1960s; once Zhou had officially announced the Four Modernisations in 1975, Deng had issued three documents setting out more specific ways in which to achieve Zhou's aims. These had been quickly condemned as 'deviationist' by the Gang of Four, who had re-named them the 'Three Poisonous Weeds'. Once the Gang had been overthrown, Deng and his pragmatic supporters began to re-introduce these ideas.

Deng's plans were intended to overcome some of the problems resulting from the Great Leap Forward and the Cultural Revolution, and to make the Chinese economy more efficient and productive. By 1976, 20 million people in China were unemployed, and 100 million were undernourished. China also had a 6.5 billion *yuan* deficit; while science, technology and the military were all old-fashioned compared to the advanced countries. All this had led to significant disenchantment among many Chinese citizens (as shown in Source 7.1), and Deng clearly hoped that successful reform would result in renewed support for the Party.

The Four Modernisations focused on four areas of the economy: agriculture, industry, science and technology, and the military. One essential difference between these policies and those that had often been implemented before 1976 was that they were based more on pragmatism than ideology. Deng and his supporters justified this by claiming that Mao's emphasis on ideology had led to negative economic results – though such criticisms tended to ignore what was achieved by Mao.

7 The People's Republic of China (1949–2005)

> **SOURCE 7.1**
>
> Major problems faced the new Deng administration: the government now had a 6.5 billion yuan deficit; 20 million Chinese were unemployed; and an estimated 100 million were undernourished. The military was woefully out of date, as was China's own technology and scientific research. Thousands of CCP members and wide segments of the population questioned the decisions of the Party leadership… If the legacy of the [Maoist] revolutionaries was to mean anything, new approaches to China's many problems were imperative… Deng and his supporters realized that without economic advances, the future position of the CCP would be untenable.
>
> Benson, L., 2002, **China Since 1949**, London, Pearson Education, p.46.

As well as affecting domestic economic policy, Deng's approach also involved the linked issue of foreign trade and relations with Western capitalist states. This had been another important factor in the struggle during the late 1960s and early 1970s between Leftists and Rightists.

China's economy in 1976

Despite some real economic gains under Mao, by 1976, the Chinese economy was suffering from many problems: inefficiency, technological backwardness, waste, low productivity, overstaffing and bureaucratic stagnation. While the political struggle – between Hua and the 'Whateverists', and Deng and the Rightists – was taking place in the period 1976–81, both factions were attempting to address some of China's economic problems. There was some agreement between both groups on the general economic policies that needed to be followed. Essentially, both groups wanted to implement the Four Modernisations by adopting more pragmatic economic policies.

Hua's approach was based on the acceptance of Zhou's comments in 1975 that revolutionary principles, if applied too rigorously, could cause economic growth to slow down or even cease altogether. Thus, while publicly expressing continued support for Maoism, Hua quietly abandoned several aspects of late Maoism. Instead, he reverted to a modified 1950s' form of early Maoism. For instance – in something similar to the Hundred Flowers campaign's initial approach to culture and education – Hua allowed films, operas and plays that had previously

Deng's economic revolution, 1976–89

been banned to be shown again, and allowed the re-appearance of literary and scholarly journals. He also allowed the publication of short stories by young writers – known as the 'wounded generation' – which described their experiences during the Cultural Revolution.

Unfortunately for him, this more relaxed approach allowed the emergence of an increasingly influential pro-Deng and anti-Maoist (and thus anti-Hua) body of opinion. While this weakened him, it strengthened Deng. This helped Deng in the mostly behind-the-scenes struggle between his 'Practice' faction (which emphasised practical outcomes over ideology and theory as the main criteria for judging the 'correctness' of economic policies) and the Hua 'Whateverist' faction.

Hua's economic policies

Initially, Hua decided to concentrate on agriculture, and several conferences were held in 1977 to decide what to do. Peasant family plots were restored, their size was increased, and subsidies were also increased, to boost agricultural production. As a result, agricultural productivity increased by 8.9% in 1978, and by 8.6% in 1979. This was *before* Deng's Household Responsibility System policy, which wasn't really widely adopted until the early 1980s, had been introduced (see Section 7.2).

In industry, wage differentials and greater specialisation were introduced for the same purpose. There was also a 10% wage increase for all, announced on 1 October 1977, at the 28th anniversary of the Communist Revolution.

As Source 7.2 shows, these changes led to intense debate among historians, economists and political commentators over the implications of these policies for the future direction of the Chinese Revolution. For example, both Burton and Bettelheim (an economics professor) were supporters of Mao but came to differ over what Deng's intentions were. Bettelheim had earlier resigned as president of the Franco-Chinese Friendship Association because of his concerns over the policies of the new leadership of the CCP.

7 The People's Republic of China (1949–2005)

QUESTION

Given the origin and possible purpose of Source 7.2, what are its value and limitations for historians trying to study Deng's intentions during the period 1976–78?

ACTIVITY

Using this and the previous chapter, try to identify and then list the names of the 'capitalist roaders' referred to in Source 7.2.

SOURCE 7.2

And let's not be too quick to label those [leaders of the CCP] who do not quite measure up... as 'revisionists,' 'capitalist roaders,' or what have you... the present leadership... is at this very moment implementing new regulations to alleviate the economic insecurity of city-dwellers in the lowest income categories through a re-adjustment of wage scales.

In your letter you raise the specter of the advances of the Cultural Revolution being wiped away. Some of its products will indeed be dropped, others modified – some for the right reasons, some not. And since classes and class struggle are going to be with us for some time to come, it's even conceivable that a revisionist line – a real revisionist line – might gain the upper hand for a time... But could the really important gains of the Cultural Revolution ever be submerged for long? Not a chance! ... They infuse Chairman Hua Kuo-feng's speeches.

Extracts from an Open Letter, dated 1 October 1977, by Neil Burton, a Canadian working in China, to Charles Bettelheim, a French economics professor, on the likely course of China following the defeat of the Gang of Four. In Bettelheim, C. and Burton, N., 1978, **China Since Mao,** *New York, Monthly Review Press, pp.34–5*

Even at this stage, Hua's economic policies were largely based on policy documents Deng had drawn up in the autumn of 1975, before his temporary fall in 1976. These included a big increase in the amount of modern technology purchased abroad. But Hua also claimed to be continuing Mao's legacy. In early 1977, Hua proclaimed his 'Whateverist'

Deng's economic revolution, 1976–89

position. This eventually played a part in his downfall, as most senior people in the Party, government and army had been unhappy about the Cultural Revolution, and increasingly supported Deng, who wanted to give some kind of justice to its victims. Yet, Hua's main support base was precisely those in the lower levels who had risen during the Cultural Revolution. Hua and Deng had been united in bringing down the Gang of Four – but once this had been accomplished in 1976, there was little to keep them together – and Deng's supporters were stronger and more numerous.

The Ten-Year Plan

When Deng fell from favour in 1976, as a result of the Qingming Festival (see Chapter 6), the introduction of further and deeper reform was put on hold. However, as early as 1977 (when Deng was again restored to his positions), there were moves towards implementing some of those reforms favoured by Deng. These in turn led to further political changes. Under Hua, at the 11th Party Congress in August 1977, Deng made a speech reiterating the importance of the Four Modernisations.

Figure 7.1: Chinese leaders at the 11th. Party Congress, August 1977: Hua Guofeng is on the left, with Deng Xiaoping in the centre.

In February 1978, Hua announced an ambitious new Ten-Year Plan, to cover the period 1976–85. This was designed to implement the 'Four Modernisations', and its basic principles were incorporated into the Party constitution in August 1978. This economic plan was largely based on a document drafted for the State Council by Deng in 1975. It focused on specific sectors of China's economy, especially heavy

7 The People's Republic of China (1949–2005)

industry, where state control would retain socialist principles, while relaxing such principles in smaller enterprises.

The intention was to create 120 massive industrial projects. Targets were set for the period 1978–85, with the aim of greatly increasing production. Steel production, for example, had fallen significantly as a result of the Great Leap Forward. It had been 21 million tons in 1973, but was to increase to 60 million tons by 1985, and to 180 million tons by 1999. High targets were also set for oil, petroleum, coal and non-ferrous metals, electricity, railways and water transportation.

It would require massive public works in order to provide the necessary infrastructure to meet these ambitious targets. This could not happen, however, without the modernisation of agriculture – by improving irrigation and mechanisation, a more efficient agriculture would release workers for industry. According to Hua, China's industry would catch up with the world's most advanced nations by 2000.

Significantly, Deng was put in charge of carrying out these reforms, and he soon announced that 100 000 construction projects would be implemented, at a cost of 54 billion yuan. However, the targets were too ambitious, and the costs too high – Hua had not developed any plan to raise the massive sums needed to invest in this expansion. The first year of the plan alone had cost 37% of GDP – this was too high a figure for the government to sustain. Consequently, the Ten-Year Plan soon proved unworkable. Its problems played a significant role in Hua's downfall and the rise of Deng – even though Deng had been closely associated with the Plan.

The end of the Ten-Year Plan

The Third Plenum of the CC in December 1978 was a turning point, as Deng was appointed the chairman of the People's Political Consultative Conference. As well as confirming his return to top-level politics, this post was crucial as it carried the main responsibility for carrying out economic reform. The meeting also saw a significant number of Deng's supporters elected to the CC and the Politburo. This gave Deng effective control of both these bodies and thus of the Party as a whole.

While most of Hua's supporters at first remained in post, they lost many of their main economic and political responsibilities. As stated in Source 7.3, the Third Plenum of December 1978 also accepted Deng's own plan to implement the 'Four Modernisations', which stepped up

Deng's economic revolution, 1976–89

and replaced Hua's economic policies. Thus, Deng's economic reform programme effectively began in 1979. The most dramatic indication of Deng's supremacy in economics came in June 1979, when the Ten-Year Plan was dropped.

> **SOURCE 7.3**
>
> …the Third Plenum of the Central Committee of the CCP… proved to be a landmark in China's post-Mao reformation. The decisions reached at the plenum meant a new departure for the People's Republic of China… [The] resolutions of the Third Plenum clearly meant that the Cultural Revolution had been abandoned. Deng Xiaoping's personal success at the plenum, in obtaining the full support of the CCP for his proposals, also showed that he was now the outstanding figure in Chinese politics. This was soon recognised by the CCP by its conferring on him the honorary title of 'paramount leader'. This had no specific functions attached to it but was all the more powerful because of that. He feigned humility by declining to accept formal positions while knowing that he had the influence and connections to remain in control of developments. He was now in a position to begin what was to become known as the Deng revolution.
>
> Lynch, M., 2008, *The People's Republic of China, 1949–76*, London, Hodder Education, pp. 156–7.

KEY CONCEPTS QUESTION

Significance: Why was Deng's appointment as Chairman of the People's Political Consultative Conference so important?

ACTIVITY

Carry out some further research on Hua's economic policies, and those favoured by Deng, in the period 1976–79. Then draw up a table with two columns (headed 'Hua' and 'Deng') briefly summarising their economic policies. Then produce a mindmap which displays the main differences and similarities.

7 The People's Republic of China (1949–2005)

7.2 What were the main features of Deng's 'Revolution', 1979–89?

Deng's main approach to economics was pragmatic, and several slogans were associated with the period of his influence, which lasted until 1992. These included: '*It doesn't matter if a cat is black or white, as long as it catches mice*'; '*To get rich is glorious*'; and '*Not introducing reforms will take us down a blind alley*'. The evidence suggests that a *democratic socialist* alternative to the centralised command economy was never seriously considered. What *was* on the agenda were various schemes for economic decentralisation, and the introduction – to a greater or lesser extent – of 'market' mechanisms.

However, there has been – and continues to be – considerable debate about the ultimate aims of Deng and his supporters. Some, such as Carl Riskin, stress the number of Deng's supporters who seemed captivated by the 'wonders of the market'; while Charles Bettelheim (in Source 7.4) argues that Deng was intent on moving back to capitalism. On the other hand, others – such as Maurice Meisner – argue strongly that while Deng had no intention of building socialist democracy in China, he also had no desire to restore capitalism.

According to Meisner, Deng's aim was not to restore capitalism, but to decentralise the inefficient centrally controlled command economy, in which government bodies made most of the economic decisions about investments and production levels. This, in Deng's opinion, would eventually create the conditions for socialism.

Many of Deng's supporters were encouraged in part by the reform communists in Hungary and Yugoslavia who had adopted 'socialist market' models in the 1970s – these had apparently introduced market mechanisms without weakening Party control of the 'commanding heights' of the economy. Later, though, such changes in those two countries soon led to a weakening of political control and the fall of those Communist governments in 1989.

Deng's economic revolution, 1976–89

SOURCE 7.4

...the political changes which have taken place in China since October 1976... have become clearer than they were: in particular, it is more obvious what policy has triumphed as a result of the elimination of the Four, namely a bourgeois [capitalist] policy and not a proletarian one...

Secondly, alongside the announcement that the Cultural Revolution is over, the measures which have been taken since more than a year ago, and the themes expounded in official speeches and in the press, constitute a de facto negation of the Cultural Revolution. There has been a veritable leap backward. These two aspects of the present situation are obviously not accidental. They are the product of profound tendencies, the result of a certain relation of forces between classes and also of a political line which forms part of this relation of forces and reacts upon it.

Extracts from Charles Bettelheim's response, The Great Leap Backward, dated 3 March 1978, to Neil Burton's open letter on the likely course of China following the defeat of the Gang of Four. In Bettelheim, C. and Burton, N., 1978, **China Since Mao**, *New York, Monthly Review Press, pp.38–9.*

Deng's economic approach

In June 1979, Deng persuaded the government to announce a three-year period in which some aspects of the Ten-Year Plan would be 'modified' – though the main aspects of the Four Modernisations would be retained.

This time, however, Deng wanted to concentrate on agriculture, light industry and consumer goods, rather than heavy industry. In particular, he believed that by encouraging farmers and factory workers to become rich, and allowing them more freedom and initiative, they would work harder and so help increase production and efficiency.

Like Gorbachev in the Soviet Union, he also believed that for these economic reform plans to work, it would be necessary to reduce the central bureaucracy's power over some aspects of the planning system. The aim – as explained in Source 7.5 – was to make the state bureaucracy the servant, rather than the master, of the economy.

The People's Republic of China (1949–2005)

SOURCE 7.5

Thus, in the discussions among Communist leaders and intellectuals in the politically victorious Deng camp around the time of the Third Plenum, a genuinely socialist alternative to the command economy was never seriously considered. Only reformist measures which could be accommodated within the existing political system were discussed. These included various schemes for economic decentralization and the introduction of market mechanisms…

The decentralization of economic administration and decision making… posed no threat to general Communist rule… Nor was the market the mortal threat to the Communist political system that it was assumed to be by many foreign observers…

That a market economy inevitably breeds capitalist social relationships, and all the inequitable consequences of capitalism, was well known to China's Communist leaders in the late 1970s. But Deng Xiaoping and his reformist associates did not envision a capitalist future for China… most did not champion a market economy or a capitalist regime because of their intrinsic virtues. Rather, they saw the mechanism of the market as a means to eventual socialist ends, as the most efficient way to break down the stifling system of centralized state planning and to speed up the development of modern productive forces, thereby creating the essential material foundations for a future socialist society.

Meisner, M., 1991, **Mao's China and After: A History of the People's Republic.** *New York, The Free Press, pp.451–2.*

QUESTION

Meisner, in Source 7.5, suggests that Deng was attempting to create a more decentralised – but not a more democratic – economic system, in order to achieve a developed socialist economy. In view of the current situation in China, do you think Deng's belief that his market reforms would not end in the restoration of capitalism was a realistic one?

Deng's economic revolution, 1976–89

Implementing the Four Modernisations

To put his long-held economic reform ideas into practice, Deng readjusted the Ten-Year Plan's goals: 348 heavy industry projects, and 4800 smaller ones, were put on hold; though many of the core ideas were retained. In particular, he decided to concentrate on short-term projects that could earn foreign capital, which would then be used to finance other projects. This approach was facilitated by Zhou and Mao's decision, in the early 1970s, to 'open up' relations with the US and the West. It thus became possible for China to export goods to non-communist countries, and to receive some foreign investment capital for its own projects. This generated extra capital to make more improvements, though there were still problems with energy and transportation.

These changes were accompanied by various techniques, which began to raise the question of whether or not the new leaders of China were still communists. These techniques included incentives and bonuses; allowing peasant farmers to grow crops on small leased commune plots, and to sell any surplus produce for profit to the state; and also allowing more scope for individual initiatives in industrial and scientific sectors. The following sections will focus on the two Modernisations that relate to the economy: agriculture and industry.

Agriculture

After the initial setbacks suffered by the industrial aspects of the Ten-Year Plan, the leadership decided that agriculture was the economic sector most in need of modernisation. This area became Deng's main concern during the period 1978–84. Although China's population had increased rapidly between 1955 and 1977, and thus so too had total grain production, the per capita figure was still at the same level. In addition, 80% of China's people were still based in the countryside, making China still a largely agricultural economy.

A more efficient and productive agriculture would release people to work in the factories. So the leadership's plan was to encourage peasants to move away from traditional methods (based on extensive manual labour), and instead to adopt mechanised farming. To assist these moves, incentives, and plans for diversification, were approved.

7 The People's Republic of China (1949–2005)

The first steps had been taken in December 1978, when the vast communes (set up in 1958 by the Great Leap Forward) were broken up into smaller production units. The policy of collectivisation was maintained: this had been a core element of the 1949 Revolution and, although not very efficient, could not easily be abandoned. However, Deng began to persuade the bureaucrats that the production units should be allowed more freedom to make decisions. He also substantially raised the subsidies and prices paid to farmers for their agricultural products.

Central planning continued, with the government setting targets and quotas, and issuing directives on how to achieve greater productivity. The plan was to increase agricultural production by 4–5% per year, and to increase food production to 400 million tons by 1985. The plan also aimed to mechanise 85% of farming, promote a greater use of chemical fertilisers and to improve irrigation of fields. In addition, the government wanted to improve the distribution of food products – so 12 commodity and food base areas were created.

Household Responsibility System

In 1979, the government resurrected a plan from the 1950s, which had been stopped by Mao. The Household Responsibility System (HRS), was officially adopted by the June 1980 CC meeting – and has been seen as the first attempt to introduce capitalism into the countryside. Deng ensured that one of his closest supporters, Wan Li, was put in charge of the new plan.

> ### Wan Li (1916–2015):
> Wan joined the CCP in 1936 and, after 1949, held a variety of important government and Party positions. He was purged during the Cultural Revolution; after being rehabilitated, he was put in charge of Anhui province, where he reformed agriculture via what became known as the 'Household Responsibility System'. During the 1980s, he was a strong supporter of Deng's economic reforms.

Deng's economic revolution, 1976–89

> In 1980, he became vice-premier, and supported Hu Yaobang and Zhao Ziyang in rolling out the Household Responsibility System to the rest of China. In 1988, after his appointment to the Standing Committee of the Politburo was blocked by conservatives/'leftists', he accepted the post of chairman of the Standing Committee of the National People's Congress.
>
> While he was sympathetic to some political liberalisation, he eventually gave his reluctant support to the suppression of the Tiananmen Square demonstrations in June 1989. He played an increasingly limited role thereafter, and retired in 1993.

At first, Wan applied it to the Anhui province – where, in 1978, 18 peasant families in Xiaogang village had unilaterally decided (in defiance of the local authorities) to implement what they called a 'responsibility system', in order to increase production. After it proved successful, it helped persuade those in the Central Committee who were doubtful of Deng's reform ideas, that it should be applied to the whole country.

Though there was still no private ownership of land, the HRS meant each farming family would be able to rent a plot of commune land they could use – to an extent – as they wanted. In late 1982, a new state constitution transferred the administrative functions of communes to township or county governments, which were to be the new units of central state administration. These were called *xiang*, and they effectively replaced the communes. Each *xiang* still had to meet state food production quotas, but this was now to be done by individuals and their families, who contributed their share of the local quota. Once they had met this, and paid their taxes, they were free to sell any surplus produce for private profit.

Families then contracted annually with their local *xiang* to provide a certain amount of work, and to plant a specified amount and type of crops. A fixed quota would then go back to the commune in return for being able to lease the land. In 1984, the lease was increased to 15 years. Families would control their own labour any way they wished, and were free to keep or sell any surplus produce, either to the commune or in the local market.

7 The People's Republic of China (1949–2005)

> **QUESTION**
> What were the main aspects of the Household Responsibility System?

Figure 7.2: A 'free market', where families could sell their own farm produce, in Kasha, a city in Xinjiang, western China.

In 1980, the government decided to set aside 15% of agricultural land for this scheme of family plots, instead of the previous 5%. This effectively resulted in the virtual dismantling of the communes established by the Great Leap Forward, with farmers having more and more control over the land they farmed. Although it began as a voluntary scheme, it soon became compulsory.

By 1983, over 90% of farming households were involved in the scheme, and it was official policy '*to make the peasants rich*'. These changes led to a significant increase in living standards for the rural population, although there were regional variations. In 1983, the government allowed families

Deng's economic revolution, 1976–89

to rent out 'their' lease – and also allowed farmers and workshop owners to hire wage labourers. Thus, new classes of sub-tenants and wage labourers reappeared in rural China, after having been abolished under Mao.

Industry

Deng hoped that the Ten Year Plan would result in a vastly improved infrastructure, and a level of industrialisation that would be at least as good – and hopefully superior – to what had taken place in the decades after 1949. In addition, the leadership wanted to catch up with, and even exceed, the industrial development of the advanced capitalist states in the West. However, industry proved more difficult to reform than agriculture. This was partly because the industrial workers had been the main beneficiaries of the 1949 Revolution. Each worker was hired as part of a *danwei* (work unit), and could ensure his children would be employed when old enough. This led to high job security, reasonable wages, and social wage benefits such as subsidised housing, medical care, pensions and other benefits.

Deng's economic reforms in industry involved two phases: Phase 1, 1978–84, and Phase 2, begun in October 1984.

Phase 1, 1978–84

These reforms were partly meant to 'improve the attitudes' of industrial workers: in practice, this meant getting them to give up their relatively privileged position. The reforms also involved moving away from detailed central planning to less restrictive guidelines.

The process was overseen by Zhao Ziyang, another strong supporter of Deng. He had been Party Secretary in Sichuan province, where he had applied a 'responsibility' system similar to the one that Wan was introducing in Anhui. The success of his 'Sichuan Experiment' led him, in 1980, to be appointed to the State Council. In September 1980 he became premier in place of Hua Guofeng, who slipped into the background.

Zhao's methods were then applied to industry. Over 400 000 factories were given more 'responsibility' (i.e. more freedom and independence) to set wages and prices, and produce goods, which the state would then buy. Any surplus over the quota set could then be sold for a profit. This was then applied to China as a whole.

7 The People's Republic of China (1949–2005)

Similar to the HRS in agriculture, the Industrial Responsibility System created by the government was based on establishing a supervisory body for each State-Owned Enterprise (SOE). Each SOE (or factory) had a contractual agreement, under which part of the production and/or profits would go to the state, with the surplus being kept by the SOE. This created an incentive to improve productivity. Later, contracts were used to try to address the issue of quality as well.

By 1980, 6 600 reformed SOEs had been created. However, workers were dubious about the reforms, as the existing system had provided them with job security, along with many social benefits such as housing and medical care. Even factory managers were not keen on the idea of a market-based system – especially those in heavy industry.

The 'Open Door' policy

It had soon become obvious that China's economy alone could not generate all the capital investment funds needed to fulfil the ambitious goals of the Ten-Year Plan. As early as 1979, targets had been revised downwards and, in practice, the Ten-Year Plan was largely set aside. The earlier rapprochement with the US, resulting from Nixon's visit in 1972, was thus very helpful, as it led to increased trade and especially much-needed foreign investments.

When the UN recognised the People's Republic of China in October 1971 – as the US no longer vetoed it – China's isolation ended. Moves were then made to open up China even further to Western countries. It is this area more than any other that supports the argument that China was gradually becoming capitalist. Between 1971 and 1974, China's foreign trade increased by more than 300% – most of it with non-communist countries. Foreign trade increased even further under Hua's rule. From 1978–88, under Deng's supervision, it increased by over 400%, and continued to rise thereafter.

In December 1978, the Party officially adopted the 'Open Door' policy, to open up China to the world even more. By engaging in trade with the West, China could earn cash from exports – and develop and/or import science, technology, capital and managerial skills.

Deng and his supporters decided to diversify exports, raise the quality of goods, devalue the *yuan* (which would make Chinese exports cheaper, and thus easier to sell), and build up currency reserves. Beginning in 1978, China began to link its currency – known officially since

Deng's economic revolution, 1976–89

1949 as the renminbi ('people's currency'), but usually referred to as the yuan – to foreign exchange rates, in order to facilitate trading in the international currency markets. Until 2005, its exchange rate was linked to the $US. Later, in 1980, China secured its first loans from the International Monetary Fund and the World Bank. This provided money to upgrade industrial machinery and set up new enterprises.

Many Western nations quickly saw the advantages of moving into the massive new Chinese market – first Japan and Taiwan, soon followed by West Germany and the US. Hong Kong, with its connections to both China and the West, was able to take advantage of this new policy. By adopting capitalist-friendly policies, Deng hoped Taiwan – which also had a thriving market economy – might eventually be returned to China.

China's leaders still felt that more foreign capital was needed for the country's economy to be fully modernised and expanded. So, while trying to maintain state ownership of the 'commanding heights' of the economy, they tried various ways to encourage Western firms to invest in China. However, it was decided that all joint ventures with foreign firms had to be at least 50% Chinese-owned. This would allow China to retain control over its economy.

QUESTION
Why was the 'Open Door' policy seen as being important for China's rapid economic development?

Special Economic Zones

In 1979, the government also created Special Economic Zones (SEZs) in coastal areas in the south of China. Here, economic policies were more 'liberal' (i.e. more friendly to capitalist economic mechanisms) than in the rest of the country. This included special tax concessions: 15% tax was waived for the first two years of profitability, and 50% exemptions for years three and four; and no import duties were applied to production materials or equipment.

7 The People's Republic of China (1949–2005)

Figure 7.3: China's administrative regions and Special Economic Zones, as well as Hong Kong, Macao and Taiwan.

These zones were almost like 'states within a state', as they were given regional autonomy – non-residents needed special permission and an internal passport to travel to them. This was because Deng was also aware that the SEZs would become more and more like capitalist Hong Kong, and that workers there would come into contact with Western ideas. Hence the policy of limiting access for other Chinese people, so that 'bad influences' – such as democracy – would not spread to the rest of the country.

Inside the SEZs, the government built roads, railways and port facilities to help attract foreign companies. These companies liked the idea of a large pool of disciplined, educated but relatively cheap workers and the promise of profit-friendly regulations and policies.

The aim of these zones was to increase the chances of direct foreign investment, and expand the import of advanced modern technology.

Deng's economic revolution, 1976–89

Figure 7.4: Shenzen, the first Special Economic Zone created in China in 1980.

The SEZs also gave China access to important world export markets. It was also hoped that local Chinese managers – including those who had studied abroad – would learn the latest management methods from these foreign firms; while workers would learn how to use the latest technology and machinery.

The first ones established were in 1979, in the Guangdong and Fujian provinces; they were in Shenzhen (just across the border with Hong Kong) and Zhuhai (near Macao) in the south, and in Shantou and Xaimen (across from Taiwan) in the north. These were approved by the National People's Congress in August 1980. In the 1980s, a fifth was established on Hainan Island, off the southern coast.

KEY CONCEPTS ACTIVITY

Change and continuity: Carry out further research on the SEZs of the 1980s, using the internet and whatever books are available to you. In particular, try to evaluate the extent to which wages and working conditions have changed in these areas; and then compare your findings with what the situation in the rest of China was like during this period.

7 The People's Republic of China (1949–2005)

Criticism and Deng's response

These policy directions led to a resurgence of concerns about 'taking the capitalist road' in the Party. Several leaders feared they would lead to the restoration of capitalism. Others feared that foreign domination of China – which had existed in the 19th and early 20th centuries – would soon reappear. The ending of foreign domination had been one of the main achievements of the 1949 Chinese Communist Revolution.

In 1980, Deng responded to this growing criticism by resigning his formal positions of power (officially on account of his age), thereby forcing potential opponents (most of whom were of a similar age) to do the same. In this way, he was able to remove from power those who opposed his economic policies. Their places were taken by younger, more pragmatically minded leaders. However, Deng remained incredibly powerful, informally, as the behind-the-scene 'paramount leader'. His approach seemed to be based on the Marxist view that capitalism provides the base for the construction of socialism. In fact, as early as September 1956, at the 8th Party Congress, Deng had argued that class divisions – and thus class struggle – had been virtually eliminated. He had thus argued that all that was left to deal with was China's backward productive forces in order to be able to move on to advanced socialism.

Deng's power was further consolidated by the events of 1981, which included the ending of the trial of the Gang of Four and the passing of the resolution that Mao was '70% good and 30% bad', which made it possible to move forward and away from Maoism. Deng's power was also strengthened by Hua's resignation as Party Chairman.

By 1982, when Deng had secured full control of both Party and government, he was able to push ahead with the policies he favoured, which were intended to make China wealthier and so able to advance to full socialism.

Communism or capitalism?

To achieve his aims, Deng favoured introducing aspects of a 'free' market economy, which would enable China to compete with the West in production and economic efficiency. He therefore pushed for Western-style, capitalist industrial policies. This does not necessarily mean, however, that Deng and his supporters were capitalists – the accusation thrown against them by the Maoists and Leftists in the period before 1976.

Deng's economic revolution, 1976–89

Indeed, Marx – and until Lenin's death in 1924, Soviet communist leaders – had always said that socialism could only emerge in developed capitalist economies. Deng argued his policies were necessary as China still had feudal hang-overs. However, such policies began a still on-going debate about whether China has now become a capitalist country in all but name.

Deng's approach was based on the concept of 'economics in control', rather than the Maoist idea of 'politics in control'. In other words, economic pragmatism was more important than political dogma (or 'Practice' versus 'Whatever'). In September 1982, the 12th Congress of the CCP approved Deng's economic plans, as well as various personnel changes. He was then in a position to introduce the second phase of his plans for industry.

> **DISCUSSION POINT**
>
> Do you think that Deng's use of market mechanisms, and allowing the existence of privately owned firms and enterprises, automatically meant that China was likely to become a fully developed capitalist economy? To discuss this in any depth, you will need to do some research on key terminology and definitions – such as 'capitalism', 'socialism' and 'market mechanisms'.

Industry phase 2, 1984–89

In October 1984, the 'Resolution on the Reform of the Economic System' began Phase 2. This further reduced state control over enterprises, though they still remained under public ownership. Deng also made it clear that unprofitable enterprises would be closed down. To make profits easier, the state tax on enterprise profits was reduced from 55% to 33% in 1983–84.

This emphasised that ownership and management were two separate aspects, and that managers could be given some freedom in selecting ways to improve production. In particular, it allowed private groups to lease small- and medium-sized enterprises, though the largest ones remained under direct government control. The government also introduced a legal framework that protected private investment. This meant more people were prepared to put money into enterprises. As the incomes of many people increased during this early period, there was an

7 The People's Republic of China (1949–2005)

increased demand for more consumer goods, which provided a stimulus for small family-based enterprises.

Seventh Five-Year Plan

In June 1984, Deng had made a speech at a meeting with a Japanese delegation, at which he had said that China was 'building socialism with a specifically Chinese character' (see Source 7.6).

SOURCE 7.6

What is socialism and what is Marxism? We were not quite clear about this in the past. Marxism attaches utmost importance to developing the productive forces... Therefore, the fundamental task for the socialist stage is to develop the productive forces... Socialism means eliminating poverty. Pauperism is not socialism, still less communism...

Capitalism can only enrich less than 10 per cent of the Chinese population; it can never enrich the remaining more than 90 per cent...

Our political line is to focus on the modernization programme and on continued development of the productive forces... The minimum target of our modernization programme is to achieve a comparatively comfortable standard of living by the end of the century... To do this, we have to invigorate the domestic economy and open to the outside world...

We therefore began by invigorating the economy and adopting an open policy... We adopted this policy at the end of 1978, and after a few years it has produced the desired results. Now the recent Second Session of the Sixth National People's Congress has decided to shift the focus of reform from the countryside to the cities...

We have opened 14 large and medium-sized coastal cities. We welcome foreign investment and advanced techniques. In general, we believe that the course we have chosen, which we call building socialism with Chinese characteristics, is the right one.

Extracts from Deng's speech, **'Build socialism with Chinese characteristics'**, *30 June 1984, to the Japanese businessmen's delegation at the second session of the Council of Sino-Japanese Non-Governmental Persons.*
Source: http://english.peopledaily.com.cn/dengxp/vol3/text/c1220.html

Deng's economic revolution, 1976–89

In 1985, Deng drew up a Seventh Five-Year Plan, to cover the period 1986–90, with slightly different goals from those in the 1984 Resolution. This was officially announced in March 1986. In particular, he said he had three main aims:

1. to give more autonomy to state enterprises, and more emphasis on making a profit
2. to 'smash the iron rice bowl', and so increase the productivity of workers by introducing the fear of unemployment
3. to allow prices of goods – especially food and consumer goods – to be determined by 'market forces'.

The plan was based on the idea of removing state subsidies. This would force state enterprises to become competitive and profitable, by forcing them to cut costs and increase productivity. However, this would be at the cost of workers' wages and jobs. The reference to smashing the 'iron rice bowl' (with 'iron' meaning 'long lasting', and 'rice bowl' referring to 'living standards') meant the idea – and practice – of ending guaranteed job and wage security for industrial workers. Full employment – like the idea of a social wage that included subsidised prices for food and electricity and rents – had always been one of the main planks of Communism, and had been part of Mao's GLF.

To underline the need for competition between state enterprises, new short-term state contracts replaced the longer-term ones. Deng's approach was based on observing that when younger and reform-minded party officials had been given greater freedom to try new approaches, the results had been mostly spectacular – especially in the provinces of Sichuan and Guangdong.

His main aims, as set out in the new Plan, were to:

- increase gross agricultural and industrial output by 38% over the period of the Plan – at an average growth rate of 6.7% per year (4% for agriculture and 7.5% for industry)
- increase gross national output by 44%, at a yearly average of 7.5%
- increase import and export volumes by 35% by 1990
- expand both foreign investment and the import of advanced technology

7 The People's Republic of China (1949–2005)

- increase food and consumer goods consumption for China's population by 5% a year
- spread the 9-year compulsory education system, in order to train 5 million professionals – twice the level of the previous plan.

However, as Gorbachev in the USSR discovered, having ambitious aims and plans doesn't mean that they can be implemented. Nor, if they are implemented, does it necessarily mean that they will be successful.

> **ACTIVITY**
>
> Carry out some further research on Deng's main economic policies from 1978 to 1989. Then draw up a table to summarise the main points under these three headings:
>
> - Agriculture
> - Industry
> - Foreign trade and investment.

7.3 How successful were Deng's economic reforms?

According to official government figures, Deng's reforms were highly successful, with tremendous results and achievements. While to a large extent this seems to be have been true, the overall results were mixed. Government statistics claimed an average annual growth rate of 11% for agriculture and industry. By 1985, China's GNP was 778 billion *yuan*. In certain sectors of the economy, the growth rates were even higher – especially in the heavy industry areas of steel, coal, oil and electricity. By 1985, government investment in publicly owned enterprises had reached 530 billion *yuan*.

Agriculture

Deng had argued that any significant reform of the Chinese economy would have to start with agriculture. Under him, the family came to

Deng's economic revolution, 1976–89

replace the commune as the economic unit of production – and farmers were now rewarded by how hard they worked for themselves rather than for the community as a whole.

According to official statistics, agricultural productivity increased by 15%, above the targets set by the Ten-Year Plan – and 5% of that increase was down the HRS policy. Production increased by an average of 6.7% each year, and grain output rose to 500 billion kilograms in 1996. This made China the largest agricultural producer in the world – based on the world's largest smallholder farming system.

Given the successes of the HRS, it has continued to the present day.

Year	Grain production (millions of tonnes)	Meat production (millions of tonnes)	Index of gross output compared to base of 100 in 1952
1978	304.8	8.6	229.6
1979	332.1	10.6	249.4
1980	320.6	12.1	259.1
1981	325.0	12.6	276.2
1982	354.5	13.5	306.8
1983	387.3	14.0	330.7
1984	407.3	15.4	373.1
1985	379.1	17.6	385.7
1986	391.5	19.2	398.9
1987	404.7	19.9	422.0
1988	394.1	21.9	438.5
1989	407.8	23.3	452.0

Figure 7.6: China's agricultural production statistics, 1978–89. Lynch, M. 2008, *The People's Republic of China 1949-76*, London, Hodder, p.160.

Township and Village Enterprises (TVEs)

The increases in agricultural production resulting from these new policies allowed more farmers to leave their family plots. However, they mostly stayed local, becoming involved in developing local factories or the revival of local crafts. These are known as 'Township and Village Enterprises' (TVEs).

7 The People's Republic of China (1949–2005)

Figure 7.7: A Township and Village Enterprise in rural China.

By 1989, these new small-scale industries accounted for 58% of the total value of rural output. Over 25% of TVEs were run by rural women, allowing them to make a huge contribution to family incomes. Overall, by 1984, official figures claimed 4 million people were employed or self-employed in these industries, with more than 32 million in urban collective enterprises.

It was through these, rather than through standard farming, that rural living standards initially improved. Yet most of these were in fact owned by and/or managed by private capitalists and local governments – all operating on a capitalist basis in both the national and international markets.

De-collectivisation

Agricultural land use in China had clearly been privatised by Deng's reforms. However, land *ownership* – in theory – had not, as land remained in state hands. Once leases expired, the land reverted to the state. Thus, many people were reluctant to put much effort into improving their land, or to invest in long-term projects to give better yields.

Deng's economic revolution, 1976–89

As a result, many farmers stuck to traditional methods, rather than embracing the modern equipment and techniques wanted by the government. Consequently, leases were increased from one year to 15 years, then to 30 years and, after 1984, to 50 years. Farmers who did not want to farm their plots were allowed to rent them out to other farmers. More controversially, Deng allowed land-lease contracts to be passed on to farmers' children – thus creating almost a *de facto* free market in land, with land dealt with as if it were virtually private property that could be 'inherited'.

Stagnation

After 1984–85, growth in grain production actually declined, as farmers found it more profitable to grow those crops receiving higher subsidies – such as rice. Meanwhile, others were still reluctant to put massive effort into land which, ultimately, they did not own. This led to food shortages, and wide fluctuations in price and, in turn, to much anger in some rural areas as living standards began to fall.

Agricultural production then virtually stagnated. The changes in the countryside also gave rise to problems for the official 'one-child policy'. This had been adopted in 1980, to fight 'the enemy within the womb', in an attempt to slow down China's rapidly growing population. It imposed penalties on women and families who had more than one child.

However, the new freedom to 'pass' land on to children down the years led rural families to want more children – especially sons which, despite women having equal rights, were still seen in many areas as the 'natural' owners of farms. These traditional outlooks about inheritance led to abortions and the infanticide of girl babies.

So, in 1985, the government relaxed the 'one-child policy': in effect, allowing families to have two children. Yet, this undid the original plan to stabilise China's population at 1.2 billion by 2000. Later, in March 2011, the government announced that the 'one-child policy' would officially end in 2015.

There were also some severe implications for the environment resulting from industrial expansion, including pollution of the air and rivers, deforestation and subsequent flooding in many areas. These problems were compounded by rapid industrial growth, and later fed into the growing political demands of various movements for more democracy.

7 The People's Republic of China (1949–2005)

Industry

As Figure 7.8 shows, Deng's industrial policies and reforms had a significant impact on China's GDP and manufacturing output. However, because of continued reluctance by many officials to fully implement the reforms, by 1990, over 50% of industry was still directly controlled by the state.

Year	GDP (in billions of Yuan)	Annual GDP growth rate (%)	Annual inflation rate (%)	Annual manufacturing output growth rate (%)
1979	732.6	7.6	6.1	8.6
1980	790.5	7.9	-1.5	11.9
1981	826.1	4.5	7.0	1.6
1982	896.3	8.5	11.5	5.5
1983	987.7	10.2	8.3	9.2
1984	1130.9	14.5	12.9	14.5
1985	1276.8	12.9	1.8	18.1
1986	1385.4	8.5	3.3	8.3
1987	1539.1	11.1	4.7	12.7
1988	1713.1	11.3	2.5	15.8
1989	1786.7	4.3	3.1	4.9

Figure 7.8: China's industrial performance, 1979–89. From Lynch, M. 2008. *The People's Republic of China 1949–76*. London, UK. Hodder, p 162.

Losing the 'iron rice bowl'

It took time for entrepreneurs to find opportunities to make profits, but soon small workshops and businesses emerged. These small businesses then hired workers and operated in what was essentially a market economy framework. However, many workers were reluctant to lose their 'iron rice bowl', which was seen as a positive gain from the Communist Revolution of 1949. Consequently, there was often obstruction and lack of cooperation, which meant it took longer to implement the reforms. It was not until 1986 that the government was able to put in place a labour-contract scheme that linked wages to effort and productivity. Even then, it only applied to new employees – not those already employed. The government also provided unemployment

Deng's economic revolution, 1976–89

insurance to encourage acceptance. However, even as late as 1992, only 20% of the 80 million employees in SOEs were covered by the new contract.

These problems also helped contribute to the student-led democracy demonstrations that occurred in China in 1989. As in Poland and Czechoslovakia, these demonstrations were increasingly supported by disgruntled workers.

The impact of Special Economic Zones

The SEZs caused various problems – including the sometimes savage exploitation of Chinese workers and reduction of trade union rights. However, initially, they led to a significant increase in direct foreign investment in China. At first, funds came mostly from Hong Kong and Taiwan, and China also received considerable aid from elsewhere abroad. The success of the SEZs – especially the one at Shenzhen – led the government to authorize 14 other coastal towns to offer special privileges to foreign investors. Soon, almost the entire Chinese coast had been opened up in this way, along with some inland regions. The SEZs have had a much bigger impact on China's industrial economy than Deng's other reforms.

Year	Imports	Exports
1978	10.9	9.8
1979	15.7	13.7
1980	20.0	18.1
1981	22.0	22.0
1982	19.3	22.3
1983	21.4	22.2
1984	27.4	26.1
1985	42.3	27.4
1986	42.9	30.9
1987	43.2	39.4
1988	55.3	47.5
1989	59.1	52.5

Figure 7.9: China's Foreign Trade, 1978–89. From Lynch, M. 2008. **The People's Republic of China 1949–76**. London, UK. Hodder, p 161.

7 The People's Republic of China (1949–2005)

At first, the main types of work carried out in the SEZs was basic manufacturing, with foreign firms using Chinese workers as cheap labour for unskilled work. Also, most of the goods were then sold in China, rather than being exported as Deng had planned. However, eventually, skill levels increased, along with the quality of goods and exports. Some Party leaders who were initially sceptical of these developments soon became less critical. Instead, they made profitable connections with foreign joint venture partners. They also found jobs for their relatives in the SEZs, where wages – though low by international standards – were higher than in the rest of China.

The result of Deng's industrial reforms – especially the SEZs – was a dramatic increase in China's international trade. Between 1978 and 1989, exports grew by over 500%, and foreign investment increased by 400%.

However, as Source 7.7 shows, the rapid economic growth and industrial expansion created some serious economic problems, and to limited improvements in living standards in comparison to those of other developing Asian nations.

SOURCE 7.7

Instituting the responsibility system, increasing the role of the market in determining economic activity, 'opening to the world', and other changes have pushed growth of the gross national product to an overheated 13 per cent by 1984, the highest rate of any country in the world. But continued growth too rapid for the economy to support and assimilate without severe penalties has led to economic conditions often characterised today as 'chaos'.

Over the nine years 1979–1987 China's state revenue and per capita income approximately doubled… but there are numerous and serious economic imbalances within the overall situation… In fact, China, with a GNP in 1987 of US$277.50 per capita, ranked in the bottom 20 per cent of nations, and its peoples have not experienced the even greater growth of affluence found in some other Asian countries.

Ethridge, J. M., 1990, **China's Unfinished Revolution: Problems and Prospects Since Mao**, San Francisco, China Books, p.46

Deng's economic revolution, 1976–89

In addition, young specialists, often trained abroad, found it difficult to apply their new knowledge to China's more old-fashioned equipment. Meanwhile, older workers – many of whom had received little education during the Cultural Revolution – were resentful of these younger workers, who got promotions. In addition, despite greater consumer choice and better quality goods, the impact of inflation on real wages led to resentment.

The 'Open Door' policy necessarily favoured coastal towns and areas. This led to many wanting to move from rural areas to the coast. In addition, the rapid economic growth put increasing pressures on China's infrastructure. For instance, there were problems with transporting large quantities of raw materials to the factories, which hampered manufacturing.

The impact of high unemployment and inflation led to declining living standards for many, and an increase in worker discontent and even unrest. In the SEZs, workers were often employed on short-term contracts, to avoid giving them the same benefits as full-time workers. If they objected to the worsening working conditions, there were plenty of poor unemployed migrant workers ready to take their place. Also, the huge concentration on economic growth and increased production led to a deterioration of the environment – soon, pollution and environmental issues began to become important to many younger Chinese people.

QUESTION
What negative impacts have the industrial reforms of the 1980s had on the urban workforce – both inside and outside the SEZs?

Unemployment and poverty

Inflation became a serious problem; from late 1988 this forced the government to slow down economic growth. This led to high unemployment (officially said to be 20% in the cities) and reduced living standards.

7 The People's Republic of China (1949–2005)

One result of this was a widening of the gap between rich and poor – especially in rural areas. The de-collectivisation of agriculture showed that about half of the 400 million who worked on the land were surplus to requirements. About 100 million eventually found work in the TEVs. There, they usually did not receive the benefits enjoyed by those in state enterprises, such as medical care and retirement pensions. In addition, their wages were lower, even though their working hours were longer.

The remaining 100 million either became under-employed casual wage labourers getting irregular work, or they became a mass migrant labour force, moving to the cities, living in shanty towns and working for very low wages – or ending up in prostitution or criminal activities.

Figure 7.10: A slum area in Shanghai in the 1980s.

Many of China's cities also saw the re-emergence of stark contrasts (typical of capitalist states in the West) between rich and poor – as mentioned by Source 7.8. For instance, many of those working for private concerns were paid subsistence wages, while begging and prostitution – virtually eradicated under Mao – reappeared.

Deng's economic revolution, 1976–89

SOURCE 7.8

...Premier Zhao Ziyang's 'coastal strategy,' which loosened central financial controls over local governments after 1985 and encouraged regionalism, vastly expanded opportunities for official profiteering and the growth of bureaucratic capitalism, especially along the southern coast and in the Yangzi delta. A new urban bourgeoisie thus began to take shape in the mid 1980s, a class which in addition to bureaucratic capitalists included the rapidly growing number of large and small private entrepreneurs... they are socially and economically distinct from the great majority of the urban population... their distinctiveness as a class in Chinese society expresses itself in a taste for luxury – and the means to satisfy those tastes in expensive restaurants and nightclubs, in new and spacious apartments, and in exclusive boutiques... And the contrast between wealth and poverty in Chinese cities today is probably as great, and certainly as glaring, as it is in the metropolitan areas of most Western and Third World capitalist countries. The Dengist prediction that 'some must get rich first' has come to pass with a vengeance.

Meisner, M., 1991, **Mao's China and After: A History of the People's Republic**, New York, The Free Press, p.477.

China's debt

Deng's reforms at first led to increased borrowing. By 1989, China's external debt was almost US$ 45 000 million. This was a major transformation, as China had been a debt-free nation before the 'Open Door' policy. By world standards, its debt is relatively modest. However, it meant that China was now increasingly dependent on fluctuations in the – capitalist – world market.

China also became subject to economic pressures from international (but US-controlled) lending organisations such as the IMF and the World Bank, to reduce social spending and to adopt policies to benefit foreign firms investing in Chinese industry. Such organisations were not renowned for favouring the establishment of socialist societies.

7 The People's Republic of China (1949–2005)

> **Theory of Knowledge**
>
> History and ethics:
>
> *'Property is theft'* – this famous quotation is from P-J Proudhon (1809–65), who first raised the question whether the concept of private property is ethical. Do economic policies and principles adopted and enforced by a society – such as whether property should be privately or socially owned – affect the ethics and morality of society? Consider, for example, human rights, justice, social responsibility, equality and freedom. Is it possible to argue that one economic system is, in principle, more just than another?

Corruption

The various economic developments – and even the problems associated with the 'one-child policy' – resulted in growing corruption among Party and government officials.

As well as often flouting the 'one-child policy', they also began to benefit from links with Western businesses. As the Party élites became more bureaucratised and less revolutionary, many began to award themselves various perks which allowed them to live privileged lives. For instance, their children automatically got into universities, and were exempted from military service. Also, local and national officials took commissions and bribes from foreign firms for arranging deals in the SEZs.

This corruption and profiteering became so prevalent that it gave rise to a new term, *guan dao* ('official profiteers'). In 1985, the governor of Hainan Island, who got round the regulations for limiting the importation of motor vehicles, was dismissed. In the following years, there were several prosecutions of high-ranking officials for corruption. The children of leading Party members – even those of Deng and Zhao – were sometimes involved. While some of the money ended up in private Swiss bank accounts, a lot was invested in private enterprises in China itself by these budding Chinese capitalists. The emergence of these 'crown princes and princesses' led to growing anger.

Deng's economic revolution, 1976–89

Despite the slower-than-planned progress, and all the difficulties and negative features mentioned in this chapter, China nonetheless made significant progress in terms of modernisation and increased efficiency. By 1989, as a result of these economic policies, it seemed that China was set to become a leading industrial nation by 2040.

However, in the late 1980s, as Deng continued pushing through his economic policies, the increasing discontent among workers combined with political discontent among students. The growing dissatisfaction culminated in the pro-democracy movement and the 1989 protests in Tiananmen Square. These political issues will be examined in the following chapter.

7 The People's Republic of China (1949–2005)

Paper 3 exam practice

Question

Examine the impact of Deng Xiaoping's economic reforms between 1978 and 1989. **[15 marks]**

Skill

Using your own knowledge analytically and combining it with awareness of historical debate.

Examiner's tips

Always remember that historical knowledge and analysis should be the *core* of your answer – details of historical debate are desirable extras. However, where it is relevant, the integration of relevant knowledge about historical debates/or interpretations, with reference to individual historians, will help push your answer up into the higher bands.

Assuming that you have read the question carefully, drawn up a plan, worked out your line of argument/approach and written your introductory paragraph, you should be able to avoid both irrelevant material and simple narrative. Your task now is to follow your plan by writing a series of linked paragraphs that contain relevant analysis, precise supporting information based on your own knowledge and, where relevant, brief references to historical debate interpretations.

For this question, you will need to:

- give a *brief* explanation of the problems facing China in 1978
- offer a brief resumé of Deng's main aims
- outline the main economic policies implemented under Deng during the period 1978–89
- provide a consistently analytical and balanced examination of both the positive and negative *impact/ results* of his various policies.

Such a topic, which has been the subject of some historical debate, will also give you the chance to refer to different historians' views.

Common mistakes

Some students, aware of an existing historical debate – and that extra marks can be gained by showing this – sometimes just simply write things like: 'Historian x says … and historian y says…' However, they make no attempt to evaluate the different views (for example, has one historian had access to more/better information than another, perhaps because he/she was writing at a later date?); nor is this information integrated into their answer by being pinned to the question. Another weak use of historical debate is to write things like: 'Historian x is biased because she is American.' Such basic comments will not be given credit – what's needed is explicit understanding of historians' views, and/or the application of precise own knowledge to *evaluate* the strengths/weaknesses of these views.

Remember to refer to the simplified Paper 3 mark scheme in Chapter 10.

Sample paragraphs containing analysis and historical debate

From about 1978 until 1989, Deng was the main driving force behind the economic policies introduced by China's government – in fact, he continued to have considerable influence on economic issues until 1992. In December 1978, the Third Plenum of CCP's Central Committee appointed Deng to the position of chairman of the People's Political Consultative Conference, recognised him as 'paramount leader', and accepted his economic plans to implement the Four Modernisations. This put him in a strong position to carry through what, according to historians such as M. Lynch, became known as the 'Deng Revolution'.

As historians such as L. Benson have pointed out, China faced many problems at the time of Mao's death in 1976. These included out-dated technology, a massive deficit (of over 6 billion yuan), 20 million unemployed, and over 100 million people who were undernourished. It was problems such as these that Deng was determined to overcome, by making China into a prosperous industrial nation to rival those in the West.

Overall, Deng's policies had a big impact on three main areas of China's economy: agriculture, industry and foreign trade and investment. However, while most historians accept that China witnessed significant – and often spectacular – growth between 1978 and 1989, opinion is divided over what impact his policies have had on the nature of the Chinese state. In particular, there is a

7 The People's Republic of China (1949–2005)

sharp debate over the question of whether or not his economic reforms – regardless of his aims – transformed China into a capitalist state of some kind.

> **EXAMINER COMMENT**
> This is a good example of one way of using historians' views. The main focus of the answer is properly concerned with using precise own knowledge to address the demands of the question. The candidate has also provided some brief but relevant knowledge of historical debate that is smoothly integrated into the answer; however, there is no attempt yet at evaluating these views.

As regards agriculture, Deng's various reforms from 1978 – which were intended to move China's peasant farmers to adopt mechanised farming methods, in order to increase total production and to release agricultural workers for employment in industry – had a significant impact. In particular, the Household Responsibility System was adopted in 1980. This allowed peasant families to rent or lease plots of land from the communes. In the main, they could use the land as they wished – provided a quota of their produce was given to the commune. They were then free to keep or sell any surplus. To encourage these farmers to improve the land and so produce more, leases were gradually extended – first to 15 years and then, in 1984, to 50 years.

One immediate impact was to virtually dismantle the commune system established by Mao in the Great Leap Forward. In 1980, Deng decided that 15% of all commune lands should be leased out and, by 1983, over 90% of farming households were part of this new scheme. In that year, the government also allowed peasants to rent out 'their' lease to others, and to employ wage labourers. This was a massive social impact as it led to the emergence of sub-tenants and agricultural wage labourers in rural China – these had been effectively abolished under Mao.

However, economically, such reforms led – according to official statistics – to great increases in agricultural productivity. Annual increases averaged nearly 7%, resulting in total grain output rising from about 300 million tonnes in 1978 to just over 400 million tonnes in 1989. Most of this increase was said to be the result of the HRS, and so it was continued.

In addition, Deng's agricultural reforms had the desired result of releasing large numbers from agricultural work. However, most stayed in their rural areas, to develop or work in local factories or craft industries which grew up as part of the Township and Village Enterprise (TVE) scheme. By 1984, the government claimed that more than 4 million people were employed in these small-scale industries; by 1989, they were accounting for almost 60% of total rural output. In addition, these small industries had an impact on the position of women, with over a quarter of TVEs being run by women…

[There then follows examples – supported by precise own knowledge – of both the positive and the negative economic and social impacts of Deng's industrial policies, and of the 'Open Door' policy as regards foreign trade and investment. However, these sections – like the one on agriculture – make no reference to relevant historians and/or their views.]

However, as well as the obvious economic and social impact of Deng's economic policies during this period, there is also a much-debated one concerning the political impact of his economic reforms. This relates to what China has – or has not – become as a result of his policies. The economist, C. Bettelheim, for instance, argued as early as 1978 that what was taking place in China was a 'Great Leap Backward' from Mao's goals of socialism and communism.

This is partly challenged by historians such as M. Meisner, who has argued that, although a bureaucratic capitalist class emerged in the SEZs, China itself did not become a fully-formed capitalist economy. Instead, what Deng did was to use de-centralisation and certain market mechanisms to modernise China's centralised command economy…

EXAMINER COMMENT

In addition to a brief reference to the views of two other historians/commentators, these paragraphs – like the others – have analysis supported by good own knowledge.

Activity

In this chapter, the focus is on writing an answer that is analytical, and well-supported by precise own knowledge, and one that – where relevant – refers to historical interpretations/debates. So, using the information from this chapter, and any other sources of information available to you, try to answer one of the following Practice Paper 3 questions using these skills.

7 The People's Republic of China (1949–2005)

Paper 3 practice questions

1 Discuss the political and economic reasons why Hua Guofeng was gradually forced out of power by Deng and his supporters.

2 Evaluate the results of Deng's attempts to reform agriculture in China in the period 1976–89.

3 Examine the ways in which Deng attempted to reform China's industrial economy in the period 1979–89.

4 To what extent was Mao's economic legacy abandoned by the CCP in the years 1976–89?

5 'The decisions to adopt an 'Open Door' policy towards the West, and to create Special Economic Zones, showed that Deng and his supporters were intent on restoring capitalism in China.' To what extent do you agree with this statement?

Political developments under Deng, 1976–89

8 The People's Republic of China (1949–2005)

Introduction

From Mao's death in September 1976 until 1978, the power struggle between 'Leftists' and 'Rightists' continued, with various factions among the top Party and government leaders manoeuvring for overall control. By 1978, it was clear that Deng and his supporters were winning the first rounds, although it was not until 1980–81 that this was fully consolidated.

As was noted in Chapter 7, one reason for Deng's economic reforms was to secure the power of the CCP which it was felt had been damaged by the events of the Cultural Revolution and the policies of the Gang of Four. The period after 1976 would show that although Deng's political policies seemed to fluctuate from liberal to authoritarian, there was in fact a consistent desire to uphold the one-party system.

The first intimations of Deng's approach to politics were seen during the campaign against the Gang of Four: allowing protesters to place, on what became known as Democracy Wall, 'big-character' posters which attacked his political opponents, and called for his re-instatement to leadership positions. However, this was not an indication of his *underlying* political style, and his political legacy is likely to be most remembered as one of repression, not liberalism – as illustrated by the forceful suppression of the Democracy Movement's protests in Tiananmen Square on 4 June 1989.

TIMELINE

1978 **Nov:** Start of Democracy Wall

Dec: Wei Jingsheng's 'Fifth Modernisation'

1979 **Mar:** Arrest of Wei; Deng's 'Four Cardinal Principles'

Oct: Wei's show trial

Dec: Democracy Wall closed down

1980 **Feb:** 'Four Big Rights' abolished

Aug: Third Plenum, 5th National People's Congress

1982 **Sep:** 12th National Party Congress: older leaders 'retired'

1984 **Apr:** Reagan's visit to China

1985 **Sep:** National Conference of Party Delegates; more 'retirements' of older members

Political developments under Deng, 1976–89

1986 Nov: National People's Congress: electoral reforms for local congresses

Dec: Student demonstrations

1987 Jan: Fall of Hu

1989 Jan: Fang Lizhi's Open Letter

Apr: Death of Hu; student demonstrations and protests in Tiananmen Square; start of Democracy Movement

May: Zhao says student demands are reasonable; protests increase; start of hunger strike; Gorbachev's visit; martial law declared

Jun: Military used to crush protests in Tiananmen Square; arrests and executions of ringleaders; Zhao dismissed – replaced by Jiang Zemin.

KEY QUESTIONS
- What was Deng's political approach in the period 1976–79?
- Why did political unrest re-emerge in the period 1980–87?
- What led to the Tiananmen Square Massacre of June 1989?

Overview

- Once the Gang of Four had been overthrown in 1976, and Deng had been rehabilitated once again, it seemed as though he favoured a more liberal political approach.
- At first, a Democracy Wall in Beijing was tolerated – but when students moved from attacking the Gang of Four to criticising Deng, and demanding democracy, his attitudes began to change. In December 1979, Democracy Wall was closed down.
- During the 1980s, Deng's political approach varied from some limited liberalisation to campaigns against 'bourgeois liberalisation'. While he carried out some reforms to the Party – including replacing older leaders with younger ones – he made it clear that he would maintain the CCP's monopoly of political power.
- However, his implementation of liberal economic policies increasingly resulted in demands from intellectuals and students for a

The People's Republic of China (1949–2005)

similar liberalisation of politics. Meanwhile, from 1985 the effects of his economic policies – and of growing signs of corruption – were creating distress and dissatisfaction among many workers and peasants.

- From late 1986, student protests again began to spread, with many calling for democracy. These Democracy Movement protests tailed off in early 1987 – but because of his support of pro-democracy intellectuals, Hu Yaobang was dismissed as General-Secretary of the CCP.
- Some protests occurred again in 1988 and, in January 1989, Fang Lizhi, a leading intellectual, issued an Open Letter calling for the release of political prisoners.
- This, and the death of Hu in April 1989, began a rapidly expanding number of student protests – the most famous of which took place in Tiananmen Square in Beijing. By May, these protests were often a million strong; and were increasingly supported by workers.
- After much debate and hesitation, Deng's government declared martial law, and the PLA was sent in to suppress the protests and clear the Square – with significant loss of life.
- Afterwards, there were many arrests of ringleaders, and executions of workers who had joined the protests. Deng had made it clear that he had no intention of adopting a more democratic political system.

Figure 8.1: The growing confrontation between protestors and soldiers in Tiananmen Square, June 1989.

Political developments under Deng, 1976–89

8.1 What was Deng's political approach in the period 1976–79?

After the rise of Hua Guofeng and the fall of the Gang of Four, there was at first a political relaxation or 'loosening', and a more open approach. Many of those who had either been imprisoned or 'sent down to the countryside' during the Cultural Revolution were released or allowed to return home. Several important leaders – including Deng – were rehabilitated.

Democracy Wall, 1976–80

One manifestation of this political relaxation was that, in several universities, students began to put up 'big-character' posters (known as *dazibao*, and easily read when pasted on walls) calling for rapid moves towards political liberalisation. These included a large number of posters attacking Jiang in the period from the fall of the Gang of Four to the conclusion of their trials. China's new government was happy at first to allow people to have their say about recent events. In November 1978, in the centre of Beijing, on a wall in Xidan Street, near the Forbidden City and Tiananmen Square, students (and later workers) put up 'big character' posters, letters, and poems. This wall soon became known as 'Democracy Wall'.

Following the line of the new government, which was to 'seek truth from facts', people used the wall to give their views about what had happened in China in the period since 1967 – and about a whole range of other things. Such people included former Red Guards and those who had missed out on formal education during the 'Ten Wasted Years' of the Cultural Revolution. However, during that turmoil, they had learned how to organise political action, and they used this to spread their ideas and form networks.

As at first most of their posters criticised the Gang of Four – and even Mao – the government tolerated them. In fact, Deng even encouraged them, as it helped him in his struggle against his opponents in the Party – especially the Leftists who were reluctant to adopt new economic policies. Many of these posters supported his return to power, and

8 The People's Republic of China (1949–2005)

supported the Four Modernisations, while some began to criticise Hua – Deng was thus happy for the Wall to continue. He also approved of the posters that called for a reappraisal of the April 5th Movement of 1976 (see Chapter 6). Some of these posters now called for the protests to be re-termed 'revolutionary' rather than 'counter-revolutionary'.

At first, this only really affected people living in Beijing, but news of Democracy Wall spread to other parts of China, and foreign journalists reported what these posters said. Especially important was the BBC World Service, which was listened to by many Chinese people.

In December 1978, when some posters began to criticise Deng, the government still took no action – and what later became known as the Democracy Movement can be seen as having begun at this point. Then the protests widened, with a number of pro-democracy activists publishing pamphlets and even underground magazines. Some magazines – such as *Beijing Spring* – sold 100 000 copies to Chinese people. These increasingly called for more far-reaching changes, and some even began to criticise the government, the Party as a whole and the socialist system itself.

Figure 8.2: In December 1978, posters criticising Deng appeared on Democracy Wall.

Political developments under Deng, 1976–89

Their main calls were for freedom, political self-determination and human rights. These pro-democracy activists even addressed appeals to Western leaders and countries – such as US president Jimmy Carter – asking them to condemn human rights abuses in China.

This was a step too far for Deng, as he did not support increased democracy. In addition, large numbers began to arrive in Beijing from rural areas to call attention to abuses of power and corruption by Party officials, and to present petitions asking the government for redress. When this did not happen, they began to gather in Tiananmen Square and organise marches and protest demonstrations. Unlike the earlier phase, which had been directed against abuses in the period before 1976, they were now criticising the very recent past and the present.

Despite Deng's intentions, his various economic polices – and especially the opening up to the West – implemented as part of the Four 'Modernisations', soon led to the rise of open political dissent, with the demand for the 'Fifth Modernisation' – political democracy – being raised. In particular, many students and intellectuals believed that the economic reforms should be accompanied by political reforms that would increase democracy.

The 'Fifth Modernisation'

The most famous of all these pro-democracy pamphlets during this period was the 'Fifth Modernisation', by **Wei Jingsheng**.

> ### Wei Jingsheng (b. 1950):
> Wei was a worker, and had been a Red Guard. Imprisoned in 1979, he was released in 1993. He then resumed his criticisms, and was sentenced to another 14 years in 1995 – this time for 'conspiracy to subvert the government' ('counter-revolution' had been removed as an offence). He was released in 1997, and went into exile.

In it, he argued that for full modernisation to succeed in China, there needed to be a Fifth Modernisation – democracy – to ensure that the economic changes worked. Intellectuals like him saw the economic reforms as an opportunity to reform the political system as well. Wei openly criticised Deng and his policies in a series of articles – he even claimed Deng was becoming a fascist dictator, and that therefore his power should be restricted. On 5 December 1978, in a 'big-character'

The People's Republic of China (1949–2005)

poster (Source 8.1), Wei called for this 'Fifth Modernisation' to be granted, in order create full modernisation.

> **SOURCE 8.1**
>
> After the arrest of the Gang of Four, people eagerly hoped that Vice-Chairman Deng, the so-called 'restorer of capitalism,' would once again appear as a great towering banner… However, to the people's regret, the hated old political system has not changed, and even any talk about the much hoped for democracy and freedom is forbidden…
>
> Why Democracy?… Others have conducted careful analyses and indicated on the Democracy Wall how much better is democracy than autocracy…
>
> People should have democracy… Do the people have democracy now? No. Do they want to be masters of their own destiny? Definitely yes… Freedom and happiness are our sole objectives in accomplishing modernization. Without this fifth modernization all others are merely another promise…
>
> Today… the people have… a clear orientation, and they have a real leader. This leader is the democratic banner, which is [sic] now taken on a new significance. Xidan Democracy Wall has become the first battlefield in the people's fight against reactionaries… Let us unite under this great and real banner and march toward modernization for the sake of the people's peace, happiness, rights and freedom!
>
> Extracts from Wei Jingsheng's **'The Fifth Modernisation'**.
> From: www.rjgeib.com

Consequently, on 29 March 1979, Wei was arrested – at his brief show trial in October, he was found guilty of treason and sentenced to 15 years' imprisonment in solitary confinement. He can thus be seen as the first martyr in what became known as the 'Democracy Movement'.

Deng decided to make it clear that despite economic reforms, demands for democracy were an example of 'bourgeois liberalism', from which the Chinese people needed protection. So, on 30 March 1979, he made a speech setting out the 'Four Cardinal Principles' that the Party needed to uphold as the Four Modernisations were implemented (parts of his speech are shown in Source 8.2).

Political developments under Deng, 1976–89

Sometimes also referred to as the Four Basic or Fundamental Principles, these were:

- The Socialist Road
- The Dictatorship of the proletariat
- The Leadership of the Communist Party
- Marxism-Leninism and Mao Zedong Thought.

This, he stated, was because China was aiming for *socialist* modernisation, rather than other modernisations. He saw 'bourgeois liberalisation' as leading China to capitalism; hence the need to uphold the Four Cardinal Principles, and carry out a protracted struggle against 'bourgeois liberalisation'.

SOURCE 8.2

To achieve the four modernizations and make China a powerful socialist country before the end of this century will be a gigantic task…

The Central Committee maintains that, to carry out China's four modernizations, we must uphold the Four Cardinal Principles ideologically and politically…

As we all know, far from being new, these Four Cardinal Principles have long been upheld by our Party. The Central Committee has been adhering to these principles in all its guidelines and policies adopted since the smashing of the Gang of Four, and especially since the Third Plenary Session of the Eleventh Central Committee…

To sum up, in order to achieve the four modernizations we must keep to the socialist road, uphold the dictatorship of the proletariat, uphold the leadership of the Communist Party, and uphold Marxism-Leninism and Mao Zedong Thought… The Central Committee considers that we must now repeatedly emphasize the necessity of upholding these four cardinal principles, because certain people (even if only a handful) are attempting to undermine them. In no way can such attempts be tolerated… To undermine any of the four cardinal principles is to undermine the whole cause of socialism in China, the whole cause of modernization.

Extracts from Deng's speech, 30 March 1979.
Source: www.english.peopledaily.com.cn

These, he said, were the basis of the Chinese state, could not be debated, and would not be abandoned. In part, this was a fictional attempt to

8 The People's Republic of China (1949–2005)

claim that the 'old revolutionary road' was still being followed by the Party leadership. Although, in a way, the implication was that other political issues could be debated and discussed, events soon showed that the Party, despite the various reforms, was determined to maintain its monopoly of political power.

> **QUESTION**
> Why did Deng see the Four Cardinal Principles as being so important?

By the end of 1979, Deng no longer needed the posters on Democracy Wall in his struggle against his opponents. In December, he ordered the closing down of the wall, which was moved to a more remote part of Beijing. The government then began quietly to arrest and detain, or 'send down to the countryside', the most important activists of the Democracy Movement – possibly as many as 100 000. Those from outside the main cities had their residents' permits to live in those cities revoked, in an obvious attempt to prevent urban organisation and resistance.

In February 1980, the 'Four Big Rights' – *daming* (to speak out freely), *dafang* (to air views fully), *dabianlun* (to hold great debates), and *dazibao* (to write big-character posters) – were abolished. These rights dated back to the Cultural Revolution, and had been incorporated into the 1978 constitution. This action made it illegal to put up any more wall posters, and was a clear warning to intellectuals and journalists that post-Maoist China would not allow unlimited criticism of the Party and government.

Although this forced the pro-democracy groups – and reform communists – underground, they managed to retain contact with each other and, occasionally, limited protests continued to emerge.

> **ACTIVITY**
> See what more you can find out about Wei Jingsheng. Then write a couple of sentences to explain why he called his demand for democracy the 'Fifth Modernisation'.

Political developments under Deng, 1976–89

8.2 Why did political unrest re-emerge in the period 1980–88?

The 1980s in China were, politically, rather confusing in that, at times, intellectuals were encouraged to speak out in a limited form of political liberalisation – yet it was stated that no 'bourgeois' values were to be reintroduced. By the end of the decade, Deng's regime would face its most serious challenge from national protest movements of students and workers.

Reform of the CCP

The only real political reform Deng favoured was reform of the CCP. He realised that the standing of the Party had been damaged by the various developments since 1967, and that it was necessary to make some changes to restore its credibility and authority – but not by abandoning the idea of a single-party system.

The idea of a single-party system was a Stalinist, not a Marxist, belief. The 1921 Bolshevik ban in Soviet Russia on all other parties had been intended as an extraordinary and temporary pragmatic departure from the 'norms of socialist democracy'. Thus, in the 1980s, Gorbachev in the USSR could claim that his more democratic style of politics was simply a return to Leninist practice. The CCP, despite Mao's disagreements with Stalin, was mainly organised along Stalinist lines. Deng, though breaking with Mao on economic policies, remained a Stalinist as far as socialist democracy was concerned – in other words, he opposed it.

However, he also wanted it made clear that there would be no automatic harassment of Party members with different ideas – in other words, it would not be like during the Cultural Revolution, when people were targeted for being 'revisionists' and 'capitalist roaders'. As long as the authority and leadership of the Party was accepted – and no more demands for greater political freedom were made – then Chinese citizens could be confident that they could live in peace and quiet.

8 The People's Republic of China (1949–2005)

In the struggle between pragmatists such as himself, and those 'Leftists' who did not want government policies to deviate too much from communist ideology, Deng saw the advantage of separating the very close links between Party and government. But this did not mean he was no longer a communist. What Deng – and his younger supporters – wanted was to reform the system to make it more efficient and productive. While he advocated economic policies that had Western capitalist features, he had no intention of adopting a democratic political system similar to those existing in the major capitalist states. Indeed he preferred the regimes in lesser capitalist states – such as Malaysia – which were often ruled by authoritarian systems.

His reorganisation of the Party along these lines was approved in August–September 1980 by the Third Plenum of the 5th National People's Congress. This plenum also condemned as 'liberal bourgeois views' the idea that people have the 'right to speak out freely' or 'hold great debates'.

At the top of the Party, Deng was keen to make it clear that the adoption of capitalist-style mechanisms and technologies was all part of a Chinese-style socialism. Any open renunciation of socialism would undermine the Party leadership and the Party itself – and thus the whole political and power structure in Communist China.

He was, however, aware that the Party had become isolated from the mass of the Chinese people – and that many of the Party members and officials were poorly educated and not very efficient. Yet they remained in post, even at the highest levels, because they were politically 'reliable'. In the upper reaches of the party, in the Politburo and the Central Committee, a small number of old men – including Deng himself – monopolised power.

Consequently, in 1982 (building on his previous actions in 1980), Deng began another campaign to 'encourage' senior members of the Party to retire. At the 12th National Party Congress, in September, older leading members were 'promoted' to the Central Advisory Commission – headed by Deng – and their official positions were taken by younger members. In September 1985, the National Conference of Party Delegates oversaw further retirements, so that younger and better-educated members could take their place. Similar changes were encouraged at the lower levels too.

Political developments under Deng, 1976–89

Figure 8.3: 'The Long March' – a cartoon by Kevin Kallaugher, published in *The Observer*, a British newspaper, 22 September 1985. It shows the departure of leading older members of the CCP.

> **QUESTION**
>
> In what way was the title of the cartoon in Figure 8.3 particularly ironic as regards the old CCP leaders shown heading for the exit? If in doubt, refer to the *Background* section of Chapter 1.

By 1986, a total of 1.8 million senior members had gone. Deng also supervised a 'cleansing' purge – between 1983 and 1987, the CCP expelled over 150 000 cadres (officials) for various offences (including abuse of power, and bribery and corruption). At the same time, he made steps to improve the overall educational level of cadres – as a result, over 60% of the Party membership below the Politburo soon consisted of younger men and women with college qualifications.

Many of these changes also contributed to Deng's ability to remove those who were less than enthusiastic about his economic reforms. However, underlying all these reforms of the Party, there remained Deng's commitment to his version of communism.

8 The People's Republic of China (1949–2005)

Inner-party divisions

By 1982, Deng had full control over both the government and the party. He himself never formally held any high political post, such as premier, or Chairman or General-Secretary of the CCP. Instead, he chaired important economic committees, preferring to put his supporters into the top positions – in particular Hu Yaobang and Zhao Ziyang.
By then, in fact, it seemed fairly clear that Deng would eventually be replaced either by Zhao, the premier, or by Hu, the General-Secretary of the CCP.

Hu in particular favoured a more democratic approach to dissent, and tried to protect intellectuals when Deng periodically launched attacks on 'bourgeois liberalisation' – especially during 1983–84. For example, during 1980, Hu made speeches in which he announced the rehabilitation of intellectuals (who had been known as the 'stinking ninth' – one of the groups previously singled out as 'revisionists', 'bourgeois' and 'capitalist roaders'). His reforms to the educational system restored the emphasis on improving the quality of specialist schools and of higher education, thus reversing certain aspects of the Cultural Revolution.

Under Mao, students had to have a good work record and the support of their work team before acceptance at a university. He had also placed more emphasis on a good basic education for all, rather than spending more money on the education of those who were more able. In part, this was because he had worried that the children of important Party officials were getting an advantage in schools and universities, and would thus become a new middle class, at the expense of workers and peasants.

Hu also backed the official Party newspaper, the *People's Daily*, in the early 1980s, when it promoted democratic reform and exposed official corruption. Indeed, Deng's government initially relaxed controls on newspapers, allowing them to report on certain negative aspects about life in China. In particular, several important middle-level Party leaders criticised the growing evidence of corruption. This had been a growing problem for some time. In the late 1970s, a case of corruption and embezzlement of state funds had come to light in Heilongjiang province, resulting in the trial and execution of the main guilty parties, all of whom had been leading members of the local CCP.

Political developments under Deng, 1976–89

> **QUESTION**
> Why did corruption become such a problem in China during the 1980s?

This support for greater political freedom was shared by Zhao. Having lost position during the Cultural Revolution, Zhao had been restored by Mao in 1972, being put in charge of Guangdong province as Party Secretary. There he had quietly supported three young democratic activists known by the acronym 'Li-Yi-Zhe'. These activists were Li Zhengtian, Chen Yiyang and Wang Xizhe. They had first become known nationally in November 1974, when their pamphlet 'On Socialist Democracy and the Legal System' was put on a wall in Canton, covering a hundred yards.

However, it was not Zhao's support of democratic activists that got him Deng's support, but his introduction of market-reform economic policies – this had resulted in his being elected to the Politburo and becoming premier in 1980, where he enthusiastically supported Deng's economic reforms and especially the 'Open Door' policy.

Though Deng promoted these two, he did not share their approach to greater political democracy. On the contrary, as regards politics, Deng was as conservative politically as he was 'progressive' economically. As he saw it, if China's economy was going to be modernised successfully, it needed internal political stability – he was not alone in believing that the chaos of the Cultural Revolution had impeded both economic and educational progress. What he wanted was for China to turn its back on political debates, and instead get on with economic transformation – he believed that politics was less important than turning China into a modern and powerful country, and so should be subordinated to that task.

Renewal of student activism, 1986–87

During a visit to China in April 1984, US president Ronald Reagan made two speeches, which included references to 'freedom' and 'trust in the people'. Despite government attempts to censor these, it appears that uncensored translations of the speeches began to circulate in China.

The People's Republic of China (1949–2005)

These, as well as the earlier newspaper articles against corruption, helped resurrect the pro-democracy groups. In 1985, a 17 000-strong student demonstration at the élite China University of Science and Technology (CUST) in Hefei, in Anhui province, called for greater reform – especially political reform. Most of the students here were the children of high-ranking officials and prominent intellectuals.

In May 1986 (on the 30th anniversary of Mao's launch of the Hundred Flowers campaign), Deng ended another more repressive period – during which **Wang Ruoshui**, a democratic Marxist, had been dismissed in 1983 as managing editor of the *People's Daily* – by launching another period of political relaxation.

> ### Wang Ruoshui (1926–2002):
> Wang studied philosophy in the late 1940s, became a Marxist philosopher and joined the CCP before its victory in 1949, and became the political theory editor on the ***People's Daily***. He was originally a Maoist, but later became an exponent of Marxist humanism and liberalism. His beliefs and his journalism led to his losing this editorial job and to being expelled from the CCP in 1987, in one of Deng's campaigns against 'bourgeois liberalism'.

This encouraged ideological flexibility and stressed the need for 'political reform'. In the summer of 1986, Wang had his treatise 'On the Marxist Philosophy of Man' published in a Shanghai newspaper, in which he stressed the democratic and humanitarian strands of Marxist philosophy and politics.

In November 1986, the National People's Congress introduced some changes to the election of candidates to local congresses. More student demonstrations were held – ostensibly to encourage more students to get involved in local government. However, they soon moved on to demanding better living standards and the need for greater freedom. At first, the government concentrated on simply dispersing the demonstrations, without arresting the organisers.

The students were supported by Professor Fang Lizhi and, more circumspectly, by intellectuals associated with Hu Yaobang.

Political developments under Deng, 1976–89

> **Fang Lizhi (b. 1936):**
>
> Fang was a popular astrophysics professor and Vice President at CUST in Hefei, and an outspoken activist for democratic reform. As a result of his support of the student protests in 1986–87, he was expelled from the CCP and, on 5 June, the day after the Tiananmen Square massacre, he sought asylum in the US embassy in Beijing.

In a speech delivered on 18 November (see Source 8.3), Fang made the point that China would only be able to develop towards modernity if there were freedom to think freely. He also said socialism had failed, and that for modernisation to work, it would be necessary to adopt Westernisation as well.

SOURCE 8.3

…I have to judge this era [since 1949] a failure. This is not my opinion only… many of our leaders are also admitting as much, saying that socialism is in trouble everywhere. Since the end of World War II, socialist countries have by and large not been successful… Are the things done in the name of socialism actually socialist? We have to take a fresh look at these questions and the first step in that process is to free our minds from the narrow confines of orthodox Marxism.

We've talked about the need for modernization and reform, so now let's consider democracy… the word 'democracy' is quite clear, and it is poles apart from 'loosening up'. If you want to understand democracy, look at how people understand it in the developed countries… In democratic countries, democracy begins with the individual. I am the master, and the government is responsible to me… If you want reform – and there are more reforms needed in our political institutions than I have time to talk about – the most crucial thing of all is to have a democratic mentality and a democratic spirit.

Extracts from Fang Lizhi's speech of 18 November 1986, in Fang, L., 1990, (trans. Williams, J. H.), **Bringing Down the Great Wall: Writings on Science, Culture and Democracy in China**, *New York, W.W Norton, pp.157–88*

8 The People's Republic of China (1949–2005)

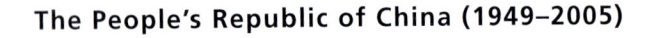

> **QUESTION**
> Why would Deng and his supporters have been against Fang's speech?

> **DISCUSSION POINT**
> How far is the idea of 'actually existing' democracy in the West, as was held by intellectuals such as Fang, an 'ideal' which, in reality, often falls far short of what China's Democracy Movement thought democracy to mean? Try to identify some specific examples to make your points.

During December 1986, in the leading universities of Hefei, Shanghai and Wuhan, students called for even greater changes to the electoral system – in Hefei, on 5 December, about 3000 students of CUST demonstrated for greater reforms. On 20 December 1986, over 50 000 demonstrated in Shanghai – this time, there were minor clashes with the police. Deng and his supporters were particularly worried by the fact that, in Shanghai and one or two other places, the student demonstrations had attracted the support of some workers.

These student pro-democracy protests then spread to Beijing. Many students were concerned about the relatively slow pace of expansion of job opportunities for the growing number of graduates as the Chinese economy began to slow down in the mid 1980s. In the late 1970s, along with the removal of the need to perform manual labour to get into university, there had been a rapid expansion of university places. Now, however, graduates were finding it difficult to get jobs.

Such student discontent has often been a critical factor in pre-revolutionary and revolutionary situations – including China in 1919. As hope and idealism tend to be more of a feature of youth than of middle-age, young people – especially those who continue their education – are often attracted to revolutionary movements. Especially if they live in a society that tends to ignore or exclude the young, and where power is in the hands of middle-aged – or even older – people.

Political developments under Deng, 1976–89

Deng condemned these protests in January 1987, dismissing them as the work of a small number of 'anti-socials'. The government then dismissed Fang, giving him a new post in Beijing, where the authorities could monitor him more effectively. However, he continued to speak out – some saw him as a Chinese equivalent of Andrei Sakharov in the USSR. Other prominent dissidents were the journalists Lin Binyan and Wang Ruoshui. Both of these had continued to investigate cases of corruption among government and Party officials, even after Wang's removal from his editorial position – and both were expelled from the CCP and their posts. However, despite these government actions, intellectuals continued to speak out in favour of democracy. They were encouraged in part by some sympathetic comments made by Hu, the General Secretary of the CCP.

As exams began in January, the 1986 pro-democracy student movement mostly faded away. The main ringleaders were arrested, although the small number of students arrested were soon released. However, the regime was tougher on the workers who had joined them – many of these were given prison sentences for 'counter-revolution.' Deng's government then launched a new campaign against 'bourgeois liberalisation' in 1987– his third 'witch hunt' (the other two were in 1980 and 1983).

The fall of Hu

Deng decided that these protests required a new purge – and the most prominent victim was Hu Yaobang. In January 1987, Hu – who had criticised the slow pace of political reform and had supported some of the students' demands for political liberalisation – was dismissed as General-Secretary, though he remained on the Politburo. In fact, it seems that Deng had decided on this move in late 1986, as Hu's exposure of corruption among the children of senior Party leaders, and his close ties to democratic intellectuals, had angered several senior Party leaders.

He had also criticised recent reforms to higher education: these said two years of assigned labour were necessary before graduates could start work; and that 30% of each graduating class had to accept jobs assigned to them by the government. These were seen for what they were – measures to try to limit student access to dissident intellectuals and lecturers, and so limit the spread of protest.

8 The People's Republic of China (1949–2005)

Deng had first planned to remove Hu – who, in 1986, had suggested that Deng was too old and should therefore resign – at the Thirteenth Party Congress, due in the autumn of 1987. However, the events of the winter 1986–87 made Deng decide to act earlier. So Hu was dismissed at an informal meeting of Deng and a group of the most senior Party 'elders' who soon became known as the 'Gang of Old', after being forced to admit he had made 'serious mistakes'. Officially, it was announced that the Politburo had dismissed him. His dismissal and treatment made him a hero to many students who later became very active in the Democracy Movement in the late 1980s.

He was replaced by Zhao Ziyang – Zhao's place as premier being taken by **Li Peng**, who was more of a conservative. These changes of leadership were later formally approved by the Thirteenth Party Congress in late October 1987. It was at this Congress that Deng retired from the Standing Committee of the Politburo – forcing other elderly members to resign as well. This action, as well as removing possible opponents, also reduced the average age of Committee members from 77 to 63. Of the older ones, only Zhao remained.

> **Li Peng (b. 1928):**
>
> Li was a hardliner, who was totally opposed to making concessions to the democracy movement. Hence the growing conflict between him and Zhao. In particular, Li disapproved of Zhao's idea of including trades unions and student organisations in discussions over economic and political reform. Instead, Li supported Deng's continuing belief that the CCP needed to retain an authoritarian political system to keep control of the economic reforms.

However, Deng remained chair of the Military Affairs Commission, as well as 'paramount leader'. He also retained great influence through the establishment of the 'retired' senior Party elders as a 'Gang of Old'. Deng and this group continued to exert great influence informally, behind the scenes. Deng reiterated that Western-style democracy was not part of the modernisation programme – in part, because of China's vast size and its mixed population, and the low educational level of the majority. Thus the leadership of the Communist Party was still essential – without that, there could be 'no building of socialism.'

Political developments under Deng, 1976–89

Continuing unrest

These actions in 1987 were a clear signal from the government about its attitude to the student demonstrations. Though fewer, these continued – they protested not only against the new reforms of higher education, but also about student grants (or stipends), which were low, and poor living conditions. In 1988, student organisers circulated a petition calling for greater reform. Encouraged and inspired by intellectuals such as Fang, and some radical student leaders, these demands soon included calls for democracy. The summer of 1988 saw another wave of student demonstrations in cities across China. But they were not joined by workers or peasants and, as exam time approached, the numbers involved declined. However, unrest in the universities continued in the new academic year 1988–89.

These protests worried Deng, who seems to have feared another power struggle between his pragmatist 'faction', and the more hard-line Maoists in the Party. He managed to get several more of these to retire on age grounds – though Deng, at 83, had no intention of stepping down. Essentially, as described by Immanuel C.Y. Hsu, Deng was an odd mixture of an economic progressive and a political conservative – as noted previously, he saw the market mechanisms and Western technology as a means to strengthen the Chinese economy and to strengthen Communist rule. Michael Lynch, too, sees him as someone who was a reformer but only in the economy – in politics, he was a CCP hardliner. Hence an eventual show-down between Deng and the democracy activists was almost inevitable.

Impact of Deng's economic reforms

What helped make the later protests of 1988–89 so serious compared to the 1986 protests was the greater number of workers who joined with the students. This was largely the result of the impact of Deng's economic policies on living standards.

As seen in Chapter 7, one of the results of Deng's moves to greater freedom for enterprises was less state involvement in guaranteeing basic necessities for Chinese peasants and industrial workers. In the state industrial sector, greater freedom for the State Owned Enterprises (SOEs) had meant growing unemployment, while industrial workers also lost their food coupons, free health care and free education. In addition, inflation and rising food prices – in early 1985, the cost of

8 The People's Republic of China (1949–2005)

basic necessities increased by 30% – were reducing real wages, especially for factory workers and lower-level government employees.

One result of all this was a change in public attitudes to Deng's reforms – by 1985, there was a growing feeling that things were going wrong, and by 1989, Deng's popularity among the people was much lower than it had been in the late 1970s and early 1980s. It also began to produce divisions within the CCP – especially between Deng and Chen Yun, an old-style economic planner, who felt that market mechanisms should only play a supplementary role.

At first, Deng tried to avoid any direct confrontations with those voicing political or economic criticisms. He had been observing events in Poland, where the rise of Solidarity (an unofficial independent trade union that began to organise strikes against Poland's Communist government) in 1980 had led to the introduction of martial law – this was something he wished to avoid for China. However, despite such concerns, Deng had no intention of reversing his economic policies.

Nonetheless, as these economic policies were pushed through, the social impact increased – by early autumn 1988, inflation in the main cities had reached 30% a year, the economy was out of control, and the government imposed further austerity measures, which reduced spending on social services and kept wages low – which particularly hit the TVEs. By late 1988, living standards for many had dropped dramatically – resulting in an increasing number of workers' strikes and 'slow-downs' in factories; while in rural areas, as farmers found the purchase of expensive fertilizers increasingly difficult, and rural industrial jobs were lost, there were clashes with local officials. Renewed student activism saw protests spread into the city streets, and illegal 'big-character' posters began to appear in the winter of 1988–89.

KEY CONCEPTS QUESTION

Causation and consequence: Why did Deng's economic reforms result in many workers joining students in the growing political unrest of 1988–89?

Political developments under Deng, 1976–89

Neo-Authoritarianism

One response of the authorities was to send police abroad to learn the latest crowd control and anti-riot techniques. Another was to work out some ideological backing for the practical results of Deng's programme – combining an essentially capitalist market economy with the continued political dictatorship of the CCP. The intellectuals who developed the new 'politics' became known as the 'new authoritarians'. They argued that the experiences of places such as Taiwan and Singapore showed that in order to achieve rapid modern economic development it was necessary to have states that were strong enough to 'tame the masses' and 'discipline the working population' (or, as Source 8.4 describes them, '*the victims of the transition to a market economy*') who suffered as a consequence.

SOURCE 8.4

…China could not afford democracy, which would bring the chaos of Party politics and disruptive protests by the victims of the transition to a market economy, thus delaying China's modernization. Political democracy was not ruled out entirely, but the neo-authoritarians said it presupposed a highly developed economy and a viable capitalist class. This did not yet exist, and thus democracy was put off until an indefinite time in the future…

Neo-authoritarian doctrines, tacitly endorsed by Party General Secretary Zhao Ziyang and based on the ideas of Deng Xiaoping, or so its proponents claimed, brought criticism from democratic Marxist intellectuals. Many democratic Marxists, such as Su Shaozhi, had been associated with ousted Party head Hu Yaobang, and thus now found themselves in political limbo, increasingly in opposition to both Deng Xiaoping and Zhao Ziyang.

Meisner, M., 1999, **Mao's China and After: A History of the People's Republic.** *New York, The Free Press, p. 494.*

QUESTION

Why were Deng's economy policies likely to lead to 'disruptive protests'?

8 The People's Republic of China (1949–2005)

This political debate revealed how things had moved on since 1978, when Deng's re-emergence was seen by many intellectuals as ushering in 'socialist democracy'. Both sides of the debate accepted the need for a market (ie. essentially capitalist) economy – the difference was over whether the regime should be democratic or authoritarian. Deng's supporters had come to accept a capitalist autocracy.

> **ACTIVITY**
>
> Try to find out the names of those who belonged to the inner Party group known as the 'Gang of Old'. Then write a couple of paragraphs to explain why students might have seen their moves as a significant obstacle to demands for increased democracy in China.

8.3 What led to the Tiananmen Square Massacre of June 1989?

Developments in the second half of 1988 rapidly snowballed into the well-known confrontation in Tiananmen Square in June 1989.

Democracy salons

During the summer and autumn of 1988, democratic Marxists and intellectuals who had been dismissed or sidelined following the disturbances of 1986–87 held informal lectures at Beijing University and elsewhere. The most famous of these discussion groups – known as 'democracy salons' (named after those that had contributed to the start of the French Revolution of 1789) – was organised by Wang Dan, an undergraduate history student at Beijing University. These meetings discussed aspects of democracy and politics, and attracted growing numbers.

In December 1988, Su Shaozhi, a prominent Marxist theoretician, who had been sacked from his post of head of the Marx-Lenin-Mao Institute after the fall of Hu, attacked the new official ideology of Deng's regime,

Political developments under Deng, 1976–89

and called for an open debate about the various strands of Western Marxism. This placed greater emphasis on the democratic and libertarian aspects of Marxism than did the authoritarian Chinese version of Marxism-Leninism, and had always been banned in Communist China. Then, on 6 January 1989, Fang Lizhi wrote an Open Letter to Deng, calling for the release of Wei Jingsheng and other political prisoners. In it, he argued that this would be a good way to celebrate the 40th anniversary of the foundation of the People's Republic, the 70th anniversary of the May Fourth Movement – and the bicentennial of the French Revolution, which had proclaimed '*liberty, equality and fraternity*'. This inspired an unprecedented number of intellectuals to issue similar appeals for a general amnesty for all political prisoners.

By early 1989 the 'democracy salons' of 1988 had transformed into regular democracy discussion groups in Beijing University. At the same time, secret political groups were organised in Beijing and other universities to plan their own unofficial demonstrations to mark the 1919 May Fourth Movement anniversary.

The death of Hu

In the end, things moved faster because of the unexpected death of Hu Yaobang. His death, on 15 April 1989, was rumoured to be the result of his removal from office and the subsequent 'self-criticism' he had to undergo at the hands of 'anti-reformers' in the Party. His death became the catalyst for the dramatic events in Tiananmen Square in June 1989.

Hu's death provided an opportunity for renewed dissent, as part of the tradition of 'mourning the dead to criticise the living'. There were several marches and rallies, especially in Beijing (10 000 strong in Beijing's Tiananmen Square on 16 April) and Shanghai (1000 strong), in which people spoke in favour of change. These calls covered a range of issues, including freedom of information and a free press.

As the days went by, the marches and demonstrations grew larger – some students staged a sit-in at the Great Hall of the People, demanding that representatives of the National People's Congress receive their petitions calling for democratic rights such as free organisation and freedom of the press, and condemning corruption and nepotism. Others – joined by some workers – tried to break into the old Forbidden City (where top Party leaders had their homes) – but were met by police and

The People's Republic of China (1949–2005)

clashes took place. Meanwhile, the numbers in Tiananmen Square grew, as students were joined by workers and others.

Figure 8.4: Soldiers keep student demonstrators away from the official memorial for Hu Yaobang at the Great Hall of the People, where the service was being held.

The Politburo decided against giving into the students' demands, and fixed 22 April as the official day of mourning. As Li Peng and other government officials tried to go into the official ceremony, three students attempted to give him a petition demanding political liberalisation. However, Li and the others refused to accept the petition. By then, over 100 000 were standing in the Square in a silent protest against Deng's regime; and more than 1 million lined the streets to watch the funeral procession.

The government issued a ban on demonstrations and called for them to end; Zhao, who might have argued against this, was away in North Korea on an official visit. The pro-democracy activists ignored the ban and, after their mass memorial service on 22 April, began a number of sit-ins and boycotts of university classes. These started on 24 April – and were soon joined by many non-students, including significant numbers of workers. The protests, which continued throughout April, called for greater democracy and an end to corruption among officials.

Political developments under Deng, 1976–89

The People's Daily editorial, 26 April

Student leaders then announced the formation of an 'Autonomous Federation' to coordinate student activities. In particular, they declared a student 'strike', while some students began to make speeches on street corners appealing to ordinary citizens to support their calls for democracy and denouncements of corruption.

Deng was increasingly annoyed – writing in an editorial in *The People's Daily* on 26 April, Deng denounced the protesters as a small handful of plotters who were aiming to cause chaos and undo the leadership of the CCP and the socialist system, and who must be crushed. Even though the editorial had forbidden the students to associate with workers and peasants, transport workers showed solidarity with the students by not collecting fares as they travelled to Beijing from over 40 universities across China. The students – especially those who had made great efforts to show their loyalty to the CCP and socialism – were angered by the editorial, and became more united and determined. However, concerned that they might be repressed any time soon, they called for dialogue with top government and Party leaders.

The 'Beijing Spring'

The next day, 27 April, over 100 000 students from the various campuses in Beijing broke through the police and militia cordons intended to keep them from leaving their universities. Others marched through the streets of Beijing for over 12 hours, with approval expressed by many local residents (about 500 000 onlookers gave their support via food and money, and even by joining them), and then went to Tiananmen Square. This was the largest demonstration since the death of Zhou in April 1976 – the Democracy Movement's actions on 27 April were seen as the start of the 'Beijing Spring', and the beginning of a new era of democracy for China.

This was similar to the 'Prague Spring' in Czechoslovakia in 1968. It is important to note that many other Chinese cities – such as Shanghai, Wuhan, Guangzhou and Xian – were also the scenes of demonstrations and protests. Several travelled to Beijing to record the speeches for democracy – along with music by China's main rock bands – and then returned to play them to protesters in their areas. Workers increasingly joined the students in mass demonstrations which, like the ones in the capital, called for greater political reform.

8 The People's Republic of China (1949–2005)

Splits in the CCP

The actions of the students began to lead to a split in the CCP leadership, with several now wanting to back down from Deng's uncompromising attitude. These divisions widened on 30 April, when Zhao returned from North Korea. Evidence suggests that the relationship between Deng and Zhao had been deteriorating since the start of the year, with Deng becoming increasingly suspicious of Zhao's links with pro-democracy intellectuals.

Unpopular because of his pushing of the new economic policies, and with his two sons' involvement in corruption, Zhao seems to have calculated that he was about to be dismissed. He therefore decided to support those CCP leaders who wanted compromise with the students. This put him on an unavoidable collision course with Deng.

While this struggle over what to do went on for much of May, the Democracy Movement was able to continue to spread and grow – and to organise a demonstration in Tiananmen Square, outside the headquarters of the CCP.

Tiananmen Square, May–June 1989

On his return, Zhao tried to appease the protesters, without having to use force, and suggested opening a dialogue with the student leaders. He also suggested that *The People's Daily* had gone too far in attacking the protesters – but he was very much in a minority in the Politburo. His attitude, similar to that of Hu in 1986–87, led to a growing conflict with Premier Li Peng.

On the anniversary of the May 4th Movement, 1919 – when a Chinese student protested against the World War I treaties that allowed Japan to take over German concessions in China – Zhao characterised the students' demands as 'reasonable', and urged that they be implemented in democratic fashion and by legal means. However, the majority of student leaders were no longer prepared to cooperate with sympathetic government leaders like Zhao, and instead increased their protests, holding another mass demonstration of over 60 000 in the capital, which the police were unable to control, shortly followed by another, 300 000 strong rally in Tiananmen Square. This involved students from all over China, and also several non-student groups – older intellectuals, journalists and workers.

Political developments under Deng, 1976–89

Though Zhao made no contact with the student leaders, he did support their demand for a retraction of the 26 April editorial and called for democratic negotiations with the students. But Deng – and the 'Gang of Old' (most of whom, like Deng, had been victims of the Cultural Revolution) – still refused any compromise, and managed to get the support of most of the generals of the PLA.

The hunger strike

By 13 May, the students had filled Tiananmen Square with makeshift camps. However, by then, a split in the students had begun to emerge. The split was essentially between the older graduate students who had started the Democracy Movement, and who wanted to work with leaders such as Zhao, and younger more radical ones who wanted nothing to do with the existing leadership, which they distrusted.

This split helped Deng win the upper-hand within the Party leadership. On 14 May, a group of about 300–500 students marched into the Square and, surrounded by thousands of supporters, began a hunger strike which had been called by students such as Wang Dan and Wuer Kaixi. These students belonged to the group opposed to compromise with the CCP leaders.

The hunger strikers' morale was boosted by visits by China's main rock bands, which often performed impromptu rock concerts. This merely increased the numbers of those in the Square. For the first time, government leaders made contact with student leaders, urging them to end the hunger strike – as Gorbachev was due to arrive the next day.

Gorbachev's impact

Just as Gorbachev's policies and statements since 1985 had encouraged reform communists and others in Eastern Europe (leading to an increasing reduction of communist influence and power), so too were many Chinese influenced by his ideas of *perestroika* – especially those of greater openness (*glasnost*) and democracy (*demokratizatsiya*). In the spring of 1989, it seemed that several East European satellites were moving towards ending single-party rule – this encouraged optimistic hopes among Chinese pro-democracy activists.

The students thus had no intention of calling off their protests – on the contrary, they were emboldened by the presence of world TV crews and journalists, who had arrived early to cover Gorbachev's visit to China. This visit – the first Sino-Soviet summit since 1959 and the start of the

8 The People's Republic of China (1949–2005)

split between Mao and Khrushchev – was seen as very important by the leaders of the Chinese government.

Consequently, the protests were becoming known world-wide, turning a national problem into an international embarrassment for the CCP leaders. The students also believed that the imminent arrival of the Soviet leader would tie the government's hands, and that therefore it would not carry out any repression during Gorbachev's visit.

When he arrived on 15 May, the students ignored orders to disperse, and were joined by 500 000 people. By 17 May, there were 1 million protesters in the Square (now including members of the CCP, government office workers, policemen and even PLA cadets), calling for democratic reforms and the resignation of Deng.

The protests were so huge that Deng was forced to abandon part of the official schedule. The official reception was moved to Beijing airport, and his tour of the Forbidden City and a wreath-laying ceremony in Tiananmen Square were cancelled. Gorbachev was then kept in indoor meetings until his departure for Shanghai on 18 May. All this was seen as hugely embarrassing, and it strengthened the hands of the hardliners who called for strong measures to end the protests.

On 18 May, Li Peng agreed to a televised interview with student leaders such as Wang Dan and Wuer Kaixi – including some of the hunger strikers. The students continued to raise the issues of greater democracy, and the need for the government and Party to listen to the people about what should happen next in China. However, the Politburo had already decided that there would be no real dialogue, and that no concessions would be made.

Instead, that day, the Politburo decided to declare martial law. Though apparently some other members were reluctant, they did not want to oppose the 'paramount leader', so only Zhao voted against.

Zhao's speech

On 19 May, at 4.50 am, on the day Gorbachev was due to leave China, Zhao visited the demonstrators in the Square to call on them to end their hunger strike – Figure 8.5 shows him with megaphone in hand. He also apologised – tearfully – for the actions of the Politburo, and (as Source 8.5 shows) admitted that mistakes had been made and that the students' criticisms were justified.

Political developments under Deng, 1976–89

Figure 8.5: Zhao (centre, holding the megaphone) talks to students in Tiananmen Square, 19 May 1989, in what turned out to be his last public appearance.

SOURCE 8.5

Students, we came too late. Sorry, students. Whatever you say and criticise about us is deserved. My purpose here now is not to ask for your forgiveness… You have been on a hunger strike for six days, and it's now the seventh day. You cannot go on like this… Now what is most important is to end this hunger strike. I know, you are doing this in the hope that the Party and the government will give a most satisfactory answer for what you are asking for. I feel, our channel for dialogue is open, and some problems need to be resolved through a process…

You are still young and have much time ahead of you. You should live healthily to see the day that the Four Modernisations… of China are realised… Now the situation is very dire as you all know, the Party and nation are very anxious, the whole society is worried… You mean well, and have the interests of our country at heart, but if this goes on, it will go out of control and will have various adverse effects… If you stop

8 The People's Republic of China (1949–2005)

> the hunger strike, the government will not close the door on dialogue, definitely not! What you have proposed, we can continue to discuss. It is slow, but some issues are being broached… All the vigour that you have as young people, we understand as we too were young once, we too protested and we too laid on the tracks without considering the consequences.
>
> Finally I ask again sincerely that you calmly think about what happens from now on. A lot of things can be resolved. I hope that you will end the hunger strike soon and I thank you.
>
> *Extracts from Zhao's speech, taken from: www.theasiamag.com/*

ACTIVITY

Look on YouTube to see footage of Zhao making this speech. Can you think of a prominent political figure in your own country who has personally intervened in this way in such a large protest?

Martial law

On the evening of 19 May, Li Peng broadcast a speech announcing that the government was declaring martial law, in order to deal with the 'rioting' students. PLA units were ordered to take up positions in Beijing, but did not enforce martial law. The students reacted by resuming the hunger strike, which they had only just suspended. In Beijing, local people were able to disarm these PLA, as many soldiers were sympathetic and unwilling to use force against the protesters.

On Sunday 21 May, over 1 million people protested and, on 23 May, an equally large number of protesters gathered, and many workers and citizens helped construct barricades and road blocks across streets to prevent military action. Factories went on strike and transport in Beijing was severely disrupted. Workers and students plastered walls with posters, leaflets were produced and distributed, and street-corner speeches were made.

At the same time, the Democracy Movement spread to even more towns and cities. The Standing Committee of National People's Congress declared its support for the students, and called for martial law to be repealed; while several retired PLA generals issued an Open Letter to Deng, pointing out that the PLA belonged to the people and could not 'stand in opposition to the people'.

By then, some protesters wanted to end the demonstrations altogether and disperse, as suggested by several sympathetic professors who wanted to avoid a bloody confrontation. After some serious discussions, the students decided to end the hunger strike, but to continue occupying the Square.

These developments led to serious continuing divisions over what to do, and so delayed immediate government orders to disperse the protesters from the Square. Deng himself was uncertain at first about how to deal with the students and their demands. However, when the students were joined by workers and ordinary citizens of Beijing, who then blocked the roads leading to the Square and so prevented the first wave of PLA troops from reaching the Square, his concerns increased.

Worryingly for the government, many soldiers were confused by the mass popular resistance – some soldiers had begun fraternising with the demonstrators, and responded to invitations to join the protesters in singing revolutionary songs. After discussions with student leaders, the commanders ordered their troops to withdraw to the outskirts of Beijing. At the same time, the protesters made increasing references to the corruption of Party leaders and officials. Then, between 27 and 30 May, art students built the *Goddess of Democracy and the Spirit of Liberty* as a symbol of their hopes and aims.

Their statue was erected opposite the official painting of Mao over the central gate at the north end of the Square. Because it was similar to the Statue of Liberty in New York, many commentators saw this as showing that students were asking for Western or capitalist-style liberal parliamentary democracy. However, many students were calling for socialist democracy, and these saw the statue as having greater connections with the French Revolution's demands for '*Liberty, Equality, Fraternity*' – the last two not generally seen as aspects of capitalism.

8 The People's Republic of China (1949–2005)

Figure 8.6: This photograph, entitled 'Goddess of Democracy versus Chairman Mao', was taken by an anonymous photographer and posted online in June 1989.

> **QUESTION**
>
> What message are the protestors trying to get across with statue in Figure 8.6? Why would it have angered many of the CCP leaders?

After its unveiling, the numbers in the Square itself stood at over 300 000, and as the protest continued, more and more people began to side with the pro-democracy protesters.

Repression

However, Deng and Li had at last decided to take strong action. On 29 May, many trade union and workers' leaders who had supported the protests were arrested. By the end of May, more politically reliable troops, numbering 200 000, from outside the capital and led by commanders especially appointed by the government, began to move to Beijing. Under this kind of pressure, the Democracy Movement began to crumble, and the large-scale marches and demonstrations ceased, with many students returning to their colleges.

Political developments under Deng, 1976–89

Soon, the number remaining in the Square had dropped to 5000 – most from outside Beijing. As the student activists faded away, the protests moved to workers' districts, which had been suffering from the market-based economic reforms.

Yet there was no real alliance between the workers and intellectuals. The latter had never shown much interest in the workers' grievances, and in fact, in the early days, students had actively sought to exclude workers, who they felt might be undisciplined and so give the authorities an excuse to take repressive action. So the 'Polish fear', which so worried the CCP leadership, was less of a problem than first thought.

By 2 June, new troops had surrounded the Square, and controlled the routes leading to and from it. The first actions began in the evening of 3 June, with the first shots being fired at 10.00 pm. Workers, students and others – using sticks, bricks and Molotov cocktails – did what they could to prevent the troops reaching the Square.

It was in the side streets, out of sight of the cameras, that most of the casualties were suffered, as workers in residential areas tried to prevent the tanks reaching the Square. Then, at midnight on 3–4 June, Deng finally ordered the army to 'take all necessary measures' to re-take control of the Square and arrest activists.

In full view of TV cameras, troops and tanks went into action, to clear the Square and end the demonstrations. Some tried to fight back, but most did not – however, all those who tried to remain in the Square were fired upon, and hundreds were killed (some put the figure of deaths at about 1500, while others go as high as 7000, with up to 10 000 injured).

Towards the end, last-minute discussions between the army officers and rock star Hou Dejian and literary critic Liu Xiaobo, allowed a group of protesters at the south end of the Square to leave – they did so, singing the *Internationale*, the anthem of the international communist movement. Consequently, there were fewer casualties in the Square itself. By midday on 4 June, the six-week occupation was over.

8 The People's Republic of China (1949–2005)

> **ACTIVITY**
>
> Look on YouTube for a report of the suppression, by BBC journalist, Kate Adie. There is also a video section on YouTube of Kate Adie's update and interviews with pro-democracy dissidents in 2009, 20 years after the events of 1989.
>
> Once you have watched these short clips, compare them with what you have read about the suppression of the pro-democracy demonstration, and then write a couple of paragraphs on their value and limitations. Explain how useful such reports are to historians studying the events in Tiananmen Square in June 1989.

There were also riots and resistance reported in 80 other cities. Nevertheless, the government was able to quickly suppress all the uprisings and protests.

According to the first official accounts, no civilians had been killed in the Square, but 23 students had been killed in fighting that took place in the surrounding streets. The government also claimed 150 soldiers had been killed and 5000 wounded.

Angry members of the crowd did attack and beat to death soldiers; but there were also unconfirmed reports that some troops against the repression had fired on those shooting the protesters. Later, official accounts said that fewer than 300 had been killed.

The government imposed a news blackout of the events in the Square. The official message by Deng, on 9 June was that the army had suppressed a 'counter-revolutionary rebellion' planned to spark a coup by 'misguided Party leaders'. Deng and the Party leadership condemned the student protests, and reaffirmed that the economic reforms would continue.

It has been argued that the recourse to live ammunition – rather than tear gas and water cannons – suggests the authorities wanted to make it clear to China's people that attempts to press for political democracy would not be tolerated.

Political developments under Deng, 1976–89

It is estimated by some that almost 5000 were arrested immediately after the events of 4 June; with 40 000 more arrested during June and July. By 17 July, 29 had been given quick trials and executed; some estimate that, eventually, several hundred were executed.

The vast majority of these were trade union activists who had tried to link workers' economic demands to the political demands for greater democracy. Thousands – most of them workers – were given long prison sentences. Students – many of whom had relatives in high places – were treated relatively leniently.

These conflicting statistics illustrate the confused situation that followed the events of 4 June. Yet, whatever the numbers might be, Deng clearly wanted to ensure no Solidarity-type movement would emerge in China that might stall his economic reforms. Members of the CCP known to be sympathetic to some of the demands were purged. As late as 2007, some activists remained in prison.

Many leaders of the protests – such as Fang Lizhi, Wang Dan, Wucr Kaixi, and Chai Ling – managed to avoid arrest, despite being on a 'most wanted' list of 21 sought by the authorities, and eventually were able to escape abroad, where they continued the Democracy Movement's struggle.

Chai Ling (b. 1966):

Chai was one of the main women leaders of the demonstrations in Tiananmen Square, and helped organise the hunger strikes towards the end of the demonstrations. Her parents were both members of the CCP, as she was. However, in 1987, she began to get involved in the demonstrations calling for greater democracy. Known as the 'general commander', she became one of the top 21 dissidents sought by the Chinese government after the Tiananmen Square massacre. She later became a Christian.

The People's Republic of China (1949–2005)

Theory of Knowledge

History, ethics and utilitarianism:

When E. H. Carr came to the end of writing his massive history of the early years of the Russian Revolution, he concluded by saying:

'the danger is not that we shall draw a veil over the enormous blots on the record of the Revolution, over its cost in human suffering, over the crimes committed in its name. The danger is that we shall be tempted to forget altogether, and to pass over in silence, its immense achievement.'

Quoted in Ali, T., (ed), 1984, The Stalinist Legacy: its Impact on Twentieth Century World Politics, Harmondsworth, Penguin Books, p 9.)

How far should the ethics of utilitarianism be applied to what happened in China under Deng in the period 1976–89 – and to what Mao achieved in China in the period 1949–76?

World reaction

Yet, despite the violence in the Square, and the repression that followed, after initial first-reactions of shock and condemnation, most democratic Western states soon began to ignore the repression and the abuses of human rights. Keen to get involved in the rapidly expanding Chinese economy, such countries wanted 'business as usual' to resume as soon as possible.

While foreign investment was halted for a time, and cultural exchanges were suspended, these were resumed relatively quickly. However, organisations such as Amnesty International did take up the cause of pro-democracy activists imprisoned by Deng's regime, and those sent to labour camps for *laogai* (reform through labour).

Political developments under Deng, 1976–89

Figure 8.7: A cartoon by Nicholas Garland, which was published in *The Independent*, a British newspaper, on 16 June 1989. The man standing in front of the tank represents Deng Xiaoping trying to prevent the truth being told about the massacre in Beijing.

Why did the pro-democracy movement fail?

Part of the reason for the failure of the movement was that the organisers were not united in what they wanted. Beyond more freedoms, and reform of the Party, there was little to unite on. This made it difficult for sympathetic members of the Party and government to negotiate with them. There was also the problem that among the protesters there were groups that wanted a violent confrontation with the authorities, who therefore had no wish to discuss and agree some compromise. The lack of unity and an agreed list of demands made it easier for Deng to claim that the repression was necessary to prevent China descending into chaos.

8 The People's Republic of China (1949–2005)

The aftermath of the 'Beijing Spring'

One early result was the dismissal, on 24 June, of Zhao (like Hu before him) as General-Secretary of the CCP, for his support for the students' demands (see Section 8.2) – he was replaced by one of Deng's loyal supporters – Jiang Zemin.

In addition, the events in Tiananmen Square also saw increased criticism of Deng and his reforms from within the CCP leadership. Those who had been unhappy at the move away from Maoism now criticised his privatisation policies, and were even able to block – for a time – further investment in the SEZs. Later that year, Deng resigned as chair of the Central Military Commission, but he remained the guiding light in Chinese politics behind the scene until his death in 1997, aged 92. By 1994, he had made something of a comeback and successfully challenged his 'conservative' opponents – and his economic policies were soon restored.

For a time, in the period immediately following Mao's death, it had not been clear in what direction China was likely to go. But by 1989, the signs were pretty clear – under Deng, there would be economic modernisation and liberalisation. However, it was also clear that there would be no 'Fifth Modernisation' – i.e. no political democratisation or liberalisation. Instead, the Chinese Communist Party – unlike almost all of those in Eastern Europe – was determined to retain control. Thus Chinese political and intellectual life after 1989 was markedly more repressive than it had been during most of the 1980s.

Persecution of dissidents was harsher, and the activities of the secret police were stepped up. Prison sentences for protest became more common, and there was much more censorship of newspapers, books and journals and films.

KEY CONCEPTS ACTIVITY

Significance: Write a couple of paragraphs to explain the significance of CCP individuals such as Hu Yaobang and Zhao Ziyang on the emerging pro-democracy movement's demands for greater democracy during 1988–89. Then draw up a list of other factors that also influenced this movement.

Political Developments under Deng, 1976–89

Paper 3 exam practice

Question

Examine the reasons for Deng's decision to disperse the protestors in Tiananmen Square in June 1989? **[15 marks]**

Skill

Writing a conclusion to your essay

Examiner's tips

Provided you have carried out all the steps recommended so far, it should be relatively easy to write one or two concluding paragraphs.

For this question, you will need to cover the following possible reasons:

- the opposition that Deng still faced within the leadership of the CCP
- the impact of his economic policies on Chinese workers' living standards, and on job opportunities for graduates
- the growth of opposition from both students and lecturers within higher education
- the extent to which the protests were being reported worldwide.

This question requires you to consider a range of different reasons/factors, and to support your analysis with precise and specific supporting knowledge – so avoid generalisations.

Also, such a question, which is asking for an evaluation/analysis of several reasons, implicitly expects you to come to some kind of judgement about which reason(s) was/were most important.

Common mistakes

Sometimes, candidates simply re-hash in their conclusion what they have written earlier – making the examiner read the same things twice! Generally, concluding paragraphs should be relatively short: the aim should be to come to a judgement/conclusion that is clearly based on what has already been written. If possible, a short but relevant quotation is a good way to round off an argument.

8 The People's Republic of China (1949–2005)

Remember to refer to the simplified Paper 3 mark scheme in Chapter 10.

Sample student conclusion

As I have shown, it is difficult to come to a single conclusion about why Deng decided to use military force to disperse the protestors in Tiananmen Square in June 1989. One important factor, I think, was the fact that, because of Gorbachev's visit, the CCP leadership were embarrassed by the large demonstrations which, they felt, showed their political weakness. This was made worse by the fact that, because reporters and television crews from around the world were present for Gorbachev's visit, the protests were being seen across the world.

More important, though, was the fact that the impact of several of his economic reforms which, by 1989, had led growing discontent among many Chinese workers – because of rising unemployment, worse working conditions and loss of social benefits for, I don't think this – of itself – was a major consideration. However, he was certainly worried by the fact that, from about 1987, many of these increasingly discontented workers began joining Democracy Movement students in their protests for greater political rights.

This was certainly a worry as – on their own – the CCP leadership had been able to control earlier student protests. But, with workers on the side of the students, there was the risk of a much wider protest movement. That this was an important factor is shown by the fact that, during the repression which followed, it was mainly workers who were either executed or given extremely long prison sentences. Equally worrying was the fact that, before the army was sent in to crush the protests, there were several cases where soldiers had fraternised with the protestors and even showed sympathy with their demands.

However, the main reason for his decision was that there was also a split emerging within the CCP leadership – not just about what to do as regards the protests, but also about whether his economic policies should be continued in their present form. Chen Yun was just one of those who'd begun to argue that the market mechanisms of Deng's economic reforms should be reduced. I think it was this – in conjunction with the worrying evidence of increasing worker participation in the protests (and signs of support among some of the military units) – that ultimately led him to declare martial law, order military action and carry out a violent repression of the protestors. It was this combination of reasons which ultimately lay behind his decision to make it clear that, under him, China would have no 'Fifth Modernisation'.

Political Developments under Deng, 1976–89

> **EXAMINER COMMENT**
> This is a good conclusion as it briefly pulls together the main threads of the argument (without simply repeating/summarising them), and then also makes a clear judgement. In addition, there is an intelligent final comment which rounds off the whole conclusion – and no doubt the core of the essay – in a memorable way.

Activity

In this chapter, the focus is on writing a useful conclusion. So, using the information from this chapter, and any other sources of information available to you, write concluding paragraphs for at least two of the following Practice Paper 3 questions. Remember – to do this, you will need to do full plans for the questions you choose.

Paper 3 practice questions

1. Discuss the reasons for, and the results of, Deng's promotion of a 'loosening' of political controls in the period 1976–79?

2. Evaluate the reasons why political unrest affected China for large parts of the 1980s.

3. 'The main reason why the Democracy Movement was defeated by the end of 1989 was because it was divided into several different factions.' To what extent do you agree with this statement?

4. Examine the impact of Deng's economic reforms on the growing political opposition in China during the late 1980s.

5. Examine the ways in which Deng attempted to retain the CCP's political monopoly in the period 1980–89.

9 Developments in China 1989–2005

Developments in China 1989–2005

Introduction

By 1989, Deng's economic policies had considerably transformed China. However, the Tiananmen protests of 1989 led to a debate within the leadership of the CCP over what direction China should take. Even the 'centre' of the Party began to divide along 'conservative' left and 'liberal' right lines, with Li Peng (a hardliner who had pushed for the PLA to suppress the protests) heading the left. He and his supporters began attempts to slow down Deng's economic reforms and, instead, to give earlier socialist aims greater prominence.

Also, despite the many prestigious construction projects in Beijing and Shanghai, many serious political and economic problems remained. Large sections of rural China still remained to be developed and, especially in the western regions, poverty and limited cultural development posed serious threats to social stability and to the rule of China's political élites.

Figure 9.1: Chinese leaders at The CCP's Sixteenth Party Congress, 2002. This Congress marked the retirement of Jiang Zemin, Li Peng and Zhu Ronjgi, with Hu confirmed as 'paramount leader'.

9 The People's Republic of China (1949–2005)

TIMELINE

1989 Nov: Jiang Zemin replaces Deng as chair of the CMC

1990 Sep: Provincial leaders oppose attempts by Chen Yun and Li Peng to slow down Deng's economic reforms

1991 Mar: Zhu Rongji becomes vice-premier

Dec: Collapse of the Soviet Union

1992 Jan: Start of Deng's 'Southern Tour'

Mar: Politburo endorses Deng's reforms

Oct: 14th Congress of CCP endorses Deng's reforms

1993 Mar: Jiang Zemin becomes president

Jul: Jiang launches campaign against corruption

1997 Jul: Britain returns Hong Kong to China

Sep: 15th Congress of CCP

1998 Mar: Zhu Rongji becomes premier

1999 May: US bomb Chinese embassy in Belgrade

Dec: Portugal returns Macao to China

2000 Feb: Jiang's 'Three Represents'

Jun: Zhengzhou strike

Oct: CCP decide Jiang, Zhu and Li to retire in 2002; US grants China PNTRT status

2001 Dec: China joins WTO

2002 Feb: US president Bush visits China

Mar: Liaoyang and Daqing strikes

Nov: 16th. Congress of CCP; Hu Jintao becomes general-secretary

2003 Mar: Hu becomes president

2005 Nov: Wen Jiabao visits Harbin after river polluted

KEY QUESTIONS

- How did China's politics change after 1989?
- What were the main economic developments after 1989?
- How far have China's leaders created a 'Harmonious Society'?
- How did China's relations with the rest of the world develop after 1989?
- To what extent was China still communist by 2005?

Developments in China 1989–2005

Overview

- After the Tiananmen protests of 1989, the 'conservative' left of the CCP – headed by Chen Yun and Li Peng – tried to slow down Deng's reforms and to place more emphasis on socialist principles and central planning. Their determination was strengthened by the collapse of the Soviet Union in December 1991.
- However, Deng and the 'liberal' right fought back and, in January 1992, Deng began his 'Southern Tour' to gain support of provincial leaders for his economic reforms.
- As a result, in March 1992, his policies were endorsed by the Politburo and, in October, by the 14th Party Congress. In March 1993, Jiang Zemin – one of Deng's supporters – became president, and the influence of the left declined under this 'third generation' of leaders.
- From 1993 onwards, Deng's economic reforms were speeded up, and China rapidly developed a market-based economy. However, although China's economy expanded greatly, various problems – such as growing inequalities, unemployment, environmental pollution and corruption – began to cause social unrest.
- Nonetheless, the market reforms continued: from March 1998, these were largely implemented by the new premier, Zhu Rongji. In December 2001, China's growing connection with the international economy was strengthened when it became a member of the World Trade Organization (WTO).
- In 2002, Jiang and Zhu retired, and a 'fourth generation' of leaders took over, headed by Hu Jintao. While China had become the second largest economy in the world – and was predicted to overtake the US in the next 20 years or so – historians are divided over whether China remains a communist country.

9 The People's Republic of China (1949–2005)

9.1 How did China's politics change after 1989?

Deng and those 'second generation' leaders who remained in power after 1989 were deeply concerned about the implications of the collapse of communism in Eastern Europe – and by the political unrest among China's students and workers during the 'Beijing Spring' of 1989, which had culminated in the Tiananmen protests. Two years later, with the collapse of the Soviet Union in 1991, China's former mentor and economic model was gone.

These events of 1989–91 heightened a debate that had been taking place among China's leaders since 1981. This was about the direction China should take, both politically and economically. Immediately after 1989, the CCP was divided on whether to move away from the economic reforms that had improved the lives of many Chinese but had also impoverished others, or to continue with those economic reforms that some saw as having precipitated the political crisis.

The 'conservative' left of the Party blamed the unrest of 1989 on the social problems – such as unemployment and economic inequalities – which had appeared following China's 'socialist market' reforms. However, to many within the 'liberal' right of the CCP, the collapse of communism in Eastern Europe and the Soviet Union – and the political and social unrest in China – were the result of political weakness and economic stagnation.

As explained in Source 9.1, the right eventually managed to reassert its dominance in 1992, and decided that, to preserve political stability and the rule of the CCP, it would be necessary to do three things:

- consolidate the Party's authority over the military
- develop closer links between the Party and the growing business sector
- establish strong economic growth.

Developments in China 1989–2005

> **SOURCE 9.1**
>
> The year 1989 in China was marked by the defeat of a group of reformists in the Communist Party leadership and the shattering of hopes of continuing political liberalization that were held by many. In retrospect, it is clear that 1989 also marked the end of one era of cautiously managed economic reform. Economic reform, as such, did not die, but when reforms resumed in earnest around 1992, they took on a new form, more resolute and in some ways harsher. The new reform pattern reinforced state and Communist Party interests, while exposing some social groups to major losses. Income grew dramatically, but inequality increased and economic life became more precarious. The post-1989 model of economic reform was one of concentrated power wielded more effectively and led to a remarkable recovery in the power of the Chinese state.
>
> Bandelj, N. and Solinger, D. J. (eds), 2012. **Socialism Vanquished, Socialism Challenged: Eastern Europe and China, 1989–2009.** Oxford. Oxford University Press. p.125

Political divisions before 1992

Even before 1989, a quiet struggle had been taking place for some time between Deng and Chen Yun over implementing the economic reforms. Chen was seen as a 'conservative' leftist, and Deng as a 'liberal' rightist as regards economic policies. Chen had initially supported Deng's policy of introducing 'market mechanisms' – though only as a way of supplementing state planning in order to modernise China's economy. As head of the Economic and Financial Commission – and thus in charge of the detailed planning of Deng's reforms – Chen had played an important role in ensuring that these early reforms were successful.

The campaign against 'bourgeois liberalisation'

However, from as early as 1980–81, Chen had begun to raise concerns about the economic reforms being implemented in relation to industry and the Special Economic Zones (see Chapter 7 and Section 9.3). Although appointed by Deng to head the Central Advisory Commission in 1982, Chen's growing concerns led him to resign his Party – though not his administrative – posts. From 1980 to 1991, Chen and his supporters mounted a campaign against what they saw as

9

The People's Republic of China (1949–2005)

dangerous capitalist-influenced social and political ideas and trends that were linked to some of the economic reforms.

In 1985, Chen warned that 'bourgeois liberalisation' attitudes were drifting from economics and were undermining political ideas and values. He felt this was weakening the Party's commitment to China remaining socialist, and argued for a determined struggle against 'mistakes' which he felt were counter to 'communist ideals and ethics', and for the dominance of the planned economy over the market economy. The left were also concerned that too much power had been devolved to the provinces, and believed this prevented central government from overseeing the national economy. As a result, Chen was increasingly seen as one of the 'conservative' left opponents of Deng's reforms.

> **QUESTION**
>
> What did Chen and the 'conservative' left mean by 'bourgeois liberalisation', and why were they concerned about this trend?

One of Deng's protégé, Zhao, had begun to replace Chen as the person pushing forward economic reform. Although Zhao frequently consulted with Chen on certain aspects, the main direction of Deng's economic policies was maintained. By 1986, it had seemed as though Deng's economic reforms were well-established; and that his supporters, Hu and Zhao, would carry them through to completion. Though Deng had resigned from most of his official posts by then, this had not meant the end of his influence. In fact, he was often consulted, and his suggestions were respected and mostly followed.

The 'conservative' leftist counter-offensive, 1989–91

However, political events just before and after the Tiananmen Square democracy protests of 1989 (see Chapter 8) led to the fall of Deng's two closest protégés. In January 1987, Hu had been forced by the 'conservative' left to resign as general-secretary of the CCP because of his limited support of the growing pro-democracy movement. Zhao, who continued as premier, took over that post as well. Then, in November 1987, Zhao himself had been replaced as premier by the

Developments in China 1989–2005

more 'conservative' Li Peng. Finally, immediately after the suppression of the Tiananmen Square protests in June 1989, Zhao – who had opposed the use of force to suppress the demonstration – was also forced to resign from his general-secretary post and was put under house arrest. The criticisms made of him were, in many ways, seen as criticisms of Deng's economic policies.

While it was clear that Deng's prestige declined after Tiananmen, he was still seen as the 'core' of the Party, and was determined to use his core status to maintain his influence. In particular, he continued to stress that the only way to develop China's economy was to marketise and join the international economy. When Deng resigned as chairman of the Central Military Commission in November 1989, he ensured his place was taken by **Jiang Zemin**.

> ### Jiang Zemin (b. 1926):
> Jiang trained as an engineer, and his political career began in the 1950s. In 1986, he was appointed mayor of Shanghai and, in 1989, following the Tiananmen Square protests, Deng ensured he replaced Zhao Ziyang as general-secretary of the CCP. In the 1990s, he became the 'paramount leader' and maintained strong central control. Though he retired as general-secretary in 2002, he retained some leadership posts until 2005, and continued to influence developments for some time after that.

Although Jiang was another of Deng's protégés, and had been promoted at his suggestion, he was seen as centrist rather than a rightist and, at first, seemed to favour using state power to set limits to the 'free market', and to help those not benefitting from the market's operations. These ideas were close to some of Chen's criticisms, and it appeared that the left of the CCP would succeed in slowing down Deng's reforms. Jiang was also loosely associated with the prime minister, Li Peng – seen as on the left of the leading group – who had been appointed to that post in 1987. In the summer of 1990, Chen and Li were able to get these ideas about increasing central control into the draft of the Eighth Five-Year Plan.

However, in September 1990, provincial Party leaders – most of whom supported Deng's economic reforms, and did not want renewed central controls as these would limit their powers in the regions – voiced strong opposition to these changes. Deng and his supporters were encouraged

9 The People's Republic of China (1949–2005)

by the responses of the provincial leaders, which strengthened their determination to counter the leftists, and to push ahead with the market-oriented economic reforms. In the spring of 1991, Deng used his influence to secure the appointment of Zhu Rongji as vice-premier – although this was balanced by the left's ability to get one of their supporters appointed as another vice-premier.

Initially, though, developments in the Soviet Union in 1991 – the failed coup against Gorbachev in August, and then the collapse of the Soviet Union in December – seemed to strengthen the hand of the left, which emphasised the need to ensure a socialist course and the dominant role of public ownership. Thus, for a time, Deng's political influence declined further.

> ### Zhu Rongji (b. 1928):
>
> Zhu's family were intellectuals and wealthy landowners but, in 1949, he joined the CCP. He graduated with a degree in electrical engineering and, from 1952 to 1958, held senior positions in the State Planning Commission. He criticised Mao's economic policies in 1957, and was expelled from the party and his posts as a 'rightist'. During the Cultural Revolution, he was purged again as a 'capitalist roader'. After Mao's death and the rise of Deng, Zhu was rehabilitated and allowed to re-join the party.
>
> In 1988, he replaced Jiang Zemin as mayor of Shanghai, where he oversaw rapid economic development – though often clashing with Li Peng. In 1990, he moved to Beijing and, in 1998, was appointed as prime minister by Jiang. His main role was to push forward China's economic reforms – although he saved some of the biggest State Owned Enterprises; smaller ones were allowed to go bankrupt. As a result, millions of workers lost their jobs and the social benefits of their 'iron rice bowl'. Zhu also took the lead in China's bid to join the World Trade Organization, and oversaw significant privatisation within China, assuming this would eventually solve the unemployment problem. He also ran strong campaigns against corruption.

Developments in China 1989–2005

> **ACTIVITY**
>
> Carry out some additional research on economic and political developments in the Soviet Union in 1991. Then, with a partner, produce a spider diagram to show the links between events in the Soviet Union and the impact these had on the debate over economic policy within the CCP.

Deng's 'Southern Tour', January–February 1992

However, in January 1992, Deng began what became known as his 'Southern Tour'. This lasted just over a month, during which he visited the Shenzen SEZ and other key areas of southern China. For Deng, his 'Tour' was a political mission in defence of his economic reform policies. It was intended as a signal that China should – and would – continue to move away from a centrally planned economy, and instead embrace a market-based system. It was, above all, part of a counter-attack against the 'conservative' leftists – although these blocked immediate press coverage of his visits and speeches, by the time he had finished his 'Tour', he had persuaded provincial leaders to support him on the need to press on with his reforms.

His 'Tour' had an immediate impact on the debate within the leadership of the CCP. At the end of February 1992, the CC issued a summary of the key points of his speeches, which was then issued to all Party members. Then, in March 1992, Jiang convened a meeting of the Politburo which fully endorsed Deng's reforms. At a subsequent meeting of the National People's Congress, the vice-chair of the CMC declared that the PLA supported Deng's economic reforms.

These successes pushed the left into making some concessions, and encouraged Jiang to swing decisively in favour of stepping up the speed of the market-based economic reforms favoured by the right. These moves made it clear that the overall influence of Deng's 'Tour' had succeeded in settling the direction of economic reform along the lines he favoured. This was confirmed in October by the Fourteenth Party Congress which endorsed the goal of creating a 'socialist market economic system', and warned of the need to guard against 'leftist' tendencies. Thus, by 1992, the main aim of Deng and what became known as the 'second generation' seemed to have been achieved –

9 The People's Republic of China (1949–2005)

the maintenance of strong authoritarian political control, and the implementation of further 'socialist market' reforms in order to build a strong economy.

> **KEY CONCEPTS QUESTION**
>
> **Significance:** What was the importance of Deng's 'Southern Tour' for the subsequent direction of China's economic policies?

Political leaderships 1992–2005

After 1992, with his economic reform programme secure, Deng played less of a role in Chinese politics. Before he died in February 1997, political discourse had begun to use the term 'political generations' to classify successive leadership groups, and was particularly linked to ideas about change and continuity.

The 'first generation' – applied retrospectively – were those leaders who had been prominent when Mao was in power, such as Liu Shaoqi, Peng Dehuai, Lin Biao and Zhou Enlai. The 'second generation' were those who held sway under Deng, following the death of Mao and the defeat of the 'Gang of Four'. These included Chen Yun, Hu Yaobang and Zhao Ziyang. From 1992 to 2005, two further distinct 'generations' of CCP leaders exercised power.

Jiang Zemin and the 'Third Generation' 1992–2003

The rule of Jiang Zemin, who had replaced Zhao Ziyang as Party secretary in 1989, really began in March 1993 when he was elected State Chairman (president) of the PRC. Since 1989, he had also been chair of the Central Military Commission – an extremely important post, which ensured ultimate Party authority over the military. His position was further strengthened in 1993, when Zhu Rongji was appointed as deputy prime minister.

In September 1994, the Fourth Plenum of CC for the first time recognised Jiang as the core of the 'third generation' leaders. At the same time, three of his supporters – who tended to support a more centrist line than Zhu's – were promoted. From then on, Jiang tried to steer a middle course between the left and the right, both of which voiced criticisms of his approach.

Developments in China 1989–2005

By the mid 1990s, Jiang – like Deng – had concluded that the lesson of the collapse of the Soviet Union in 1991 was that the Party needed to provide China's people with substantial material gains if its political control of China was to be maintained. Deng's death in 1997 – and the standing down of Li Peng as prime minister in March 1998, which allowed Zhu to take over as premier – further strengthened Jiang's hand. Although Li Peng became chairman of the National People's Congress in 1999, his position was undermined in 2000 when the vice-chair of the NPC, who was one of his protégés, was executed for corruption.

Like all previous leaders, Jiang's position was also strengthened by using his role as head of the military. He used this position to bolster his support among the military leaders by ensuring extra funding was made available for the modernisation of all branches of China's military forces.

Jiang used his power to ensure that China continued with Deng's economic reforms – and to eliminate any signs of dissent. In November 1998, the new China Democracy Party was crushed and its leaders arrested. The new Falun Gong religion – a mixture of Buddhist and Daoist teachings, along with qigong exercises – was also ruthlessly suppressed. However, although Jiang appeared to have the same status previously enjoyed by Deng, his personal authority and his power-base within the Party were not as extensive as Deng's had been.

Jiang's 'Three Represents'

Although Jiang's administration maintained stability and economic growth, his 'Three Represents' theory – first announced in February 2000 – was portrayed as being as politically important as Marxism-Leninism, the Thoughts of Mao Zedong, and Deng Xiaoping Theory. It was meant to justify his policy of admitting senior people from the business community as members of the Party. Before then, Party membership had been restricted to workers, peasants and the military.

The 'Three Represents' also changed the ideological aim of the CCP from '*protecting the interests of workers and peasants*' to that of the '*overwhelming majority of the people*'. Not surprisingly, those within the Party who remained concerned about the political implications of the economic reforms saw this as evidence of betrayal of communist principles. Although the theory was approved by the CC in October 2000, and nominally remained operative during his rule, it was quietly dropped when his period of office effectively ended in November 2003.

9 The People's Republic of China (1949–2005)

In October 2000, the main business of the CCP's CC was the adoption of the Tenth Five-Year Plan which, in particular, would focus on the relatively impoverished western regions. However, it was also concerned with organising a smooth political transition from Jiang and his team to a 'fourth generation' leadership. It decided that Jiang, Zhu Rongji and Li Peng (chair of the National People's Congress) would retire within the next two years. In fact, at the Fifteenth Party Congress in September 1997, Jiang had indicated he would retire after completing another five-year term. Though it was clear he wished to remain as 'paramount leader' beyond 2002, most Party leaders were not prepared to see him elevated to the ranks of Mao Zedong and Deng Xiaoping.

Hu Jintao and the 'Fourth-Generation Leadership'

The new 'fourth generation' leaders in 2003 were: **Hu Jintao** (vice-president), **Wen Jiabao** (vice-premier) and **Zeng Qinghong** (head of the CCP's Organisation Department). These new leaders had emerged formally at the Sixteenth Congress of the CCP in November 2002. By then, the Party was in the throes of dropping some of its ideological commitments, as well as pushing ahead with economic reforms and maintaining the Party's strictly authoritarian political control. This group remained in power until 2012, when they were succeeded by Xi Jinping, the 'paramount leader' of the 'fifth generation'.

Hu Jintao (b. 1942):

Hu studied hydroelectric engineering and, in 1984, became general secretary of the Communist Youth League. From 1988 to 1989, he was provincial party secretary in Tibet, where he imposed martial law to end political unrest. In 1992, he became a Politburo member and a member of the CC. In 1998, he became vice-president of China and, in 1999, he was appointed as vice-chairman of the Central Military Commission.

By 2002, he had emerged as Jiang's heir apparent, and succeeded him as general-secretary of the CCP later that year. The following year, he was elected president of China and in 2004, he took over as chair of the Central Military Commission. During 2012–13, he stepped down from his positions, and his place was taken by Xi Jinping, China's current 'fifth generation' leader.

Developments in China 1989–2005

> **Wen Jiabao (b. 1942):**
>
> Wen was trained in geology and engineering and, from 1985 to 1993, moved to Beijing where he became deputy-chief and then chief of the CCP's General Office. Although he was linked to Zhao Ziyang, and had accompanied him when Ziyang had visited the Tiananmen Square protestors in 1989, he managed to retain his posts. In 1993, he became a full member of the CC's Secretariat and, in 1997, he became a member of the Politburo. In 1998, he became vice-premier under Zhu Rongji; from 2003 to 2013, he was premier, and was one of the main figures pushing China's economic reforms. In particular, he tried to close the gap between the most- and least-developed regions in China.

> **Zeng Qinghong (b. 1939):**
>
> Zeng studied engineering and, in 1960, joined the CCP; during the Cultural revolution, he was one of those 'sent down' to do manual labour. Following the 1989 democracy protests, he became deputy chief of the party's Central Office, and was a close ally of Jiang Zemin and his 'Shanghai Clique', helping him consolidate his power. In 1999, he became chief of the Organisation Department, a post he held until 2002. In that year, he became a member of the CC and the Politburo – in 2003, as part of the gradual distancing of the CCP leadership from aspects of Marxism, he ordered Party meetings not to sing or play *The Internationale.* Although he retained considerable influence after Jiang's retirement, it was Hu Jintao, not he, who succeeded to Jiang's posts. In 2008, his reputation was tarnished by his son's corruption; and, in 2013, he was himself investigated concerning various corruption charges.

The two most dominant leaders were Hu, who became president, and Wen, who became prime minister. Although Zeng was not in such a powerful position, he was seen by many as a likely successor to Hu as president. Despite this seeming to sideline Wen, he in fact consolidated his position by associating himself with populist causes such as the reduction of poverty, stamping out corruption, and promoting environmental protection. However, in October 2007, Zeng unexpectedly lost his posts at the Seventeenth Congress of the CCP, following the eventual complete retirement of his patron, Jiang Zemin.

9 The People's Republic of China (1949–2005)

Hu – like previous Party leaders – realised the importance of maintaining Party control of the military. Thus, in 2004, when Jiang reluctantly retired as chair of the Central Military Commission, Hu moved quickly to strengthen his ties to senior military officers. He personally promoted several to the rank of general, and was frequently photographed at PLA functions and exercises – often wearing the 'Mao jacket' rather than his usual Western-style suit.

Figure 9.2: Hu (R), with PLA Garrison Chief Wang Jitang, inspecting PLA troops stationed in Hong Kong, which had been returned to China in 1997.

QUESTION
How did Hu strengthen his support among the PLA after 2004?

Hu, continuing a process begun by Jiang, also strengthened the CCP's links to the increasingly important business class in China. He seemed a cautious politician – but one determined to maintain the political authority of the Party. He also stressed his support for the 'one-China principle', and the aim of a peaceful reunification with Taiwan.

Developments in China 1989–2005

When he took office, Wen was seen as a rather dull, though very efficient, functionary. He had previously worked with Hu Yaobang, Zhao Ziyang and Jiang Zemin. Yet, despite having gone with Zhao to visit the hunger-striking students in Tiananmen Square in 1989, he had not been purged.

His support for closing the wealth gap, ending corruption, promoting openness and the environment made him quite popular. For instance, in November 2005, he visited Harbin to see what had been done following the pollution of the Songhua River – and accused officials for not having acted quickly enough and warned them against attempting any cover-up. He then went on record to say that the protection of the environment and public health was vital.

Figure 9.3: Premier Wen Jiabao visiting Harbin, 26 November 2005, after the pollution of the river following an explosion at a chemical plant in neighbouring Jilin Province on 13 November.

9 The People's Republic of China (1949–2005)

9.2 What were the main economic developments after 1989?

It was the continuing struggle over economic directions that led Deng, from January-February 1992, to undertake what became known as his 'Southern Tour'. The purpose was to overcome resistance to his economic reforms from 'leftists' who felt they had gone too far. Deng's aim was to defeat this opposition, and to ensure that there was sufficient support for the acceleration of these policies. Such opposition had become more obvious which from 1987 to 1991 – and Deng wished to ensure his ideas of creating a 'socialist' market economy remained in force.

In March 1992, the Politburo supported Deng's call for the speeding up of his economic reforms. As a result, in September 1992, Li Peng, the prime minister – who had been one of those attempting to slow down the pace of economic reform – toured the northwest of China, to encourage trade with the newly independent republics of former Soviet Central Asia.

From 1994, with the deaths of many of the Chen Yun camp – and Chen's own serious illness and death in 1995 – Deng's reforms seemed secure at last. This has led to some observers referring to the period from 1994 to Deng's death in 1997 as the 'Later Deng period'.

Economic developments in the 'Later Deng period'

After 1976, the state had progressively retreated from direct management of the economy. In 1978, most prices had been controlled by central government but, by the mid 1990s, the state controlled only a few prices, and over 60% of the economy was market-orientated.

Developments in China 1989–2005

Industry: the move from state- to private-owned

By 1995, considerable headway had been made in abolishing state-run enterprises. Although almost 34% of industries remained in government hands, 37% were classified as collectives, while 29% of enterprises (i.e. 25 million businesses) were privately owned and operated.

By 1996, China's State Statistical Bureau reported that 1 in 12 Chinese workers were employed in these private enterprises, which produced China's first multi-millionaires (up to 5% of private owners had incomes over 10 million yuan). By then, privately run enterprises were accounting for 14.6% of China's GDP. The state-run enterprises, which employed over 60% of China's urban workforce produced less than half of GDP. Even official statistics pointed out how the true number of private enterprises was 'hidden' – with most TVEs being, in reality, private enterprises. These changes had a big impact on the pattern of urban employment, as shown by Figure 9.4.

Figure 9.4: A graph showing changes in the share of urban employment, from state-owned enterprises to joint or private firms.

Adapted from: Bandelj, N. and Solinger, D. J. (eds), 2012. **Socialism Vanquished, Socialism Challenged: Eastern Europe and China, 1989–2009.** Oxford. Oxford University Press. p 222

9 The People's Republic of China (1949–2005)

> **QUESTION**
>
> How did the move from state to private employment affect the living and living standards of most urban employees?

By 1998, there were over 1 million private enterprises, employing over 17 million people (see Figure 9.5).

Year	Number	Employees (million)	Registered capital (billion Yuan)	Retail sales (billion Yuan)
1989	90,581	1,60	8.4	3.4
1990	98,141	1,70	9.5	4.3
1991	107,843	1,84	12.3	5.7
1992	139,633	2,32	22.1	9.1
1993	237,919	3,73	68.1	19.0
1994	432,240	6,48	144.8	51.3
1995	654,531	9,56	262.2	100.6
1996	819,252	11,70	375.2	145.9
1997	960,726	13,50	514.0	185.5
1998	1,200,978	17,10	719.8	305.9

Figure 9.5: Growth of Registered Private Enterprises, 1989–98.
Adapted from Fewsmith, J. *China since Tiananmen: the Politics of Transition.* Cambridge University Press. pp.173

> **QUESTION**
>
> How far does the evidence shown in Figures 9.4 and 9.5 suggest that, by 2005, China had ceased to be communist?

This new system was referred to by the Chinese government as 'socialism with Chinese characteristics'. But many outside – and some internal – observers saw it as an 'authoritarian capitalism' in all but name. While some aspects during the 1990s remained subject to some government controls – such as banking and internal trade – enterprises were increasingly free to expand and develop new products and markets.

Developments in China 1989–2005

Foreign trade and investment

Under Deng, foreign trade had – along with the quadrupling of the size of the Chinese economy in the same period – also increased greatly: from $38 billion in 1978, to $300 billion by 1997 (accounting for approximately 40% of domestic production). By then, foreign capital accounted for approximately 20% of all investment in fixed assets (factories and industrial plant) in China, while foreign-invested enterprises accounted for 39% of China's exports.

China also witnessed an increasing number of 'joint venture' enterprises that involved foreign investments working in partnership with Chinese public agencies. By the time of Deng's death in 1997, China was experiencing rapid economic reform under tight political control. The SEZs in particular continued to draw in foreign direct investment from Western multi-national corporations eager to take advantage of China's relatively low-paid workers.

Changes in agriculture

During the 1990s, the number of agricultural workers steadily declined as the expanding industrial economy created more employment opportunities. At the beginning of the new economic reforms, approximately 70% of Chinese workers were employed in agriculture or related industries. By 1995, this had dropped to less than 50%. As a result, the urban population grew significantly during the 1990s, and some parts of China experienced a 'feminisation of agriculture', as young men sought seasonal or permanent work in the cities, with women taking their place in agricultural work.

Many young women also went to the towns – though their work was usually low-paid factory work. Women were also more readily exploited – for instance, by employing them on short-time contracts which meant the private employers didn't have to provide them with the benefits to which long-term employees were entitled. As there were so many seeking work, any who protested were quickly and easily replaced.

Growing inequalities

All this led to increasing disparities between urban and rural areas of China, and a growing poverty gap. Most of the economic growth in the 1990s was in the urban areas in the east and south of China, and especially along the coast. While many working in urban centres benefitted from a more prosperous and modern lifestyle, rural incomes

9 The People's Republic of China (1949–2005)

improved only slowly. On average, urban workers had double the income of those still working in rural areas. Such areas also often lacked adequate electricity supplies – even elementary schools and healthcare were poor compared to urban centres.

In addition, the growing disparities between provinces and regions – and the lessening of central economic controls resulting from the move to a more market-orientated economy – have led some observers to speculate of the possible break-up of China. Such potential developments are exacerbated by ethnic tensions in those areas – such as Tibet, Xinjiang and Inner Mongolia – which lie on China's borders. The break-up of the Soviet Union in 1991 into separate states suggests that such a development is possible.

> **KEY CONCEPTS ACTIVITY**
>
> **Change and continuity:** Carry out further research on the economic developments that took place during the 'Later Deng period'. Compare your findings with the main economic policies followed from 1976 to 1992. Then write a couple of paragraphs to show how the policies in those two periods were (a) similar and (b) different.

Economic policies, 1997–2005

Although seen as uninspiring, Jiang had managed to control the pro-democracy demonstrations in Shanghai in 1989 – his political base before national leadership – without loss of life. The main task of his team was to revive confidence in China's reform programme, which had been badly shaken by the 1989 protests and the following suppression. In particular, there were concerns that foreign direct investment – vital to China's reform programme – might fall. However, spearheaded by Japan, foreign businesses quickly resumed their interest taking a share of China's growing economy.

Rather than Jiang, it was his prime minister, Zhu Rongji, – seen as on the right of the centre group of the CCP – who, according to some historians, arguably brought about the main economic changes during this period. Jiang and Zhu maintained Deng's economic reforms, with Jiang reaffirming the need to adopt modern production and management methods. At the Fifteenth Congress of the CCP in

September 1997, and the Ninth NPC in March 1998, new economic reform policies were adopted.

> **SOURCE 9.2**
>
> The biggest problem [after 1997] was that of the state-owned enterprises. In some ways, China had sidestepped the problem of the SOEs in the 1980s and early 1990s as the TVE sector grew dramatically. The SOE sector, however, did not fade away. In some ways, it actually increased in importance as the number of workers employed by SOEs rose by 40 million between 1978 and 1994. Despite the decreasing importance of SOEs in the overall economy, they continued to dominate important sectors, particularly heavy industry… By the late 1990s, it was apparent that SOE reform could not be avoided…
>
> Furthermore, there was the question of how and to what extent China's economy should be linked to the international economy… In the mid 1990s, in an effort to increase foreign investment, China had relaxed its rules on foreign ownership… Should the rules on foreign investment be relaxed even further? … Without the pressures of foreign investment, how could [SOEs] behind a wall of protection be expected to reform? Such questions were, of course, linked to China's bid to join the WTO – to what extent should China compromise in order to join the world trade body?
>
> Fewsmith, J. **China Since Tiananmen: The Politics of Transition.** Cambridge. Cambridge University Press, 2001. pp.201–02

From the 1990s, China became increasingly popular with foreign multinational companies – this was the result of China possessing, in addition to a growing domestic market, a seemingly unlimited supply of cheap labour, disciplined by official trades unions and state repression. Consequently, a massive amount of foreign investment poured into China. This, combined with large investments by China's SOEs, and the creation of new private industrial enterprises, led to a massive expansion of China's industrial development. The result was that, after a decline from 1978 to 1991 (because of the initial effects of introducing 'free' market mechanisms, which resulted in the closure of many factories and consequent unemployment), Chinese industry's share in GDP massively increased, as shown by Figure 9.6. The result was to make China the 'factory of the world'.

9 The People's Republic of China (1949–2005)

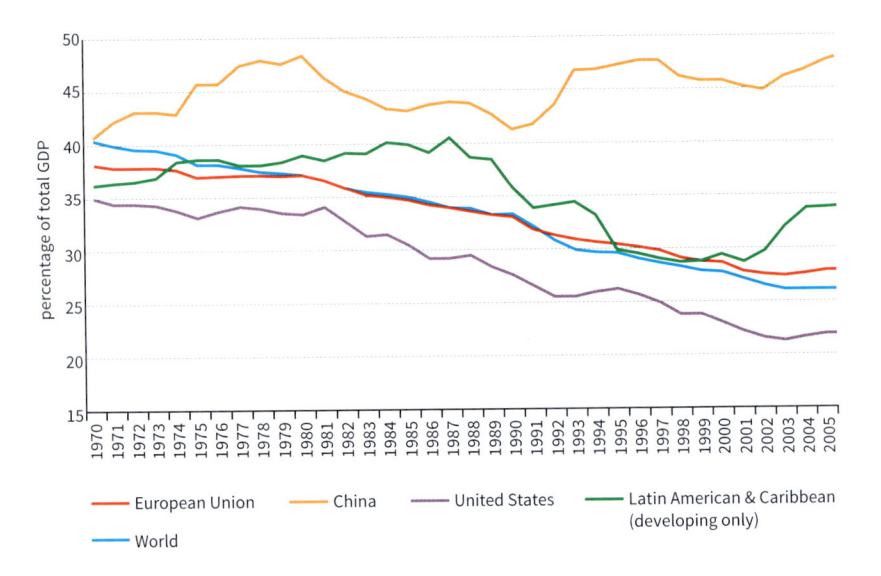

Figure 9.6: A graph showing China's increasing industrialisation and its contribution to China's economy.
Adapted from: Loong Yu, A. 2012. **China's Rise: Strength and Fragility**. Pontypool, Merlin Press. p.99

China and the World Trade Organization

As well as successfully managing the transition to a semi-market economy in Shanghai, it was Zhu who was largely responsible for China's successful application to become a member of the World Trade Organization (WTO). In November 1999, after 15 years of protracted negotiation, terms for China joining the WTO were agreed, and this took place in December 2001.

This reflected the success of China's economic modernisation – and showed that the main advanced capitalist countries felt the new China was a country with which it could do business. The Chinese leaders saw their country's acceptance as a member of the WTO as international recognition of China having become a world-class market economy and a major world power. This status was confirmed publicly in February 2002 by US president Bush's visit to Beijing, and by Jiang's return visit to the US the following October.

Developments in China 1989–2005

> **DISCUSSION POINT**
>
> The WTO, formed in 1995, had its origins in the Bretton Woods (USA) agreements in July 1944, which were intended by the US to organise the new post-war economic and financial world order – along the lines of 'free' market principles. These agreements, as well as setting up the WTO's forerunner, the General Agreement on Tariffs and Trade (GATT), also established the IMF and the World Bank. All three institutions were dominated by the US and its ideas about the need to allow free trade, remove controls on the export of capital and for 'budgetary discipline' – which often meant reductions in welfare spending. Do you think China's membership of the WTO in 2001 proves that it is now a capitalist country?

Although China was seen as a 'socialist market economy', the WTO required that China should open its doors to international financial markets. Once it was a member, advanced capitalist countries were confident that China would now be obliged to open its commercial and financial sectors to their overseas businesses and banks. One of the consequences of China's membership has been that the various private firms in China are increasingly free to directly conduct foreign trade, without central government controls. Another gain for China was that when Taiwan joined in January 2002, it did not do so as the 'Republic of China', but as the Customs Territory of Taiwan, Penghu, Jinmen and Mazu.

Before 2002, acquisitions and mergers (A & M) accounted for 20% of all Chinese overseas investments. Since then, as Figure 9.7 shows, A & M has become an increasingly significant proportion of all Chinese outward Foreign Direct Investment (FDI) – this is seen as the quickest way to expand globally.

Year	New investment	A & M
2003	82.0%	18.0%
2004	68.2%	31.8%
2005	47.0%	53.0%

Figure 9.7: A table showing China's investments and acquisitions abroad in the early years of the twenty-first century. Adapted from: Loong Yu, A. 2012. **China's Rise: Strength and Fragility.** Pontypool, Merlin Press. p.77

9 The People's Republic of China (1949–2005)

> **ACTIVITY**
> Carry out some further research on the main economic policies followed from 1989 to 2005. Then draw up a table to summarise the main points under these three headings:
> - agriculture
> - industry
> - foreign trade and investment.

However, this growing integration in the global capitalist economy poses real dangers for China's economy. The Asian Crisis of October 1997, which saw massive falls in stock markets, caused serious problems for several Chinese companies. The government was able to overcome these by massive state bail-outs, and by the fact that it still retained some capital controls. Nonetheless, membership of the WTO, which entails acceptance of the neo-liberal principle of abolishing all capital controls, makes China much more vulnerable to international capitalist crises.

9.3 How far have China's leaders created a 'Harmonious Society'?

China's rulers have been faced with several serious political and social problems since 1989. Many of these were associated with China's economic growth, and included:

- unemployment and industrial unrest
- environmental degradation
- corruption.

Nonetheless, at the end of 2005, the government issued its plans for the future development of China – apart from increased prosperity in order to achieve a 'comfortably off' society by 2020, this stressed the need for peaceful development and harmony.

Developments in China 1989–2005

The corruption problems resulted in a growing number of large-scale protests, demonstrations and even riots in rural areas – some of which ended in violence – rather than the desired 'harmonious society'. In the 1990s, the authorities officially acknowledged that tens of thousands of major protests had broken out across China because of such problems. The highest number – 17 900 – of 'mass incidents' took place in 2005, along with 87 000 smaller 'public order disturbances'. The fact that such social unrest is officially admitted by the authorities – which have always tried to create a 'harmonious society' – indicates how serious this problem is becoming.

Of particular growing significance, the economic reforms have created an industrial working class that now comprises more than 40% of the total Chinese working population, along with a service-sector working class that comprises a further 20%. Although there is as yet no clear political consciousness uniting these groups, their mounting dissatisfaction with the economic and environmental impact of the market reforms is creating real problems for China's ruling bureaucratic caste.

Although the percentage of absolute poor in China has declined dramatically since 1981 (from 86% to 8%), inequality of income has increased dramatically – the Gini coefficient (which takes zero as indicating perfect income equality, and one as showing extreme inequality) shows a rise from 0.25 in 1985 to 0.47 by 2005. This put China among the most unequal societies in the world – and on a par with the US. Dissatisfaction with such glaring inequalities, combined with problems of unemployment, created increasing unrest among China's working classes.

Unemployment and industrial unrest

From the mid 1980s, Deng's policies of market reforms – including privatisations of SOEs – resulted in over 40 million workers losing their jobs during the mid 1990s. The number of unemployed and disaffected workers was especially marked in northeastern China, which had a large number of industrial and manufacturing cities dependent on state-run enterprises. The younger members of the unemployed often moved to join the 'floating population' in search of work (see Section 7.3), but older workers and those with family responsibilities were unable to do so.

9 The People's Republic of China (1949–2005)

As a result, many unemployed workers staged protest demonstrations. The growing problem of unemployment and under-employment (of workers who could only find occasional part-time work) had been a major reason why Chinese workers had joined the pro-democracy demonstrators in 1989.

After 1989, following several years of relative industrial peace, China's working class became increasingly dissatisfied, with tens of thousands of workers' protests taking place since the mid 1990s. Since 2000, labour unrest – often against the privatisation of SOEs – became a major problem, and a potential threat to political stability.

In June 2000, the workers at the state-owned Zhengzhou Paper Mill defied the official All China Federation of Trade Unions (ACFTU) and the Staff and Workers' Representative Council (SWRC) and launched resistance against plans by a private stock-holding company to shut the mill down and sell the land for residential development. Workers were particularly angered by evidence of corruption between the managers and the company wishing to buy the land.

The workers took over the mill and, despite initial police repression, eventually forced the local authorities to abandon the planned sell-off in 2001. The workers took over the management and, in 2002, formed it into a cooperative company. This struggle – and the government concessions – led to a dozen SOEs in Zhengzhou cancelling privatisation deals over the next few years.

Other examples of workers' resistance to privatisation and job losses include the Liaoyang Metal Factory struggle from 2000 to 2002, during which, in March 2002, the workers tried to establish cross-factory organisation and joint struggles, and the Daqing oilfield workers' struggle against job losses, also in March 2002 (see Sources 9.3 and 9.4).

Developments in China 1989–2005

SOURCE 9.3

The 2002 Daqing oilfield workers' struggle was important not only for its size and duration, but also for its organization… Up until the late 1990s the oilfield had enabled China to be self-sufficient in its oil supply for decades. China's accession to the WTO in 2001 was conditional upon the opening of all important branches of its economic sector in 2007, including oil. Hence Beijing started a deep restructuring of the oil industry in order to make it competitive with foreign oil giants. Immense downsizing was on the agenda, which subsequently led to as many as 600000 oil workers being sacked within a few years at the turn of the century.

On 1 March 2002, 3000 oil workers demonstrated in front of the managing bureau of the Daqing oilfield and at one point broke into it. Over the following days the workers actions continued to escalate and at a peak more than 50000 demonstrated openly…

The climax of the one-month-long struggle was on 4 March when 20000 workers first assembled in Tieren Square and then marched to the railway station to block the trains.

Loong Yu, A. 2012. **China's Rise: Strength and Fragility.** *Pontypool, Merlin Press. pp.150–51*

A common theme among these strikers was a feeling that the CCP had betrayed the purpose of the 1949 Revolution, and that corruption was also a serious problem – as Sources 9.4 and 9.5 show:

SOURCE 9.4

We have got to get rid of this corruption! I am 57 and a communist party member. I joined back in '65 because I believed the party's aim was to secure the welfare of the people. What I see now is that they are not providing welfare to the people, so we ordinary people have to rely on ourselves to protect our right to a livelihood.

The views of one of the Daqing strikers, from T. Leung, **China Labour Bulletin**, *2 June 2002. The* **China Labour Bulletin** *is a journal – and an organisation – that promotes and defends workers' rights in the PRC, and was founded in 1994 by labour activist Han Dongfang.*

The People's Republic of China (1949–2005)

> **SOURCE 9.5**
>
> We are barely eating enough, while the officials and managers are very comfortably off. For the past year they have been carrying out this 'reduce staff and increase efficiency' policy, while at the same time [giving themselves] hundreds and thousands of yuan in bonuses. It's corruption that allows them to live in 200-plus square metres though they don't do anything for ordinary people. Take the chief of police and top cadres like him. They live in special houses. Daqing now has a squad of 800 People's Armed Police (PAP) to guard the leaders' housing compounds round-the-clock. These people are scared to sleep at night.
>
> *The views of another Daqing striker, from T. Leung,* **China Labour Bulletin**, *2 June 2002.*

QUESTION

What are the value and limitations of Sources 9.4 and 9.5 for historians studying the impact of China's 'free' market economic reforms on ordinary Chinese workers?

In fact, 2002 saw a massive increase in workers' struggles – mostly in the northeastern provinces where market reforms had led to the closure of many firms and increased unemployment against the impact of market economic reforms.

As part of these struggles, many workers bypassed the official, government-controlled trade union, and instead set up their own organisations – similar in many ways to the Workers' Autonomous Federations (WAFs) that had been formed during the pro-democracy unrest in 1989. Most of these struggles, however, were unsuccessful.

Developments in China 1989–2005

Figure 9.8: One of the many workers' protests and strikes in China in the spring of 2002.

> **QUESTION**
>
> Why were there so many strikes and protests by workers in the late 1990s and the early years of the 21st century? Why did this cause concern among the leadership of the CCP?

While, in the long term, the government believes continued economic growth will eventually absorb the unemployed, in the short term, they try to use nationalism and pride in the economic achievements – and the fact that some sectors of the working class have seen some improvements in living standards – as a way of gaining public support for the economic reforms.

China's 'Floating Population'

Until the 1980s, the government had tried to keep people in rural areas, in order to prevent the emergence of massive urban conurbations which were seen as having too many social and political problems. But this all changed as a result of the reforms of the 1980s. By the 1990s, with the new freedom to travel, many young men left rural areas to seek temporary work in industrial centres as a way of increasing family

9 The People's Republic of China (1949–2005)

incomes by taking construction or factory jobs. These seasonal workers – who often took the jobs of full-time workers sacked from the SOEs in the mid 1990s – became known as the 'floating population'. Because they were classified as being only temporary workers, they were often housed in makeshift shelters on the various construction sites – when one project finished, they moved on to the next one.

As China's economy continued to expand, many women also began to make the move to such urban areas. However, this floating population was increasingly seen by the authorities and local residents as being prone to petty crime and unrest. Yet, the numbers of such people were increased by the move to ensure state-run enterprises made profits. State, as well as the growing number of private, firms sacked older workers so they could replace them with younger – and cheaper – workers. Female workers were encouraged to take early retirement at 50, instead of the official age of 55 – but the loss of a family's total income often caused financial problems.

Environmental protection

One of the political problems thrown up by China's rapid economic development since 1949 has been pollution which, as well as having a serious impact on public health, has led to political protests which the CCP and the government have been forced to address. Earlier policies – such as the Great Leap Forward – had already had serious impacts, including de-forestation which led to increased flooding in many parts of China. From the mid 1970s, economic expansion and urbanisation led to higher usage of coal and motor cars, both of which increased emissions and pollution levels. In particular, almost two-thirds of China's population lack sufficient fresh water supplies, while almost a third of China's population lack access to clean drinking water.

In addition, industrial waste – including even poisonous chemicals – frequently polluted waterways and drinking water. Even in rural areas, the pollution of waterways also became a problem. Apart from the continued use of untreated human faeces as a fertiliser, the increased use of chemical fertilisers and insecticides – in order to harvest crops on marginal lands – also often polluted rivers and streams.

In 1998, the government responded by setting up the State Environment Protection Administration to improve air and water quality. It enforced existing laws, and in several cases imposed fines on

Developments in China 1989–2005

polluters. However, given the continued push for economic growth, these fines often failed to end the polluting practices. In addition, major projects that are intended to modernise China and increase living standards often had serious implications for the environment.

For instance, the construction of the Three Gorges Dam on the Yangtze River (completed in 2012), to provide hydroelectric power, required the relocation of 1.3 million people, and the flooding of farmland. Although intended to provide 10% of all China's electrical power needs, it also caused significant ecological changes, and remains a controversial topic within China.

Corruption

Public criticism of corruption among Party and state officials, which was largely absent during the radical Maoist period, has become increasingly vocal during the reform period. This has become a serious concern for Chinese leaders – despite several harsh sentences (including even death sentences), the problem continues to cause protest and social unrest. One significant development has been the emergence of *guandao* – officials who use their positions to engage in speculation.

Projects such as the Three Gorges Dam are also linked to the increasing problem of corruption. In 1999, Zhu Rongji visited the dam and warned those responsible for its construction that they must not allow shoddy construction. The government was particularly sensitive to political criticism of the project, which was spearheaded by Li Peng: the Chinese journalist Dai Qing was jailed in 1989 for criticising the project on environmental grounds. Despite her imprisonment, criticisms continued.

To help diffuse the internal political climate, Jiang decided in July 1993 to launch a major campaign against corruption in national politics. To begin with, attempts were made to persuade corrupt officials to confess their crimes, in return for leniency. From the end of 1994, the authorities then cracked down hard – especially against those at the very top of Party and government structures who used their positions to enrich themselves, relatives and friends.

Yet, despite frequent reporting of the trials and execution of the worst offenders, corruption has continued into the 21st century. As a result, Hu Jintao also acted on this problem, and the leadership see this problem – if not stamped out – as potentially threatening their

9 The People's Republic of China (1949–2005)

continued political power. Such concerns are increased by evidence that the PLA – the final resort for dealing with mass protest in China – might not be as politically reliable as in the past. Apart from a significant reduction in the size of the PLA, many soldiers were unhappy about their role in the suppression of the 1989 pro-democracy protests, while some sections of the PLA have even become drawn into the disputes over the nature and direction of the economic reforms.

Increased affluence, and the much greater availability of Western consumer goods, has led to increased corruption among officials. While some took money in return for 'turning a blind eye' to shoddy materials or construction methods, others embezzled millions of *yuan* from state enterprises, or took millions in bribes from Chinese or foreign private companies. This caused political unrest among ordinary Chinese people who often suffered as a result of such corruption – it had been one of the factors behind the 1989 protests.

Apart from corrupt urban officials, an additional problem in rural areas was that many officials often increased the number of taxes and levies farming families were expected to pay. This created great resentment – especially as many were convinced that these 'occasional' taxes were pocketed by corrupt officials. In 2004, the National People's Congress drew attention to officials who, in many rural areas, were issuing peasants and those working away on construction sites with paper slips instead of cash.

Yet, the response of many authorities was generally to arrest the main leaders of the protests, while many of the officials remained in place. Although after the high number of rural protests against the unpopular land tax in 2005, the government agreed to end it. By then, however, other protests were taking place against the compulsory sale of farming land to developers in deals that involved official corruption.

However, during the 1990s, the CCP allowed a more open process of elections to develop in local areas. This had first begun in 1988, as a result of the Organic Law of Villagers' Committees – but had been slowed by the 1989 protests. Nonetheless, these continued in the 1990s, with all adults in a village entitled to vote and stand for election to their village committees, for a three-year term of office. In 1997, the CCP leadership reaffirmed its commitment to such competitive elections – where they took place, local people were often able to remove the most incompetent or corrupt officials.

Developments in China 1989–2005

Despite these measures, corruption was not ended. Corruption also affected education, with officials and wealthy factory owners ensuring their children went to the best schools and universities. Consequently, a new educated élite began to emerge, which was increasingly linked to the wealth or official positions of parents. In particular, such families often ensure their children attend overseas universities – mostly for post-graduate studies which, until the late 1980s, were not available at the majority of Chinese universities.

Corruption and increased wealth have also led to some serious crime problems. Apart from drug traffickers exploiting the development of long-distance trade within China, and increased international trade, one of the evils of pre-revolutionary China has returned to reform China. During the Maoist period, the exploitation of women in the prostitution 'industry' had virtually disappeared. However, the increased affluence after 1976 saw this problem re-emerge. Despite severe penalties, this has continued beyond the 1990s – most recently, the trafficking of women into the international sex-trade has also become a problem. In addition, urban gangs often kidnap 'brides' who are then 'sold' to men wanting a wife.

9.4 How did China's relations with the rest of the world develop after 1989?

Though the collapse of the USSR in 1991 left the USA as the only global superpower, China remained a nuclear power controlled by a communist Party. With a large population and a rapidly expanding economy, which has made it the second largest economy in the world, China clearly has the potential to become a rival superpower in the very near future – especially as, unlike the USSR, it has been able to modernise the economy without making any fundamental changes to its political structures.

After Deng's death in 1997, president Jiang took a particular interest in foreign policy, and his understanding of international relations was probably deeper than that of any previous leaders. His command of

9 The People's Republic of China (1949–2005)

English meant he was at ease during foreign visits – these trips, such as his visit to the US in 1997, enhanced his status within China.

China and the US

Despite the improvement in relations between these two countries since Nixon's visit to China in 1972, tensions remained, with political disputes occurring at various points. In May 1999, during the US-led NATO military intervention against Serbia, the Chinese Embassy in Belgrade was bombed, and three Chinese journalists were killed. Although the CIA said it was an accident as they'd been using outdated maps, there was a suspicion in China that it was deliberate as China had eventually opposed NATO's intervention, which had not received UN approval.

In China, students and intellectuals protested outside foreign embassies, claiming the bombing was just another example of the West's attempts to 'humiliate' and 'contain' China. One impact of this crisis was on the political balance of strength within the Party leadership. Li Peng – with some support from senior PLA leaders – used his position within the Politburo to attack Zhu Rongji who, despite the bombing, had decided to go ahead with a planned trip to the US. Although the main attack was on Zhu, it could also be seen as an attempt to reduce Jiang's influence. The situation improved at the end of the year, with the US paying compensation to the families of those killed, and to the Chinese government for the damage done to their embassy.

Also in 1999, there were allegations that a Chinese-born US scientist had been passing nuclear secrets to China; and in April 2001, a collision took place over Hainan Island between a US Navy reconnaissance plane (which appeared to be within Chinese airspace) and a Chinese fighter. Although the Chinese pilot was killed, none of the US personnel died and, after ten days, were released.

The US plane, however, was kept for several weeks – the assumption was that the Chinese assessed and even removed certain items of advanced technology. Because both countries were keen for trade agreements, diplomatic relations were maintained, and a negotiated settlement was reached quite quickly. Though nationalist feelings were roused in China by the US refusal to apologise or pay compensation to the family of the dead Chinese pilot.

Yet, despite these problems, in October 2000 the US granted China 'permanent normal trade relations' (PNTR) status, which ended the

Developments in China 1989–2005

official US policy of withholding certain trade privileges because of China's human rights record, and its rule in Tibet.

Figure 9.9: US president George W. Bush and Jiang Zemin, during the former's visit to China in February 2002, a year after China had become a member of the WTO.

'China Rising'

As early as 1984, Britain – which quickly saw China as an emerging economic power – had signed an agreement with China to return Hong Kong (which, since the mid 19th century, had been ceded to Britain for 99 years) to Chinese rule. This took place in July 1997, under a policy of 'one country, two systems', with Hong Kong being peacefully integrated into the south China economic region as a Special Administrative Region (SAR). In December 1999, Macao – a Portuguese colony since 1557 – was also returned to China, and also became a Special Administrative Region.

9 The People's Republic of China (1949–2005)

Foreign joint venture companies in these two regions were then encouraged to set up factories in mainland China. From the late 1980s, Taiwan investors put billions of dollars into China as a result of China adopting capitalist-friendly policies. Deng, and subsequent Chinese leaders, hoped Taiwan – which also had a thriving market economy – might eventually be returned to China. As a first step, in 2001, China agreed to direct trade with Taiwan.

As Source 9.6 shows, historians and political observers are divided over what directions 'China Rising' might take in the 21st century. Ross Munro, for instance, has argued that an increasingly wealthy and nationalistic China intends to dominate Asia – and will be prepared to militarily resist any attempts by the US to block its advance. On the other hand, Ezra Vogel, has argued that China can be integrated into what is essentially a US-dominated global capitalism.

> **SOURCE 9.6**
>
> … China's government has 'played ball' with the West consistently since the 1980s on international issues – in the UN, with the WTO. Despite fear-mongering in the commercial [US] press and from our own politicians wishing to distract us from our domestic challenges, reform China has been a good neighbour internationally… Indeed, as we have seen, China has been too good a neighbour by refusing to protect its own citizens from the labor abuses of the neo-liberal globalized 'outsourcing' of sweatshop factories.
>
> This is not the picture we get of China from the major Western media. Instead, we are told that China Rising is a threat to the US's military might, to Europe's economic balance, and to world energy resources.
>
> Cheek, T. 2006. **Living With Reform: China Since 1989.** London. Zed Books. p.140

Whatever direction is taken, China will still be a potential threat to US global hegemony (dominance). According to an IMF report, China's economy will overtake the USA's in 2017 – though World Bank studies predict either 2020 or even 2030 as the most likely dates for this to happen. This would enable China to challenge US interest – not just in Asia, but across the world. However, in many other ways, China is still a developing country, with much lower average incomes than in the US – and still faces many social problems from the move to a market

Developments in China 1989–2005

economy. These will make it hard for China's government to achieve genuine – as opposed to an imposed – 'harmony'.

9.5 To what extent was China still communist by 2005?

By 2005, it seemed to many observers that communism in China had been overthrown – not by the people, as in Eastern Europe, but by the CCP itself. When the economic reforms first began after 1976, Party leaders claimed they were creating a specifically Chinese version of socialism: '*socialism with Chinese characteristics*'. Yet within 20 years, Marxist or communist political principles had, in practice, ceased to be a significant factor in the new China – despite occasional half-hearted attempts to revive the 'Spirit of Yan'an' (see Chapter 1).

This process was in part linked to the collapse of the Soviet Union in 1991. Many Chinese saw this as proof that communism – or at least the Stalinist version of Marxism-Leninism – was not the way to modernise their country. From the 1980s, China's leaders increasingly appealed to patriotism and nationalism in place of the Marxist principles and theories that had been frequently mentioned before 1976.

As the economic reforms took effect, those who benefitted from the new economic freedoms were more concerned with improving their standard of living than any adherence to communist principles. Many were even prepared to accept the lack of political democracy, as long as they continued to benefit from economic growth.

Such attitudes were strongest among the new social groups that emerged in the 1980s and 1990s. In particular, two groups have become particularly influential. First, an élite group of managers and technical experts have become an increasingly important political force. Many of these people – increasingly referred to as the 'princelings' by ordinary Chinese – are the children of senior Party, military and government officials: though very often joining the CCP, they are much more concerned with the techniques needed for economic modernisation than with political theories such as Marxism and communism.

9 The People's Republic of China (1949–2005)

The other group is made up of private entrepreneurs who, released from Maoist restrictions on private enterprise, have formed a sizeable *nouveau riche* class. Many have become multi-millionaires who, as well as openly enjoying a lavish lifestyle, have responded positively to CCP efforts to forge ever-closer links with them.

China and communism

The communist regime in China – unlike those in the Soviet Union and Eastern Europe – seemed to have been able to overcome many of the economic problems it faced *and* maintain its authoritarian one-party rule. Yet, many observers have argued that the ruling party and government were communist in name only. Though it appeared to have successfully overcome the economic problems (stagnation and low productivity) that had greatly contributed to the collapse of communism in Europe, it seemed the government had only been able to do so by rapidly turning China into a capitalist economy.

Thus, many have argued that 'communism' had ended in China, too. Instead, several historians and political observers have argued that, by the early 21st century, China had become either a state capitalist or an authoritarian capitalist economy. Some – such as Maurice Meisner and Au Loong Yu – have preferred to describe the new China as a bureaucratic capitalist economy. According to them, China's bureaucracy has succeeded in combining the exercise of state power and capital accumulation – functions that in 'normal' capitalist societies are performed by two distinct social groups: bureaucrats and capitalists.

Under bureaucratic capitalism, the bureaucrats use their political dominance to ensure that they – and their cronies – monopolise the most profitable sectors of the nation's economy, though also allowing private capitalists to share in some of the profits. Whatever label is used, many seem convinced that the leadership of the CCP and the state bureaucracy have succeeded in restoring capitalism in China.

As evidence of this, such historians cite a World Bank report that shows that wages as a share of GDP declined from 53% in 1998 to 41.4% in 2005 – achieved by ensuring that workers have no independent trade unions, establishing a barracks-like factory regime and quickly repressing all strikes and protests. This has helped create a relatively docile workforce.

Developments in China 1989–2005

In fact, although China's leaders since 1989 have, in practice dropped many of the socialist goals of the 1949 Revolution, the attraction of Marxism – and even Maoism – continues for some. As China becomes increasingly drawn into the global capitalist economy, it may well find itself experiencing the periodic crises that seem to hit capitalism every 20–25 years.

As has been seen, the economic reform programme since 1976 has led to an increasing number of strikes and protests. If the standard of living declines as a result of economic crises, such protests seem likely to increase. Furthermore, the undemocratic political system existing in China continues to alienate large sections of society.

Theory of knowledge

History and historical perspective:

When Zhou Enlai was asked his assessment of the French Revolution of 1789, he replied: *'It is too early to tell'*. Several historians have noted that revolutions do not usually result in balanced appraisals – it usually takes several generations before the bitterness of ideological battles and disappointments has faded enough to allow the historical record to be looked at dispassionately. Do you think it possible to make definite judgement now about whether China remains a communist state or has, instead, become a capitalist economy?

The end of history?

The economic policies followed by China since the early 1980s – along with the collapse of the East European regimes during 1989, and of the Soviet Union in 1991 – have led some historians and commentators to argue that this heralded the end of the 'Great Contest' between capitalism and communism, which had lasted for almost 75 years, following the Bolshevik Revolution in Russia in 1917. Thus Francis Fukuyama, a US official, announced that the 'end of history' had arrived. By this, he meant the final victory of 'liberal' capitalism over Marxism and communist (or other radical) movements based – to one degree or another – on this political philosophy.

Certainly, after 1991, communism remained the official ideology of only a handful of states. Apart from China (which seemed to many

9 The People's Republic of China (1949–2005)

observers to be quickly applying capitalist economic policies), the only other states to retain it were North Korea, Cuba and Vietnam – and of these, the latter two had also begun moving towards some kind of market-based economic reforms, once aid from the Soviet Union had ceased. History's verdict on communism as a general political theory and practice thus seemed, at best, to be mixed.

The idea of communism

However, Fukuyama's claims that Marxism and communism had been permanently defeated and consigned to the 'dustbin of history', and that capitalism was now secure, might – given world poverty, ecological crises, and the 2008 financial crash and its aftermath – prove to be a rather premature judgement.

Despite the evident crises of communism – as shown by the developments in China after 1976, as well as by the collapse of the communist states of Europe during 1988–91 – some historians argue that these events do not necessarily mark the end of Marxism, communism or the 'Great Contest'. In particular, they point out that Marxist theory and communist practice originally arose from conditions of poverty, the destruction of war and strong desires for liberty, fairness and equality. While it could be argued that most people in the developed world enjoy these freedoms and conditions, this is hardly true for the majority of the world's population.

With the continuing authoritarian rule of the CCP in China, as well as the collapse of the USSR and its satellite regimes in Eastern Europe, commentators have suggested that a newer, more liberal and libertarian, version of communism might re-emerge to challenge the global economic interests of US and Western capitalism, and of Chinese 'authoritarian capitalism'.

In fact, for several observers, Marxism – in its original version – is simply a logical extension of the more radical socialist interpretation, first given by Babeuf (1760–97), to the French Revolution's ideals of *'liberty, equality and fraternity'*. Significantly perhaps, two hundred years later, in 1989, the demand for the full implementation of these ideals formed the core demands of the crowds in Tiananmen Square, Beijing. Thus, as Source 9.7 argues, it may be rather too early for historians to proclaim the death and funeral of communism.

SOURCE 9.7

We have to take the long view of the historical process... For as long as contemporary capitalism, a system based on exploitation and inequality and recurring crises, not to mention its impact on the fragile economy of the planet, continues to exist, the possibility of anti-capitalist movements taking power cannot be ruled out... The duels between the possessors and the dispossessed continue, taking new forms.

Ali, T., 2009, **The Idea of Communism**, *London, Seagull Books, pp. 112–4*

9 The People's Republic of China (1949–2005)

Summary activity

Copy the spider diagram below to show the main political, economic and social developments in China from 1989 to 2005. Then, using the information from this chapter, and any other sources available to you, complete the diagram. Make sure you include, where relevant, brief comments about different historical debates/ interpretations.

- POLITICAL DEVELOPMENTS
- ECONOMIC DEVELOPMENTS
- CHINA, 1989–2005
- SOCIAL PROBLEMS
- CHINA IN 2005

Practice Paper 3 questions

1. To what extent did the fall of Hu Yaobang and Zhao Ziyang mark the victory of the 'conservative' leftists in the CCP over Deng's economic reforms?

2. Evaluate the factors that led to Deng Xiaoping's 'Southern Tour' in 1992.

3 Discuss the most important economic developments in China in the period 1989–2005.

4 Examine the reasons why significant social problems arose in China during the period 1989–2005.

5 'By 2005, it was clear that the Chinese Communist Party had moved China to a form of authoritarian capitalism.' To what extent do you agree with this statement?

10 Exam practice

Introduction

You have now completed your study of the main events and developments of the People's Republic of China during the period 1949–2005. You have also had the chance to examine the various historical debates and differing historical interpretations that surround some of these developments.

In the previous chapters, you have encountered examples of Paper 3-type essay questions, with examiner's tips. You have also had some basic practice in answering such questions. In this chapter, these tips and skills will be developed in more depth. Longer examples of possible student answers are provided, accompanied by examiner's comments which should increase your understanding of what examiners are looking for when they mark your essays. Following each question and answer, you will find tasks to give you further practice in the skills needed to gain the higher marks in this exam.

IB History Paper 3 exam questions and skills

Those of you following HL Option 3 – *History of Asia and Oceania* – will have studied in depth three of the eighteen sections available for this HL Option. *The People's Republic of China 1949–2005* is one of those sections. For Paper 3, two questions are set from each of the 18 sections, giving 36 questions in total; and you have to answer three of these.

Each question has a specific mark scheme. However, the 'generic' mark scheme in the *IB History Guide* gives you a good general idea of what examiners are looking for in order to be able to put answers into the higher bands. In particular, you will need to acquire reasonably precise historical knowledge so that you can address issues such as cause and effect, change and continuity, and so that you can explain historical developments in a clear, coherent, well-supported and relevant way. You will also need to understand relevant historical debates and

10 The People's Republic of China (1949–2005)

interpretations; you will need to be able to refer to these and critically evaluate them.

Essay planning

Make sure you read each question *carefully*, noting all the important key or 'command' words – you might find it useful to highlight them on your question paper. You can then produce a rough plan (for example a spider diagram) of *each* of the three essays you intend to attempt, *before* you start to write your answers: that way, you will soon know whether you have enough own knowledge to answer them adequately. Next, refer back to the wording of each question – this will help you see whether or not you are responding to *all* its various demands/aspects. In addition, if you run short of time towards the end of your exam, you will at least be able to jot down in note form – and in a clear and structured way – the key issues/points you would have gone on to address. It is thus far better to do the planning at the *start* of the exam; that is, *before* you panic should you suddenly realise you haven't time to finish your last essay.

Relevance to the question

Remember, too, to keep your answers relevant and focused on the question – don't go outside the dates mentioned in the question, or write answers on subjects not identified in that question. Also, don't just *describe* the events or developments – sometimes, students just focus on one key word, date or individual, and then write down everything they know about it. Instead, select your own knowledge carefully, and pin the relevant information to the key features raised by the question. Finally, if the question asks for 'reasons' and 'effects', 'continuity and change', 'successes and failures' or 'nature and development' make sure you deal with all the parts of the question. Otherwise, you will limit yourself to half marks at best.

Examiner's tips

For Paper 3 answers, examiners are looking for well-structured arguments that:

- are consistently relevant/linked to the question
- offer clear/precise analysis/evaluation

Exam practice

- are supported by the deployment of accurate, precise and relevant own knowledge
- offer a balanced judgement
- refer to different historical debates/interpretations or to relevant historians and, where relevant, offer some critical evaluation of these.

Simplified mark scheme

Band		Marks
1	**Consistently clear understanding of and focus** on the question, with **all main aspects addressed**. Answer is **fully analytical, balanced** and **well-structured/organised**. Own knowledge is **detailed, accurate and relevant**, with events placed **in their historical context**. There is **developed critical analysis**, and **sound understanding of historical concepts**. Examples used are **relevant**, and used effectively **to support analysis/evaluation**. The answer also integrates **evaluation of different historical debates/perspectives**. All/almost all of the main points are **substantiated**, and the answer reaches a **clear/reasoned/consistent judgement/conclusion**.	13–15
2	**Clear understanding of the question**, and most of its **main aspects are addressed**. Answer is mostly **well-structured and developed**, though, with **some repetition/lack of clarity** in places. Supporting **own knowledge mostly relevant/accurate**, and events are placed **in their historical context**. The answer is **mainly analytical**, with relevant examples **used to support critical analysis/evaluation**. There is **some understanding/evaluation of historical concepts and debates/perspectives**. Most of the main points **are substantiated**, and the answer offers a **consistent conclusion**.	10–12

10 The People's Republic of China (1949–2005)

Band		Marks
3	**Demands of the question are understood** – but some aspects **not fully developed/ addressed. Mostly relevant/accurate supporting own knowledge,** and events generally placed **in their historical context.** Some attempts at analysis/evaluation but these are limited/not sustained/ inconsistent.	7–9
4	**Some understanding** of the question. **Some relevant own knowledge,** with some factors identified – but with **limited explanation. Some attempts at analysis,** but answer **lacks clarity/coherence, and is mainly description/narrative.**	4–6
5	**Limited understanding of/focus on** the question. **Short/generalised** answer, with very **little accurate/relevant own knowledge.** Some **unsupported assertions,** with **no real analysis.**	0–3

Student answers

The extracts from student answers that follow will have brief examiner comments at some points, and a longer overall comment at the end. Those parts of student answers that are particularly strong and well-focused (e.g. demonstrations of precise and relevant own knowledge, or examination of historical interpretations) will be highlighted in red. Errors/confusions/irrelevance/loss of focus will be highlighted in blue. In this way, students should find it easier to follow why marks were awarded or withheld.

Exam practice

Question 1

'By 1957, Mao's economic policies had been successful in fully modernising the Chinese economy.' To what extent do you agree with this statement? **[15 marks]**

Skills
- Factual knowledge and understanding
- Structured, analytical and balanced argument
- Awareness/understanding/evaluation of historical interpretations
- Clear and balanced judgement.

Examiner's tip

Look carefully at the wording of this question, which asks you to consider the view that Mao's economic policies from 1949 to 1957 had succeeded in modernising the Chinese economy. This means you would need to show both how the statement is true and how it is not true. Thus, remember, it is perfectly all right for you to challenge the view – as long as you support your arguments with relevant and precise own knowledge. All aspects of the question will need to be addressed in order to achieve high marks. And remember – don't just describe what Mao's economic policies were: what's needed is explicit analysis and explanation of his policies and their impact, and the extent to which these had modernised China's economy. So try to produce a balanced answer.

Student answer

While Mao's economic policies from 1949 to 1957 certainly succeeded in creating a more developed economy in China, it would be wrong to argue that he had fully modernised the Chinese economy by 1957. In fact, Mao himself clearly recognised that much more remained to be done. Although his First Five-Year Plan, which began in 1953, achieved significant increases in agricultural and industrial production, Mao launched a Second Five-Year Plan – his 'Great Leap Forward' – in 1958. His hope was that, within 15 years, China would have an economy superior to Britain's. Yet the overall impact of this new plan – made worse by bad weather and floods – actually led to widespread malnutrition and

10 The People's Republic of China (1949–2005)

even starvation in many areas of China. In addition, much of the steel produced during this period was of poor quality, and limited the effectiveness of many of the industrial projects undertaken as part of Mao's GLF.

> **EXAMINER COMMENT**
> This is a clear and well-focused introduction, containing some accurate knowledge of the topic, and indicating that the answer will adopt a balanced approach.

When Mao and the CCP came to power in 1949, they inherited many problems – including economic ones – as a result of almost 40 years of civil war and Japanese invasion. In particular, agricultural production was far less than required by China's population of over 450 million, which was growing by about 15 million a year. In addition, as well as starting from a low industrial base (most of which was foreign-owned), much of China's infrastructure (such as railway lines, bridges, ports and roads) had been destroyed. Thus much would need to be done to modernise China's economy.

Mao's first priority was agriculture. In 1950, a land reform programme was begun, which took land from China's landlords and distributed it among the peasants. However, landownership remained private and, more importantly, most farms were too small to be fully efficient. Consequently, from 1951, the government began to urge peasants to form cooperatives – as a result, within a year, grain production was 10% higher than it had been in 1936. The move to cooperatives was thus further encouraged and, by 1953, 40% of peasant farms were cooperatives. During 1955, the CCP began to urge the establishment of bigger cooperatives – known as Agricultural Producers' Cooperatives (APCs); by 1957, over 90% of peasant farms were part of APCs.

As a result, agricultural production continued to increase – for instance, the increase in 1957 was 5%. Overall, China's total food production had increased from about 110 billion kgs in 1949 to almost 200 billion kgs in 1957. Yet Mao himself did not think agriculture had been sufficiently modernised – this was one of the reasons he launched the Great Leap Forward the following year. Thus, despite significant improvements, it was clear that China's agricultural system had not been fully modernised by 1957.

Exam practice

> **EXAMINER COMMENT**
> These three paragraphs are focused on the question and have a clear argument. This is supported by some accurate and specific own knowledge, which is explicitly tied into the question, and which maintains the overall judgement made in the opening paragraph.

In 1949, Mao and the CCP were fully aware of the relative under-development of China's industrial base. In particular, as well as having little industry, most of what China did have was foreign-owned. At first, the CCP nationalised foreign-owned firms, and those owned by supporters of the GMD. However, it decided to cooperate with small-scale Chinese capitalists – these firms thus remained in private hands. This approach was mainly to ensure there was minimum disruption of the existing economy. Instead, the Communists concentrated on dealing with inflation and unemployment. Nonetheless, certain controls were placed on privately-owned firms – such as improving workers' pay and rights.

As early as January 1950, China signed a Treaty of Friendship and Mutual Aid with the Soviet Union – this promised financial and technical assistance to China over 15 years, to help it develop a modern industrial base, especially as regards heavy industry. This clearly shows that China's industrial development was going to take a lot of resources, and would take some considerable time.

However, because of China's involvement in the Korean War (which broke out in 1950), there was little surplus funding available. After the Korean War ended in 1953, Mao and the CCP drew up a Five-Year Plan, designed to run from 1953 to 1957.

[There then follow several paragraphs giving accurate/precise details of the impact/results of the Five-Year Plan by 1957]

Thus, by 1957, Mao – as with agriculture – clearly believed that, despite these undoubted increases in industrial production, much more still needed to be done in order to give China a really modern industry. These were the considerations which played a big part in his decision to launch the GLF in 1958 – in particular, to develop light industry.

10 The People's Republic of China (1949–2005)

> **EXAMINER COMMENT**
> These paragraphs are also well-focused on the question, and the details of the results of the Five-Year Plan are used to maintain and carry forward the initial argument. However, there has been no reference to historical interpretations about Mao's economic policies from 1949 to 1957.

In conclusion, therefore, it is clear that – despite significant improvements in both agricultural and industrial production by 1957 – Mao and the CCP were not satisfied that they had given China a really modern economy. Consequently, Mao pushed for his Great Leap Forward, which was meant to do so in the space of 15 years. Consequently, I disagree with the statement in the question – by 1957, China's economy had not been fully modernised.

> **EXAMINER COMMENT**
> This brief conclusion makes an explicit, valid and balanced judgement, which has been supported by plenty of accurate, precise and relevant own knowledge.

Overall examiner comments

There is a clear, consistent and supported argument, and the approach is analytical rather than descriptive. There is plentiful and accurate relevant own knowledge, and sound understanding has been shown. The answer is well-focused throughout on the demands of the question, so is good enough to be awarded a mark in Band 1. However, because there are no references to historical debate/interpretations, the answer would be placed at the bottom of Band 1 – 13 marks.

Activity

Look again at the simplified mark scheme, and the student answer above. Then try to write your own answer – including some paragraphs providing details of the results of the Five-Year Plan – which will be good enough to obtain the full 15 marks. As well as making sure you address ALL aspects of the question, try to integrate into your answer some references AND evaluation of relevant historical interpretations/perspectives.

Exam practice

Question 2

Evaluate the factors which led Mao to launch the Cultural Revolution in China in 1966. **[15 marks]**

Skills
- Factual knowledge and understanding
- Structured, analytical and balanced argument
- Awareness/understanding/evaluation of historical interpretations
- Clear and balanced judgements.

Examiner's tip

Look carefully at the wording of this question, which clearly requires you to consider – and evaluate – the range of factors that led to the start of the Cultural Revolution. Just dealing with one or two factors will not allow you to score the highest marks. In addition, the question requires you to make judgements about the relative importance of these different factors.

Student answer

The reasons behind Mao's decision to launch the Cultural Revolution in 1966 can be traced back to 1949 – and even back to the 1930s, when Mao first became a really important leader of the Chinese Communist Party. In particular, most of the reasons relate to arguments over what policies the CCP should follow – and to securing Mao's leading position within the party.

> **EXAMINER COMMENT**
> This is a brief but clear and mostly well-focused introduction, showing an awareness of some key factors involved in the launching of the Cultural Revolution in 1966.

To fully understand the reasons of factors behind Mao's decision to launch the Cultural Revolution in 1966, it is necessary to be aware of the main debates within the CCP before 1966 – including those before 1949. For instance, when the CCP was formed in 1921, Mao was not one of the main leaders – these were Chen Duxiu and Li Dazhao. More importantly, during the 1920s, he

10 The People's Republic of China (1949–2005)

came to believe that the peasants could be the basis for a communist revolution in China – this was contrary to the official line of the party.

After the break with the GMD in 1927, when Jiang Jieshi carried out massacres of communists in the main urban areas, Mao had led the survivors into the countryside of Jiangxi province where, in 1931, he had created a soviet. Within this soviet, Mao had carried out a series of reforms, including land redistribution to the peasants. When Jiang Jieshi began a series of 'Extermination Campaigns' against the Communists, the latter's Red Army had some initial successes. However, after some serious set-backs in October 1934, Mao's ideas were attacked and he was expelled from the party's Central Committee. This development made Mao very resentful – and made him determined to regain and retain his position within the party. In January 1935, the CCP held a conference at the town of Zunyi: this conference decided that Mao's ideas should be followed after all, and he was elected as party leader. From then on, he was determined to retain that power.

> **EXAMINER COMMENT**
>
> Although there is some accurate own knowledge, this is mostly **background** material, and so is not explicitly linked to the demands of the question. While making a brief reference or two to the historical context preceding 1949 is a sound idea, it is not wise to give too much information on this. What is needed is precise own knowledge of the events between 1949 and 1966 – and especially those from 1958 to 1966 – which led Mao to launch the Cultural Revolution. The amount of detail provided about developments within the CCP **before** 1949 suggests that this answer might easily slip into a narrative account – or, even worse, an essay based on mainly *irrelevant* material.

After becoming leader, Mao decided to take the survivors to the more remote northern province of Shaanxi. Once there, the survivors of the Long March established a new soviet at Yan'an, under Mao's leadership. As before, Mao pushed through many reforms in the areas the Red Army controlled – these were designed to win the support of the peasants for the CCP. While there, Mao also ensured he remained as leader.

Despite a brief ceasefire between the GMD and the CCP in 1936, the civil war had soon resumed, as Jiang Jieshi was more determined to crush the CCP than to fight the Japanese invaders. Another brief ceasefire after the end of the Second World war in August 1945 soon broke down – with Mao rejecting Stalin's

Exam practice

insistence that he should form a coalition government with the GMD. From 1946 to 1949, the civil war resumed – with the defeat of the GMD certain, Jiang Jieshi fled to Taiwan and, in October 1949, Mao proclaimed the formation of the People's Republic of China.

[There then follow several more paragraphs giving a detailed and accurate – but narrative-based – account of Mao's economic policies from 1949 to 1957]

> **EXAMINER COMMENT**
> The main comment to be made on these paragraphs is that most of the information provided is essentially *irrelevant*. The candidate is thus wasting time – and thus missing opportunities to score marks. What is needed is information about the disputes within the CCP after the failure of the 'Great Leap Forward'.

After the Five-Year Plan – and the discontent revealed by the 'Hundred Flowers' campaign – Mao decided that a new Five-Year Plan was needed. Thus, in 1958, he launched the 'Great Leap Forward', which began with China being divided up into about 25 000 large communes. This was intended to create a much more modern agricultural system and, at the same time, to bring about rapid industrialisation. For instance, he launched the 'backyard steel campaign'. However, this – and the many infrastructure construction projects – led to more time and resources being spent on industry than on agriculture. Unfortunately, bad weather and floods for two consecutive years led to poor harvests in many areas: this led to food shortages and even widespread starvation in several areas of China from 1959 to 1961.

As a result of these serious setbacks and failures, Mao and his supporters were removed from any of their positions of power during 1959. Although Mao was able to retain the post of Party Chairman, he was replaced as head of state by Liu Shaoqi, while Deng Xiaoping became Party Secretary. These latter were mainly members of the centre-right of the CCP and, in 1960, the GLF was abandoned. Instead, these communists argued for peasants to be allowed to have larger private plots. They also wanted to return to the methods of the First Five-Year Plan, which had been drawn up along lines recommended by experts from the Soviet Union.

Mao disagreed strongly with such policies, and was determined to use what influence he still retained to regain control of the CCP. As a first step, in 1962, he launched his 'Socialist Education Movement'. By then, Mao had decided

10 The People's Republic of China (1949–2005)

that experts and professional administrators had undermined the revolution in Russia – and were, under Khrushchev, restoring elements of capitalism. He also concluded that these categories were now doing the same in China – in particular, he felt that 'moderates' within the CCP, such as Liu and Deng, were trying to 'restore capitalism'. These were increasingly attacked as taking China along a 'capitalist road'.

At first, his ideas were directed towards influencing school and college students. These – especially those born after 1949 – were seen as especially important to China's future. As they had no real idea of what China had been like before 1949, he argued that, if they saw nothing wrong with Liu and Deng's policies, then capitalism would soon re-emerge in China. To begin with, his ideas gained limited support but, in 1965, he won over Lin Biao, the Minister of Defence responsible for the People's Liberation Army. Mao then decided to use the PLA as the starting point for his campaign to resume power.

As a first step, Lin Biao issued each soldier with a copy of a book entitled 'Quotations from the Thoughts of Mao Zedong'. This soon became known as the 'Little Red Book', and the 4 million soldiers of the PLA were instructed to study Mao's ideas. With this base behind him, Mao launched the Cultural Revolution in the summer of 1966.

> **EXAMINER COMMENT**
>
> The candidate has at last begun to get to grips with the main demands of the question. Although the approach is rather-narrative based, at least the material is now relevant – and, in several places, is accurate and precise. However, if time had not been wasted earlier on irrelevant material, the candidate would have had more time to provide some extra detail, analysis and evaluation – as well as referring to relevant historical debates about these issues.

Thus the main reasons for the start of the Cultural Revolution were to allow Mao and his supporters to regain the powerful position in the party and the state which they had lost in 1959–60; and to overturn economic policies which they feared would lead to the restoration of capitalism in China in the near future.

Exam practice

> **EXAMINER COMMENT**
>
> This is a sound conclusion – but hasn't been fully supported. One of the main reasons for this is that, because of the time wasted on irrelevant material, there has been no time to consider the main events and outcomes of the Cultural Revolution itself. Nor has there been any significant attempt – or opportunity – to *evaluate* the *relative importance* of the different factors.

Overall examiner comments

There is a lot of detailed and accurate own knowledge – unfortunately, until the last few paragraphs, it is *mostly irrelevant*. Even where there is relevant detail, the approach is descriptive rather than analytical and evaluative. The answer shows some understanding of, and focus on, the question; but there is no attempt to consider different historical interpretations concerning the reasons for the Cultural Revolution. Thus, overall, the demands of the question are not fully addressed; and so the answer is likely to be awarded Band 4, and only gain 6 marks at the most.

Activity

Look again at the simplified mark scheme, and the student answer above. Then try to write your own answer – including some paragraphs providing details of the Cultural Revolution and its most immediate outcomes as regards positions of power within the CCP and the Chinese state – which will be good enough to obtain the full 15 marks. In particular, try to establish the various possible reasons for the launch of the Cultural Revolution – and evaluate them as regards relative importance, and make some judgements about which one/s you think were most important. In addition, don't forget to mention and evaluate relevant historical interpretations/perspectives.

10 The People's Republic of China (1949–2005)

Question 3

Discuss the reasons for, and the results of, Deng Xiaoping's opposition to the demands of the pro-democracy movement in the period 1976–89.
[15 marks]

Skills

- Factual knowledge and understanding
- Structured, analytical and balanced argument
- Awareness/understanding/evaluation of historical interpretations.

Examiner's tip

Look carefully at the wording of this question, which asks you to consider a range of reasons and results in relation to Den Xiaoping's opposition to the pro-democracy movement in China in the period 1976–89. Just focusing on one reason and/or one result will not allow you to score the highest marks. And remember – don't just describe what happened: what's needed is explicit analysis and explanation, with precise supporting own knowledge. There are also some relevant historical debates which could be made part of the answer.

Student answer

While Deng was in favour of modernising the Chinese economy through his Four Modernisations policies, he was not in favour of introducing political democracy. Instead, he wanted to maintain a one-party state, with the CCP remaining in total control. He followed this policy all the way through this period – eventually using the PLA to violently suppress protesting students in Tiananmen Square in 1989.

> **EXAMINER COMMENT**
> This is a brief introduction, with a little supporting own knowledge, which is connected to the topic – though, as yet, nothing explicit has been said about reasons or results.

The pro-democracy movement in China really began in April 1976, with protests against the Gang of Four at the Qingming Festival, following the death of Zhou Enlai. *Though Deng was initially blamed for these protests, and so lost*

Exam practice

influence again, he was soon back in power once the Gang of Four had been arrested. He allowed students to put up posters attacking the Gang (whose trials didn't begin until 1980) and, in 1978, allowed the creation of what became known as Democracy Wall. They were allowed to put up political 'big character' posters until an activist put up a poster which attacked Deng and called for the 'Fifth Modernisation' – democracy. Deng had the man arrested, and Democracy Wall was first moved, and then closed down at the end of 1979.

At this time, Deng was involved in removing Hua Guofeng and his supporters from positions of power. This was because Hua's Ten-Year Plan was running into problems, and Deng wanted to put his Four Modernisations into operation a different way. By 1980, Deng had managed to get his own supporters into position – such as Hu Yaobang and Zhao Ziyang.

> **EXAMINER COMMENT**
>
> There is some relevant supporting own knowledge about the beginnings of the Democracy Movement – but it is rather narrative-based. In addition, there is a section at the end of the paragraph which is not really relevant.

Things quietened down after 1979, but students and intellectuals began to raise demands for democracy again in the mid 1980s. This was partly because US president Reagan had made a speech in China in 1984, which had spoken about democracy – this had been unofficially translated and circulated among students. In 1986, the protests began to grow and were backed by dissident intellectuals such as Fang Jingsheng, who wrote an Open Letter demanding the release of political prisoners. The student demonstrations in university towns increased during early 1987 – and this time, they were joined by some workers. The workers were unhappy at this time because by 1985, the early success of Deng's economic policies had begun to fade – instead, many workers were facing falling living standards because of inflation, and many were becoming unemployed as their 'iron rice bowls' were being broken by Deng's economic reforms.

These intellectuals and student demonstrations had also been given some limited support by Hu Yaobang – as a result, he was dismissed as General-Secretary, and replaced by Zhao Ziyang.

10 The People's Republic of China (1949–2005)

> **EXAMINER COMMENT**
> Again, there is some relevant and accurate own knowledge (but note the mistake over the intellectual who supported the student demonstrations in 1986–7 – he was Fang *Lizhi*; Wei Jingsheng was the author of the 'Fifth Modernisation'). However, there is also some more largely irrelevant information on why some workers were prepared to join the protests – though it could have been made relevant, by pointing out that Deng would have opposed this, because he feared dissatisfied workers allying with students, as was to happen on a much bigger scale in 1989. More worryingly, the approach is still essentially narrative-based – there are no explicit explanations of Deng's reasons for opposing demands for democracy and, while some of the results are described, they are not explicitly flagged up as results. Remember – always pay close attention to the wording of questions.

These protests of 1986–87 faded away after Hu's fall from power. However, in April 1989, Hu died unexpectedly – and this led to large demonstrations in support of him in Tiananmen Square. Intellectuals once again supported the students, who began to occupy the square. During April and May, these grew in size, with many calling for democracy. Demonstrations continued in Beijing – and elsewhere – and were not called off when Gorbachev came on an important official visit to China in mid May. This was very embarrassing for Deng and the other Chinese leaders. Later that month, the students built a statue of freedom and liberty.

This led to a split in the CCP leadership, with most supporting Deng, who wanted to suppress them – especially as their protests were getting world coverage. However, Zhao – who at first had not been that much in favour of democracy – made comments sympathetic to the students' demands. Nonetheless, martial law was declared and, after first attempts by Beijing's troops to disperse the protesters failed, Deng brought in special troops from outside the capital. On 4 June, they fired on the students, killing an unknown number – this ended the Democracy Movement's protests.

> **EXAMINER COMMENT**
> This answer has continued along the same lines – relevant own knowledge (some of it quite precise), but still essentially an account of what happened.

Exam practice

After 4 June, many students and workers were arrested – while most of the students were released after a time, several of the workers who had joined their protests were executed. One reason for the failure of the Democracy Movement's protests was because they were themselves divided. So Deng was able to avoid having to introduce democratic political reforms, and he could continue with his economic policies.

Overall examiner comments

This answer makes no real attempt to explicitly address either reasons or results – but there is plenty of precise/correct own knowledge. However, because the approach is almost entirely narrative, this supporting information has not been 'pinned' to the question. Consequently, the answer is not good enough to go higher than Band 4 – probably getting about 6 marks. To reach the higher Bands, some explicit focus on both reasons and results is needed – frustratingly, much of the information needed to do this well is already in the answer.

Also, for Band 1, it would be necessary to have some mention of relevant specific historians/historical interpretations – there are several to choose from on this topic.

Activity

Look again at the simplified mark scheme, and the student answer above. Now try to draw up a plan focused on the demands of the question. Then try to write several paragraphs which will be good enough to get into Band 1, and so obtain the full 15 marks. As well as making sure you address ALL aspects of the question, try to integrate into your answer some references AND evaluation of relevant historians/ historical interpretations.

10 The People's Republic of China (1949–2005)

Further reading

Bandelj, N. and Solinger, D. J. (eds), 2012, *Socialism Vanquished, Socialism Challenged: Eastern Europe and China, 1989–2009*, Oxford, Oxford University Press.

Benson, L., 2002, *China Since 1949*, London, Longman/Pearson.

Cheek, T. 2006, *Living with Reform: China Since 1989*, London, Zed Books.

Dillon, M., 2012. *China: A Modern History*, London, I. B. Tauris

Dillon, M. 2015, *Deng Xiaoping: The Man Who Made Modern China*, London, I. B. Tauris

Ethridge, J. M., 1990, *China's Unfinished Revolution: Problems and Prospects Since Mao*, San Francisco, China Books & Periodicals.

Evans, R., 1997, *Deng Xiaoping and the Making of Modern China*, New York, Penguin.

Fewsmith, J., 2001, *China Since Tiananmen: The Politics of Transition*, Cambridge, Cambridge University Press.

Gittings, J., 2006, *The Changing Face of China: From Mao to Market*, Oxford, Oxford University Press.

Goodman, D., 1994, *Deng Xiaoping and the Chinese Revolution*, London, Routledge.

Hsu, I., 1990, *China Without Mao: The Search for a New Order*, Oxford, Oxford University Press.

J. Fenby, 2013, *The Penguin History of Modern China*, London, Penguin Books.

Lawrance, A., 2004, *China Since 1919: Revolution and Reform*, London, Routledge.

Lynch, M., 1998, *The People's Republic of China Since 1949*, London, Hodder & Stoughton.

Meisner, M., 1999, *Mao's China and After: A History of the People's Republic*, New York, The Free Press.

Further reading

Spense, J. D., et al., 1999, The Search for Modern China, New York, W. W. Norton.

Yu, A. L., et. al., 2012, *China's Rise: Strength and Fragility*. Pontypool, Merlin Press.

Index

abortion 265
Acheson, Dean 167
Agrarian Reform Law (1950) 59–61
Agricultural Producers' Cooperatives (APCs) 70–2
agriculture *see also* land collectivization
  under Deng 249–53, 262–5, 341
  and first Five-Year Plan (1952) 66, 69
  and Great Leap Forward (GLF) (1958-61) 111–12, 113–16
  Higher Agricultural Producers' Cooperatives (HAPCs) (1956-58) 97–8
  under Hua 241, 244
  Land Reform Act (1952) 70
  Mutual Aid Teams (MATs) 70
  reforms (1949-52) 58–63
  and rural communes 108
  'speaking bitterness' meetings 61–3
  women in 341
Ali, T. 363
Anti-Rightist campaign (1957) 91–3
APCs *see* Agricultural Producers' Cooperatives (APCs)
April 5th Movement 218
Asian Crisis (1997) 346

Bandelj, N. 327
Bandung Conference (1955) 174
'Beijing Spring' (1989) 305–6
Benson, Linda 61, 99, 112, 115, 208, 209, 240

Bettelheim, Charles 241, 242, 246, 247
'big character' posters 283, 285–6, 300
border disputes 185
bureaucratic capitalism 360
Burton, Neil 241, 242

capitalism
  as base for socialism 258
  defined 30
  Mao's Socialist Education Movement (SEM) as counter to 132–7
  'National Capitalism' 64–5
  neo-liberalism 30–1
'capitalist road/capitalist roaders' 22, 47, 120, 133, 134, 139, 144, 145, 147, 148, 202, 214, 236, 258, 289, 292, 330
CCP *see* Chinese Communist Party (CCP)
Chai Ling (b. 1966) 315
Chen Boda (1904-89) 136, 140
Chen Duxiu 28
Chen Xilian 220
Chen Yiyang 293
Chen Yun (1905-95) 47, 55, 119, 300, 327, 328, 338
Chicago School of Economics 31
Chile 191
China *see also* People's Republic of China (PRC)
  before 1949 14–19
  Japanese invasion of 18–19
Chinese Communist Party (CCP) *see also* Communism; People's Republic of China (PRC)

conflict within 117–21, 150–1, 201–7, 213–30, 292–3
control of military 44–5, 336
corruption in 272–3, 291, 292, 297, 353–5
criticisms of Great Leap Forward (GLF) (1958-61) 103–5
establishment of power (1949-55) 39–58
and foreign policy changes 192–3, 205–6
generational identification of 32–3
and intelligentsia 56–8
and Jiang's 'Extermination Campaign' 16–17
National Party Congress (NPC) 46
origins of 15
purges of 54–6
and 'rectification' campaigns 48–54
reform of 289–91
response to pro-democracy protests 306
and 'Three Represents' theory 333–4
Chinese Nationalist Party *see* Guomindang (GMD)
Chinese People's Political Consultative Conference (CPPCC) 40–2
Chinese People's Volunteers (CPV) 169
Civil War 16–19
class *see* social class
Cold War 190
Comintern (Communist International) 16
Common Programme 43–4
communes 100, 102, 105–8, 110, 111, 112, 120, 250–3

386

Index

Communism *see also*
Chinese Communist
Party (CCP); Marxism
in China, after 2005
359–63
collapse of, in Eastern
Europe and Soviet
Union 326
and GMD 15–16
influence of Soviet
Union on, in China
15–16
Jiang's actions against
16–17
Leninism 26–7
Maoism 29–30
Marxism 25–6
Marxism-Leninism 27–8
in North Korea 165–6
overview 22–4
reforms under 17, 18
Stalinism 28–9
'conservatives' 22
corruption 272–3, 291, 292, 297, 347, 349–50, 353–5
CPPCC *see* Chinese
People's Political
Consultative Conference
(CPPCC)
CPV *see* Chinese People's
Volunteers (CPV)
crime 355
Cultural Revolution (1966-76)
course of 144–9
and foreign policy 184–5
and Gang of Four 204
impact of 149–50
intelligentsia as target
of 146
and Mao's legacy 212
reasons for 141–3
violence of 148
Cummings, Bruce 167
Czechoslovakia 184, 187, 305

Dai Qing 353
Dalai Lama 46, 173
de-collectivisation 264–5, 270
Democracy Movement
aftermath of 318
arrests of activists 288, 297, 312, 313, 315
CCP response to 306
democracy salons 302–3
Fifth Modernisation
285–8
*Goddess of Democracy
and the Spirit of Liberty*
311–12
Gorbachev's impact on
307–8
hunger strike 307, 309–10
Hu's support of 292, 297–8
international reaction
to 316
martial law 310–12
neo-authoritarianism as
response to 301–2
origins of 284
reasons for failure of 317
repression of 312–15
student activism 293–7, 299, 300, 304–16
and Tiananmen Square
Massacre (1989) 306–16
Zhao's support of 293, 306–7, 308–10
Democracy Wall (1976-80)
283–5, 288
Deng Xiaoping (1904-97)
agriculture under 249–53, 262–5, 341
and April 5th Movement
218–19
background 94
CCP reforms under
289–91
and Chen Yun 327
criticism of 258
and Democracy Wall
283–5, 288
economic policies 244–62, 299–300, 338–42
Five-Year Plan (1986-90)
260–2
Four Cardinal Principles
286–7
and Four Modernisation
policies 239–40, 249
and Gao Gang Affair 55
historians on 246
industry under 253–62, 266–9
and labour camps
(laojiao) 93
living standards under
252, 261, 265, 269–70, 299–300
vs. Mao 132
People's Daily editorial
305
political approach (1976-79) 283–8
and power struggles
within CCP 202, 206–7, 215
purges under 291, 297–8, 315
re-education of 147–8
re-instatement of 221
rise to power 226–9, 244, 258
on socialism 260
'Southern Tour' (1992)
331–2, 338
and Soviet relations
179–80
and Ten-Year Plan (1976-85) 244
and Third Front 182
Deutscher, I. 179
'dictatorship of the
proletariat' 31–2
Dillon, M. 41, 51, 52, 119, 153, 170, 214, 218
Ding Ling (1904-86) 74
'Double Tenth' Revolution
see 1911 Revolution

economic policies
of 1949-55 58–72
after Great Leap Forward
(GLF) (1958-61) 132–3
and Communism
359–60
conservative 'leftist' vs.
liberal 'rightist' divisions
206, 209, 327–30
under Deng 244–62, 299–300, 338–42
and Deng's 'Southern
Tour' (1992) 331–2, 338
Five-Year Plan (1952)
65–9, 97

387

The People's Republic of China (1949–2005)

Five-Year Plan (1986–90) 260–2
foreign trade and investment 254, 256–7, 261, 267–8, 316, 341, 343, 345–6, 358
under Hua 238–45
'Open Door' policy 254–5
in post-Deng period (1997-2005) 342–3
reforms (1949-52) 58–63
and social unrest 347
Ten-Year Plan (1976-85) 243–5
'transition to socialism' (1953-55) 65–9
and World Trade Organization (WTO) 344–6
economy
in 1976 240–1
Asian Crisis (1997) 346
Cultural Revolution's impact on 149
growing dominance of China's 358
national debt 271–2
before 1911 Revolution 14
education
under Communism (1949-55) 75, 77–8
and corruption 355
Hu's reforms of 292
Election Law (1953) 76
elections 354
Engels, Friedrich 22–3, 25
environmental issues *see* pollution
ethnic tensions 342
Ethridge, J.M. 268
'Extermination Campaigns' 16–17

Falun Gong religion 333
famine *see* food shortages
Fang Lizhi 294, 295, 303, 315
Feigon, Lee 95
Feng Xuefeng (1903–76) 57–8
Fewsmith, J. 343

Fifth Modernisation 285–8
'Five-Anti' campaign (1952) 53–4, 172
Five-Year Plan (1952)
and agriculture 66, 69
and industry 66, 67–9
negative effects of 97
overview 65–6
results of 67–9
Soviet assistance 66–7
and workers 69
Five-Year Plan (1986-90) 260–2
'floating population' 351–2
food shortages 71, 108, 110, 113–16, 265
foot binding 73
foreign policy
and Chinese Communist Party (CCP) 192–3, 205–6
and Cultural Revolution (1966-76) 184–5
under Jiang Zemin 355–6
under Mao 162–93
Non-Aligned Movement 174–5
Four Big Rights 288
Four Cardinal Principles 286–7
'Four Cleanups' campaign (1962) 134
Four Modernisations 206–7, 226, 239–40, 249
freedom of speech 86–90, 283–5, 292 *see also* Democracy Movement; protests; repression
Friedman, Milton 31
Fukuyama, Francis 361, 362

GAC *see* Government Administrative Council (GAC)
Gang of Four 202–5, 207, 215, 220–6
Gang of Old 298
Gao Gang (1905-54) 52, 53, 54–5, 65, 66
Gao Gang Affair 54–5
GLF *see* Great Leap Forward (GLF) (1958-61)

GMD *see* Guomindang (GMD)
Goddess of Democracy and the Spirit of Liberty 311–12
Gorbachev, Mikhail 307–8
Government Administrative Council (GAC) 44
governmental structure
under CCP regime 46–8
modern-day 19–20
one-party system 289
Great Leap Forward (GLF) (1958-61)
abandonment of 119–20
and agriculture 111–12, 113–16
CCP criticisms of 103–5
consequences of 110–21
economic policies after 132–3
implementation of 105
and industry 100, 105, 111–12
Mao's position after 120–1
overview 99–101
Soviet criticisms of 180
and women's status 112
Guomindang (GMD)
and Communism 15–16
and Jiang's 'Extermination Campaign' 16–17
members of, as targets of 'rectification' campaigns 48–9, 50–1

HAPCs *see* Higher Agricultural Producers' Cooperatives (HAPCs) (1956-58)
Hayek, Friedrich 31
health care 78–9
hegemony 31
Higher Agricultural Producers' Cooperatives (HAPCs) (1956-58) 97–8
Hobsbawm, E. 142
Hong Kong 357
Hou Dejian 313
Household Responsibility System (HRS) 250–3

388

Index

HRS *see* Household Responsibility System (HRS)
Hsu, Immanuel C.Y. 299
Hu Feng (1902–85) 57–8, 86
Hu Jintao (b. 1942) 334, 335, 336, 353
Hu Yaobang (1915-89)
  background 229
  death of 303–4
  as Deng supporter 292
  fall of 297–8, 328
  as party official 228
  and pro-democracy protests 294
Hua Guofeng (1921-2008)
  agriculture under 241, 244
  economic policies of 238–45
  fall of 227–9, 243
  and Gang of Four 220–1
  industry under 241, 243–4
  rise to power 215–16, 219, 226–7
  'Whateverists' position 227–30, 242–3
Hundred Flowers Campaign (1956-57)
  Anti-Rightist campaign (1957) 91–3
  historians on 94–6
  and Mao's legacy 212
  overview of 86–91

India 174
Industrial Responsibility System 254
industry
  under Deng 253–62, 266–9, 339–40
  expansion of, in post-Deng period 343
  and first Five-Year Plan (1952) 66, 67–9
  and Great Leap Forward (GLF) (1958-61) 100, 105, 111–12
  under Hua 241, 243–4
  reforms (1949-52) 64–5
  and rural communes 106,
107–8
  shift from state-run to private 339–40
  women in 341
inequality 211, 270–1, 341–2, 347
infanticide 73, 265
intelligentsia
  and Anti-Rightist campaign (1957) 92
  and CCP 56–8
  and Hundred Flowers Campaign (1956-57) 86–8
  'rectification' campaign against (1964) 138–9
  as target of Cultural Revolution 146
  'thought reform' of 56–7
isolationism 172, 183

Japan 18–19, 188, 190
Jiang Jieshi (1887-1975) 16–17
Jiang Qing (1914-91) 139, 140, 202, 215, 220, 221–6
  see also Gang of Four
Jiang Zemin (b. 1926)
  anti-corruption campaign 353
  background 329
  economic policies 342–3
  foreign policy under 355–6
  and political generations concept 32–3
  repressive policies of 333
  rise to power 318, 332–3
  'Three Represents' theory 333–4
Jung Chang 94

Kakuei Tanaka (1918-93) 190
Khrushchev, Nikita 30, 176, 177–80, 183
Kim Il-Sung (1912-94) 166, 167, 169
Kissinger, Henry 188
Korean War 165–72
Kosygin, Alexei 185

labour camps (*laojiao*) 93–4

land collectivisation *see also* agriculture
  Agrarian Reform Law (1950) 59–61
  de-collectivisation 264–5, 270
  under Deng 250–3
  Five-Year Plan (1952) 69
  and Great Leap Forward (GLF) (1958-61) 112
  Higher Agricultural Producers' Cooperatives (HAPCs) (1956-58) 97–8
  and rural communes 105–8
Land Reform Act (1952) 70
Lardy, Nicholas 67
'leftist' conservatives *see also* 'rightist' liberals
  defined 20–2
  and Gang of Four 204
  'leftist' vs. 'rightist' divisions in CCP 103–5, 201–2, 204
  in economic policies 206, 209, 327–30
Lenin, Vladimir Ilyich 26
Leninism 26–7
Li Peng (b. 1928) 298, 304, 306, 308, 310, 338
Li Zhengtian 293
'liberals' 22
Lin Biao (1907-71) 103, 119, 135, 145, 151, 152, 187, 188, 192
Lin Binyan 297
Lin Xiling (1935-2009) 90
Little Red Book 136–7, 144
Liu Shaoqi (1898-1969)
  background 47
  and Gao Gang Affair 54–5
  on GLF as disaster 129
  vs. Mao 132–3
  purge of 147, 184
  rise to power 104, 110, 117
  and Sino-Soviet Treaty (1950) 164
Liu Xiaobo 313
Liuism 140
living standards

389

The People's Republic of China (1949–2005)

under Communism
(1949-55) 78–9
under Deng 252, 261,
265, 269–70, 299–300
'Long March' (1934-35) 17
Loong Yu, A. 349, 360
Lushan Conference (1959)
117–19
Lynch, M. 49, 96, 224, 245,
299

Macao 357
MacArthur, Douglas 168,
170
Mandarin 77
Mao Yuanxin 207, 220
Mao Zedong (1893-1976)
after Great Leap Forward
(GLF) (1958-61) 120–1
and April 5th Movement
218
background 15
cult of personality 136–7,
143, 148, 177, 211
and Cultural Revolution
(1966-76) 141–2
death of 219–20
demystification of 227
foreign policy under
162–93
historians on 208, 210,
213
and Hua 216
and Hundred Flowers
Campaign (1956-57)
88–9, 212
and Jiang's
'Extermination
Campaign' 17
and Khrushchev 177–80
legacy of 208–13
vs. Lin Biao 151
Little Red Book 136–7,
144
on Liu 184
political views of (1961)
131–2
purges under 29–30,
54–6, 119, 127, 140, 143,
147, 149, 152
replaced as PRC chair
104, 117
Sixteen Articles 144, 145

and socialism 210–11
and Socialist Education
Movement (SEM) 132–7
and Stalin 164
on women's status 73–4
Maoism
and Great Leap Forward
(GLF) (1958-61) 101
Hua's abandonment of
240–1
vs. Liuism 140
overview 29–30
marriage 73
Marriage Law (1950) 74–5
Marx, Karl (1818-83) 22–3,
25–6
Marxism
and 'dictatorship of the
proletariat' 31–2
overview 25–6
spread of, in China 15
survival of 362
Marxism-Leninism 27–8
MATs see Mutual Aid Teams
(MATs)
May Fourth Movement 15
Meisner, Maurice 39, 50, 88,
89, 95, 121, 130–1, 133,
153, 192, 210, 238, 246,
248, 271, 301, 360
Mikoyan, Anastas 164
military see also People's
Liberation Army (PLA)
CCP control of 44–5,
336
Third Front 182–3
militia 106
Munro, Ross 358
Mutual Aid Teams (MATs)
70

'National Capitalism' 64–5
national debt 271–2
National Party Congress
(NPC) 46
neo-authoritarianism 301–2
neo-liberalism 30–1
1911 Revolution 14–16
Nixon, Richard 188
Non-Aligned Movement
174–5
NPC see National Party
Congress (NPC)

nuclear weapons 183

one-child policy 265, 272
'Open Door' policy 254–5,
269, 293 see also Special
Economic Zones (SEZs)

peasants see also workers, and
land reforms 58–63, 70–2
Peng Dehuai (1898-1974)
103, 117–19, 139, 169,
180
Peng Shuzhi 28
People's Bank 64
People's Daily newspaper
292, 305
People's Liberation Army
(PLA) see also military
and CCP 44–5
and 'Little Red Book'
136
as model for Chinese
society 135
origins of 19
political reliability of 354
People's Republic of China
(PRC) see also Chinese
Communist Party (CCP)
as bureaucratic capitalist
society 360
establishment of
Communist rule (1949-
55) 39–58
governmental structure
19–20
and Japan 190
and Korean War 168–72
origins of 19
Soviet aid to 65, 66–7,
111, 163–5
split with Soviet Union
177–85
as transitional society
212–13
and US relations 185–9,
249, 356–7
'ping pong diplomacy' 188
Pinyin 77
Poland 300
political generations 332
pollution 265, 269, 337,
352–3
poverty 269–71, 299–300,

Index

341–2 *see also* living standards
'Prague Spring' (1968) 305
PRC *see* People's Republic of China (PRC)
privatisation 339–40, 348
Project 571 affair 152–3, 188
proletariat
  defined 32
  'dictatorship of' 31–2
property rights 76
prostitution 355
protests
  after Hu's death 303–4
  April 5th Movement 218
  of corruption 347, 354
  of Five-Year Plan 89
  of Great Leap Forward (GLF) (1958-61) 104
  and Hundred Flowers Campaign (1956-57) 90
  student-led democracy demonstrations 267, 294, 296–7, 299, 300, 304–16
  Tiananmen Square Massacre (1989) 306–16
  by workers 304, 347–51
purges *see also* Cultural Revolution (1966-76); 'rectification' campaigns
  of Democracy Movement activists 288 under Deng 291, 297–8, 315
  of Gang of Four 221–6
  Gao Gang Affair 54–5
  under Mao 29–30, 54–6, 119, 127, 140, 143, 147, 149, 152
  under Stalin 28
Sufan Movement 56

Qingming Festival (1976) 217–19

Rao Shushi (1903-75) 54, 55
Reagan, Ronald 189, 293
'rectification' campaigns 48–54, 138–9, 172
Red Army 16–19 *see also* People's Liberation Army (PLA)
Red Guards 144, 146–7, 148
repression *see also* Cultural Revolution (1966-76); purges; 'thought reform'
  after Tiananmen Square Massacre (1989) 318
  Anti-Rightist campaign (1957) 91–3
  of Democracy Movement activists 288, 297, 312–15
  of Falun Gong religion 333
  labour camps (*laojiao*) 93–4
  'rectification' campaigns 48–54, 138–9, 172
Resist America campaign (1950) 172
'reunification' campaigns 45–6
'rightist' liberals *see also* 'leftist' conservatives; 'leftist' vs. 'rightist' divisions
  and Anti-Rightist campaign (1957) 91–3
  defined 20–2
  and Four Modernisations policies 206
  and Gang of Four 220, 223
  as targets of Cultural Revolution 146–7
Riskin, Carl 246
Russia *see* Soviet Union

Sakharov, Andrei 297
Schram, S. 113–14, 143
SEATO *see* South East Asia Treaty Organisation (SEATO)
Second Sino-Japanese War 18–19
SEM *see* Socialist Education Movement (SEM)
SEZs *see* Special Economic Zones (SEZs)
Shanghai Communiqué 188–9
Short, Philip 95, 130
Sino-Soviet Treaty (1950) 164–5
Sixteen Articles 144, 145
Snow, Edgar 137, 138
social class
  and landownership 59–61
  and 'speaking bitterness' meetings 61–3
social reforms 73–9
social unrest *see* Democracy Movement; protests
socialism
  capitalism as base for 258
  China as 'transitional society' 212–13
  Deng on 260
  Mao's legacy 210–11
  transition to (1953-55) 65–9
'Socialism in One Country' 28
socialist democracy 29
Socialist Education Movement (SEM) 132–7
Solinger, D.J. 327
Songhua River 337
South East Asia Treaty Organisation (SEATO) 175
Soviet Union
  aid of, to PRC 65, 66–7, 163–5
  and China-US relations 187–9, 190
  collapse of Communism in 326
  criticisms of Great Leap Forward (GLF) (1958-61) 180
  de-Stalinisation of 30
  end of support by 111, 180
  influence of, on Chinese Communism 16
  and Korean War 171–2
  'peaceful coexistence' policy 178, 181
  split with PRC 177–85
  and Taiwan 175–6
Special Economic Zones (SEZs) 255–7, 267–9, 341
Spence, Jonathan 94

391

The People's Republic of China (1949–2005)

'Spirit of Yan'an' 18–19
Stalin, Josef 28, 163, 164, 168, 176–7
Stalinism 28–9
Su Shaozhi 302
Su Zhenua 220
Sufan Movement 56
Sun Yat-sen 15
'Suppression of Counter-Revolutionaries' campaign (1950-51) 50–2
Syngman Rhee (1875-1965) 166

Taiwan 16, 165, 172, 185, 188, 345, 358
Taiwan Strait Crises 175–6, 183
Ten-Year Plan (1976-85) 243–5
Third Front 182–3
'thought reform'
 and 'Five-Anti' campaign (1952) 54
 of intelligentsia 56–7
 and 'rectification' campaigns 49
'Three Bitter Years' (1959-61) 111–12, 115, 117
'Three-Anti' campaign (1951) 52–3
Tiananmen Square Massacre (1989) 306–16
Tibet 46, 104
Township and Village Enterprises (TVEs) 111, 263–4
trade unions 69, 350
transitional society 65–9, 212–13
treaties
 Sino-Soviet Treaty of Friendship, Alliance and Mutual Assistance (1950) 65, 164–5
 South East Asia Treaty Organisation (SEATO) 175
Trotsky, Leon (1879–1940) 27, 212, 213
Trotskyism 28, 182
TVEs *see* Township and Village Enterprises (TVEs)

unemployment 269–71, 299–300, 347–51
United States
 and Korean War 165–8
 and PRC relations 185–9, 249, 356–7
 and Taiwan 172, 175–6
 and Vietnam War 184
USSR *see* Soviet Union

Vietnam 183, 184, 186, 187–8
Vogel, Ezra 358
voting rights 76

Wan Li (1916-2015) 250–1
Wang Dan 302, 307, 308, 315
Wang Dongxing (1916-2015) 207
Wang Hongwen 202, 204, 220, 221, 226
Wang Ruoshui (1926-2002) 294, 297
Wang Xizhe 293
Wei Jingsheng (b. 1950) 285, 286, 303
Wen Jiabao (b. 1942) 334, 335, 337
'Whateverists' 227–30, 242–3
women
 in agriculture 341
 and Great Leap Forward (GLF) (1958-61) 112
 in industry 341
 and rural communes 106, 107
 status of, before Communism 73
 status of, under Communism (1949-55) 73–7
 as temporary workers 352
 trafficking of 355
workers *see also* peasants
 and first Five-Year Plan (1952) 69
 'floating population'

of temporary workers 351–2
and pro-democracy protests 304, 305
social unrest among 304, 347–51
women as 112, 341
World Trade Organization (WTO) 344–6
WTO *see* World Trade Organization (WTO)
Wu Han 138, 139
Wuer Kaixi 307, 308, 315

Xi Jinping 334
Xiufen Lu 74

Yao Wenyuan 202, 203, 226
Ye Jianying (1897–1986) 219, 220

Zeng Qinghong (b. 1939) 334, 335
Zhang Chunqiao 202, 203, 221, 226
Zhao Ziyang (1919–2005)
 background 229
 dismissal of, from CCP 318, 328–9
 and industrial reforms (1978-84) 253
 as party official 228, 298
 and pro-democracy protests 293, 306–7, 308–10
Zhou Enlai (1898-1976)
 and Anti-Rightist campaign (1957) 93
 background 42
 and Cultural Revolution (1966-76) 149
 death of 213–14, 217
 and Deng's 're-education' 148
 as first premier (prime minister) 41
 and Gao Gang Affair 54–5
 and Hundred Flowers Campaign (1956-57) 86
 and power struggles within CCP 202, 206–7
 and Sino-Soviet Treaty

392

Index

(1950) 164
and Soviet border disputes 185
and 'Suppression of Counter-Revolutionaries' campaign (1950-51) 51
and US relations (1970s) 188, 192
Zhou Yang 58
Zhu De (1886-1976) 44, 213
Zhu Rongji (b. 1928) 330, 332, 342–3, 344, 353

Acknowledgements

The volume editor and publishers acknowledge the following sources of copyright material and are grateful for the permissions granted. While every effort has been made, it has not always been possible to identify the sources of all the material used, or to trace all copyright holders. If any omissions are brought to our notice we will be happy to include the appropriate acknowledgement on reprinting.

Text

Extracts from Mao's China and after: a history of the People's Republic by M. Meisner, 1999, Free Press, an imprint of Simon & Schuster;
Extracts from China: a modern history by Michael Dillon, published by I.B. Tauris, 2012, licensed via the Copyright Clearance Center;
Extracts from China Since 1949 (2nd edition, 2011), L. Benson, Copyright 2002, 2011, Taylor & Francis. Reproduced with permission of Taylor & Francis Books UK;
Extracts from The People's Republic of China 1949-76 by M. Lynch, Hodder Education, 2008

Images

Cover image. Bettmann /Getty Images; p8. Bettmann / Getty Images; p25. Chronicle / Alamy Stock Photo; p38. AFP Photography, LLC / Getty Images; p62. Bettmann / Getty Images; p67. ullstein bild / Getty Images; p76. Bettmann / Getty Images; p102. © Tate, London 2015; p107. Everett Collection Historical / Alamy Stock Photo; p116. George Silk / Getty images; p127. IFOT / Hassner / Carera Press; p137. ullstein bild / Getty Images; p146. VCG / Getty Images; p147. ullstein bild / Getty Images; p152. Sovfoto / Getty Images; p180. Keystone-France / Getty Images; p181. A 1960 Herblock Cartoon, © The Herb

Block Foundation; p186. IISH collection; p189. AFP / Getty Images; p201. Keystone / Getty Images; p216. IISH collection; p217. VCG / Getty Images; p222. IISH collection; p223. AFP / Getty Images; p243. Keystone / Getty Images; p252. Topham Picturepoint / Topfoto; p257. Samantha Sin / Getty Images; p264. STR / Getty Images; p270. AFP / Getty Images; p282. CATHERINE HENRIETTE/AFP/Getty Images; p284. AFP / Getty Images; p291. Kevin KAL Kallaugher, Kaltoons.com; p304. CATHERINE HENRIETTE / AFP / Getty Images; p309. Chip HIRES / Gamma-Rapho via Getty Images; p312. Toshio Sakai / Getty Images; p317. Nicholas Garland; p323. Peter Parks / AFP / Getty Images; p336. KIN Cheung/AFP/Getty Images; p337. Yao Dawei / AP / Press Association Images; p351. Frederic J. Brown / Getty Images; p357. Sovfoto / Getty